The Golden Lands of Thomas Hobbes

Thomas Hobbes, by J. M. Wright (ca. 1669–70). Reproduced by permission of the National Portrait Gallery, London.

THE GOLDEN LANDS OF

Thomas Hobbes

Miriam M. Reik

*"Thou great Columbus of the Golden Lands
of new Philosophies."*
Abraham Cowley

Wayne State University Press
Detroit, 1977

Library of Congress Cataloging in Publication Data

Reik, Miriam M 1938–
    The golden lands of Thomas Hobbes.

    Bibliography: p.
    Includes index.
    1. Hobbes, Thomas, 1588–1679. 2. Philosophers—
England—Biography. I. Title.
B1246.R44   192 [B]   77-3594
ISBN 0-8143-1574-7

This volume is published with the support of a grant from the American Council of
Learned Societies for publication of first or second books by scholars in the fields of the
humanities.

To the Memory of
my Parents

Contents

Illustrations

9

Abbreviations

Note on the Text

In quoting seventeenth-century manuscript sources, the original spelling and punctuation are retained, no matter how idiosyncratic. I have modernized only words which included superscript letters: "Sʳ" thus becomes "Sir," for instance, and "wᶜʰ" becomes "which."

Preface

JOHN AUBREY, Hobbes's first biographer, seems to have regarded his task as somewhat of a sacred obligation, collecting whatever scraps he could gather about his eminent subject. Since his work is in the antiquarian mode, the result is a delightful jumble of facts and observations about Hobbes, thrown together like a haphazard assemblage of relics in a chest. Any modern biography of Hobbes, however, must be in large part a history of his thought for the simple reason that he never *did* much in the active sense: he never went to war, sent ships to the New World, or became Lord Chancellor. He mainly seemed to write and think, read and talk, play tennis and music. Insofar as I have departed in some ways from the conventions of intellectual biography, a word may be in order concerning what special problems helped to determine the idea of intellectual biography here, and what method has been followed.

Those philosophers are most amenable to biographical treatment who, in the course of their lifetimes, wrote their works in the same logical sequence as one would choose for making a systematic analysis of their thought. Written in any other sequence, they automatically present to the biographer a conflict between chronological and expositional order: the one represents the truth of the calendar or fidelity to the historical events of the subject's lifetime, the other represents the inner consistency of philosophic reasoning. The two principles happily coincide in Hobbes's early years, when his youth correlates with the emergence of themes basic to his thought, and in his latest years, when he was no longer producing very novel work. For his most prolific middle years, however, the problem of unity is acute. Hobbes did not write in a conveniently logical sequence, and he furthermore chose to treat the same subjects in different connections over widely separated points of time. Finally, his spectacular longevity encompassed such a huge range of events that his life story, considered in terms of his external circumstances, more nearly approximates the condition of history than it does biography.

11

My method, in view of these problems, has been to thread a chronological line through the study, but to depart from it freely in deference to the demands of topical coherence or of a broader thematic unity. In most cases, I have therefore presented Hobbes's position on any given issue as he finally formulated it rather than disrupt its presentation by comparisons with different texts for the sake of noting changes, most of them minor. Where such changes were substantial, they have been remarked upon and references to special studies cited. This does not always conform to the procedure of a biographer, nor have my priorities always been in accord with those required by a strictly philosophic study, but with Hobbes's special problems in mind, I have measured out a somewhat different, if frequently overlapping, field to cultivate.

Since my intention was to write a study of Hobbes's life and thought, not an exhaustive account of them, his arguments are sometimes presented in a condensed form to fit within a more narrow compass, and certain areas were ruled altogether outside the province of this undertaking. Most prominently, I have not dealt with Hobbes's influence on future thought or his relevance to our own age. Criticism of his system has been included, but mostly I have allowed his contemporaries to deliver it, supplemented by references to modern scholarship where I felt it necessary. Such contemporary criticism also provides a comparison with the thought of the period by which the reader can judge how far Hobbes's thought departed from accepted ideas. I have deviated from this practice most notably in the case of Hobbes's literary ideas, about which his contemporaries had little to say explicitly, while modern scholars have had a good deal to say about his role in ushering in the poetics of the Augustan age. Moreover, the different uses of language in different fields, in this case science and poetry, are of central importance to Hobbes as well as key factors in our whole relation to the seventeenth-century authors and how we read them, so I have ventured somewhat farther afield in that area.

The writing of this essay was facilitated by a number of people and institutions which it is my pleasure to acknowledge. The Social Science Research Council made it possible for me to study relevant sources in England under a Research Fellowship in the early stages of my studies. I was greatly assisted by the staffs of both the Bodleian Library and the British Museum, and also by the staff at the Royal Society, to which I am most indebted for permission to consult its archives. I am deeply grateful to His Grace the Duke of Devonshire for granting me access to the Hobbes manuscripts in the Chatsworth Collection, and to Mr. T. S. Wragg, who was a most courteous guide to the collection. Not least, my thanks to Professor Howard Warrender, who favored me with some needed advice when I was a graduate student, and whose published work on Hobbes is a major contribution to the field for which all serious Hobbes students must be grateful. Professor Michael Oakeshott similarly requires special thanks, not only for his published scholarship, but also for the astute comments he made on a large portion of my manuscript. Most recently my work has been helped by a fellowship from the National Endowment for the Humanities, which permitted me to do further research in the history of science. Finally, I am indebted to Professor J. A. Mazzeo for his encouragement, and to Professor E. W. Taylor, whose comments on an early draft taught me something about putting together a long manuscript.

Introductory Essay

W H E N the coasts of England were ringed by beacons and bells to send out alarms at the first sign of the great Spanish fleet of 1588, and a rash of rumors warning of the pending attack had made the people pass the winter in anxious expectation, the future philosopher was born in the village of Westport by the ancient market town of Malmesbury in Wiltshire. His mother was purportedly brought into premature labor from fear of the imminent invasion, but her terror could only have been caused by just another false report. For Thomas, her son, was born on April 5, Good Friday of 1588, and the Armada was not to set sail for more than a month, nor was it finally sighted off the Scilly Isles until July. As for his father, Vicar Hobbes is described as one of the less exemplary sort of Elizabethan clergyman: having fallen asleep in church one Sunday, it was apparently not out of character for him to reveal his dream to the congregation by loudly announcing from the depths of his slumber that clubs was trump. He is said to have been a vigorous but clownish and ignorant fellow who, shortly after his son was born, brawled with another parson, fled, and finally disappeared altogether somewhere "beyond London."[1]

Hobbes later attributed to these tense and warlike circumstances of his birth his hatred of England's enemies, his love of peaceful pursuits, and his physical timidity—a trait he openly acknowledged and caught in the laconic self-designation, "Twin of Fear."[2] A panicky reaction to the Roman Catholic powers was again epidemic in England when Hobbes died in December 1679, only this time it was inspired by the prospect of a "papist" heir to the throne and by the madness of Titus Oates. The fear and upheaval caused by religious strife was a repeated theme in Hobbes's life, though not much more remained the same during its ninety-one-year span.

The settings for the first fifteen years of Hobbes's life, for instance, must be taken from the England of Drake and Raleigh, from

14

the Elizabethan courtly ideals of the *Faerie Queene,* and from the meeting of the older Shakespearean world with that of Ben Jonson in the newer forms of literature for the stage. Hobbes's last fifteen years, however, were spent in the reign of Charles II, with its strange and scandalous court, and its concept of letters that made Dryden king in poetry as well as in the theater. By this same token of long life, Hobbes's name appears slightly anomalous next to those of Francis Beaumont, George Herbert, and Drummond of Hawthornden—as if he did not quite belong to their generation—although he was born within a few years of each of them. The study of his work has become, in fact, largely the province of scholars of the Restoration and later Stuart thought instead of those of the Jacobean or early Caroline periods. It will be one of the purposes of this study to show that Hobbes does belong to the end of the Renaissance period rather than to the Restoration or the beginning of the Enlightenment in England.

These changes in scenery between the beginning and end of Hobbes's life, made still more abrupt by the bustle and clamor of the Interregnum, are awkward, but no more so than the free and easy drift imposed by time upon language. To compare Hobbes's concept of "wit" or "fancy" with that of his contemporaries, for instance, entails a simultaneous comparison with Jonson, Cowley, Rymer, and the Earl of Rochester, all of whom were his contemporaries at some time in his life. The idea of science provides a still more striking example, for its formal denotation of a body of knowledge or of a method for the investigation of nature was retained, but as the concept of the universe changed, so too the content of the word was silently reformed. The historian who wishes to relate Hobbes's thought to the advances of early modern science will find that Hobbes's infancy was concurrent with Galileo's earliest lectures at Pisa and the experiments at the Leaning Tower; he will see Hobbes at middle age pondering the Cartesian method and reading the *De Motu Cordis* by his friend William Harvey. In his old age, the philosopher may have read the issue of the *Philosophical Transactions* of the Royal Society that printed the first paper submitted by Sir Isaac Newton. At the same time, he may have seen the issue of that journal reporting the early results of experiments by Anton van Leeuwenhoek, whose remarkable powers of observation were even then in the process of creating microbiology. Even if "science" ever had a homogenous meaning at any given time, extremes of meaning met in Hobbes's life:

the "science" of Bacon, whom Hobbes served as a secretary in his youth, and the "science" of Newton's *Principia*, which was originally published a scant eight years after Hobbes's death.

Through all this change, Hobbes maintained a resolute adherence to certain philosophic ideals that underwent little in the way of radical modification, making him appear solid and sure to some, but to others merely pedantic. His very substantial corpus of work, including many different types of endeavor, is therefore no less striking for its reflection of his consistency of character than for the astuteness of his observations. It reveals those modes of thinking which, once tapped, grew dominant in his personality and which are more reliable weavers of unity in his biography than chronology is. They are fundamental qualities of his mind, as evident in the style of his prose as in the character of his philosophy.

Among these qualities, none was more characteristic than a certain drive toward systematic analysis. That he should have labored to bring all the confusion of novelty in his time into an order such that it would yield its general truths and still conform to his total conceptual view seems a wholly natural effort for him. Philosophy, he said, "the child of the world and your mind, is within yourself; perhaps not fashioned yet, but like the world its father, as it was in the beginning, a thing confused. Do, therefore, as the statuaries do, who, by hewing off that which is superfluous, do not make but find the image."[3] As Hobbes hewed ambitiously, refining the material of experience, the image of a Galatea was revealed which he, like some other innovators of that period, thought he first glimpsed in the pages of Euclid. What emerged was a logic of description, a method for defining things according to the causes of their generation, their motion and number. This entailed for him a world described in almost entirely materialistic terms and moving according to mechanistic laws, and Hobbes therefore worked diligently at the sciences of physics and geometry, which deal with the properties of matter and its motion.

The laws of motion in nature comprise the art by which God created and rules the world, and they find their analogy in man, whose principle of motion is the will. But the will has rules of its own, and Hobbes, therefore, also explored the elements of psychology. Finally, man imitated the art of God by creating an artifical body—the state—in the image of himself, the motions of which are guided by civic, not natural law. So Hobbes added the moral sciences and jurisprudence to his studies, considering in them the motions which generate civil society.

In keeping with this rudimentary outline of Hobbes's scheme, it can be seen how he arrived at a three-part goal for his philosophy, planning to write first on Matter, then on Man, and finally on the State.[4] Having once formulated the axioms of his "basic sciences," he spent more than a decade completing the scheme, yet he never found it very necessary to alter his fundamental attitudes to fit the changing times. For while his political writings plunged him into England's great historical polemic, his work touched on something still larger, and as he spun his logic out, he discovered it capable of representing ever greater segments of reality. He was elaborating, he hoped, a system which was informed by a truth and usefulness comparable to that of mathematics, and similar to it in its universal applicability and capacity for accomodating new knowledge by the implementation of given methods. In this, Hobbes was participating in that wish to employ "scientific" notions to uncover the universal law or language which underlies the various disciplines, a wish as compelling to some seventeenth-century thinkers as discovery through maritime explorations had been among the Elizabethans.

Hobbes's intellectual traits form the basis for a number of anecdotes about him and give us part of our most familiar picture of his general manner. It is the picture of a man who, when at Oxford, laboriously learned the accepted logical figures and modes, but who, being early set in his ways and critical of the exercises, would then prove the *quaestiones* in "his own way."[5] It was the same Hobbes who was sometimes dogmatic even when in error and who was occasionally stung into arrogance when challenged; his confidence in the self-evidence of his reasoning so nearly approached the sublime that disagreement with him seemed to provoke only repetition or impatience. This reputation for intolerance was aggravated by his public notoriety: the fact that his doctrines were considered novel, dangerous, and ethically repellent by society did not escape the attention of certain young courtly blades, and a kind of fashionable "Hobbism" became current among those who thought it estimable to appear fearlessly villainous. Being held responsible for their bravado, their voluptuous behavior, and the smart new doctrine they justified it with, Hobbes had little reason to thank them for their favor. His forthrightness, which might otherwise have been construed as a lack of false modesty, was now seen as boastfulness or the wish to appear original; his view of man as being dominated by self-interest and passions, which was worthy of philosophic consideration, was seen instead as a cultivated cynicism.

We are told that this blunt, rather stubborn philosopher was also both cheerful and charitable; that the quickness of intellect which made him a sharp controversialist and alert to contradiction also made him pleasantly witty in conversation. He is said to have been companionable as well, and he was therefore as highly praised by some for his personal excellence and amiability as he was widely disparaged for the opinions he publicly expressed.

These remarks on Hobbes's intellectual and social traits could be further supplemented by the remarks of contemporaries, but the surviving materials about him are ill-suited to satisfy any expectation of finding a far more intimate portrait of him than his own works provide. He seems to have left no journal or diaries to record his daily thoughts, and the gossip from the coffee-house *convivia* does not indicate his participation in that popular form of Restoration entertainment. While his name is sprinkled through the pamphlets and letters of his time, he had few official affiliations—he never belonged to the Royal Society, a university faculty, or any government office in England—so that few occasions arise to see him in capacities other than his philosophical ones. Of letters, only a few are to friends, and they are too brief. The remainder of his correspondence, like his own autobiography, pertains mainly to matters more impersonal than introspective. A man's family and his women, the other sources of romantic or psychological biography, are unknown quantities in Hobbes's case, for he tell us little about his kin, and women scarcely appear in his story. He never built a family of his own, seeming content to be absorbed into the household of his patrons, the Cavendish family, and John Aubrey remarks that he was temperate with regard to women, as he was to wine. He adds that Hobbes did not dislike women, however, an aversion considered by the philosopher to be inconsistent with "an harmonicall soule."[6] In any case, Hobbes's story certainly has no analogue to a Venetia Stanley or to a Tetty Johnson, nor even some version of the philosophically inclined Lady Conway to answer to his Henry More.

In what has been said thus far of Hobbes—of the emphatically logical cast of his mind, and of the magnitude of his public personality as compared with the paucity of detail about his private thoughts—he gives the impression of a subject more fit for a Plutarch who wishes to memorialize the character of his life, than for the author who wishes to portray the personality of a man. It is true that Hobbes was no Renaissance man, no poet-courtier-prophet-statesman-lover. He did not belong to that group of chameleon personalities who display a dazzling assortment of talents and a confusing array of activities. His talents, like his aspirations, were indeed vast, but limited to the intellectual realms, and his commentators have been aware of both the failings and advantages incident to this "one-sidedness."[7] This tenacious intellectuality does not lack changing colors: sometimes it appears to be a clear, direct, measured drive toward philosophic meaning; at other times, when Hobbes is at his most combative, he seems like some kind of mad Knight of Reason. At all times, however, he would not let loose of a thought unless it were followed to the end and hobbled in a definition.

As comments by his friends remind us and as his vigorous style confirms, emphasis on these qualities can be carried too far. Hobbes was, above all, a complicated man. It would be fallacious to assume that his penchant for logical formulation discounted the capacity for sentiment or for a certain delicacy of insight. The inner necessity to create an intellectual order is a passion and a gift all its own that excludes no other, and Hobbes had not yet encountered the Romantic bifurcation of the critical intellect and the creative understanding. He could therefore profess not only a love of reason, but also of peace (as he put it) in the company of the muses.[8] The truth may simply be that his imagination was of a kind which, more than others, worked best with those symmetrical forms most suited to imitating nature's multifarious expressions of order, rather than her just amplitude.

The Biographical Problem of the Early Years

It is not possible to complete a preliminary sketch of Hobbes's background and character without mentioning a peculiarity in his life which relates to its remarkable chronology and which is of special importance to the procedures followed by his biographers: this singularity involves the fact that Hobbes produced no manuscript entailing an idea of political science until he was past fifty years of age, and his earliest manuscript on the philosophy of science was not written much earlier (probably between 1630 and 1636). His first publication appeared when he was forty-one years old, a translation of Thucydides, and it was, in almost every respect, a typically humanist essay. Aside from his classically sparse autobiography, not much is known about the period preceding this work, and one could speak without exaggeration of the entire first forty years of his life as the "dark years" in his biography. What we do know indicates that Hobbes spent most of this time cultivating various humanistic studies. He did write an early work in science (the so-called "Short Tract"), but this followed his Thucydides, and the relationship between the two books in terms of Hobbes's intellectual development is unclear.

The troubling questions that arise from this chronology may be reduced to a single one that asks: How did the early humanist scholar become, in a seemingly abrupt manner, the author of *Leviathan* and the philosopher whose method is modelled on rigorous scientific thinking?

The question involves a number of smaller ones to be discussed at the appropriate stages, but it is difficult even to focus on these questions and impossible to answer then definitively since the basis for any reconstruction of Hobbes's thought prior to his (late) publications must fall during his first forty "dark years." His biographers have treated this difficulty in essentially two ways. The simplest way is to follow Hobbes's own indications and to assume that his philosophizing began with his discovery of Euclid, after the translation of Thucydides. In his autobiography, he speaks of this discovery as a kind of milestone and the beginning of his employment of scientific method. He treats his subsequent thoughts on motion in the same way, and any biography must take these two parts of his doctrine into account. Both Leslie Stephen[9] and John Laird[10] use this approach in their biographies of Hobbes; and the organization of their books—separation of the biographical sections from the exposition of Hobbes's ideas—seems to be at least in part determined by the fact that they do not attempt to relate Hobbes's full biography (especially the "dark years") to his works in any organic sense, though Stephen in particular does take note of some of his historical context. Another approach is represented by Leo Strauss, who does investigate Hobbes's earliest work and who correctly assumes that "philosophy" includes such endeavors as Hobbes's translation of Thucydides, but he finds that there must be a "break" between Hobbes the humanist and Hobbes the scientist. Strauss finds this break not only within the philosopher's system, arguing that his naturalism is inconsistent with his moral philosophy, but he also attempts to establish a biographical framework in support of his theory, and thus posits a humanistic (early) period in Hobbes's life, and a scientific (later) period which began with his discovery of Euclid.[11]

The question is further confused by the appearance of still another Hobbes—a "scholastic" Hobbes, the Hobbes who studied scholastic philosophy at Oxford. When speaking of the beginning of Hobbes's philosophic career, some scholars refer to his rejection of scholasticism and to a dormant interest in philosophy that did not re-awaken until his Euclid discovery, as if his interest in Thucydides had no philosophic significance at all.[12]

Hobbes scholarship like that of Howard Warrender[13] and A. E. Taylor,[14] since it confines itself to an examination of his system in isolation and without reference to his biographical circumstances, is of course under no obligation to treat this question, nor are those scholars who are largely concerned with approaching his thought by comparing him to other representative thinkers without regard to biographical points. Thus Laird writes interestingly on the ideas of Bodin in comparison to Hobbes's,[15] and Eliot (among others) finds something to compare between Hobbes and Suarez.[16] However, anyone who does work out of Hobbes's biographical material must cope with his earliest period, and because of its obscurity it is inevitable that any evaluation of early influences will involve an historical reconstruction containing elements of conjecture and of reading backwards what one sees in the later Hobbes. The alternative, of course, is to give up trying to find out what Hobbes's roots were altogether: "The Leviathan is a fantastic monster, such as is sometimes cast up, with other strange births, in political, as in marine, convulsions. It is an isolated phenomenon in English thought, without ancestry or posterity; crude, academic, and wrong."[17] But some conjectures and reconstructions are more feasible than others, and some may even be incorrect and still meaningful enough.

The most noteworthy feature of this problem of Hobbes's transition from humanist to scientist or philosopher is that Hobbes himself nowhere indicates he found it the least bit problematic, making one suspect that the difficulty is imposed on his biography by the modern mind. In this respect, the Laird-Stephen approach, which does not explicitly raise the question at all, seems most satisfactory, although it denies us an understanding of how a mentality like Hobbes's developed out of a given cultural setting; it leaves the impression that his thought, while it had an historical setting, had no roots. The alternative approach, which does raise the question, is less satisfactory in that the problem of humanist *versus* scientific philosopher is itself predicated on a division among the disciplines that did not exist in the sixteenth and seventeenth centuries and therefore always necessitates an implausible "break" between philosopher, humanist, and scientist, depending on what these roles are taken to entail.[18] It is true that Hobbes mentions certain "lucky" ideas he came upon as he approached middle age (the Euclid and his idea on motion), and these ideas were extremely important in the evolution of his philosophy and scientific thought; but it is not psychologically feasible that *any* ideas could abolish forty years' worth of exposure to the classical authors, or, if they could, that he would have found them "lucky." The unbroken interest he expressed in literary things—in his youth by his reading, Latin compositions and translations, in his late middle age by his literary criticism, and in his old age by rendering both the *Iliad* and the *Odyssey* into English—would remain unexplained.

Renaissance thinkers naturally distinguished between the faculties necessary to the different scientific and humanistic disciplines in their various proportions. They also distinguished between appropriate methods and ends for the disciplines. But none would have thought of the disciplines as other than mutually determining viewpoints that acted in concert to shape the will and approach the truth. Since this was a traditional attitude, the reconstruction of Hobbes's early life offered in the following pages is based on an analysis of the traditional relationship between the disciplines in the period and their implications. It is not based on an attempt to solve the "problem" of his transition stated in that way, as a problem. It attempts, rather, to investigate the "given" terms of thought peculiar to the years during which he was educated and to explore the channels through which his thoughts might have flowed to arrive at his scientific philosophy. Some account is given of the particular milieu in which he lived, and some attempt is made to compare his idea of science to the major trends of English scientific thinking in the Restoration. But any view that categorically finds in Hobbes either a scientific or a purely political thinker to the exclusion of his humanistic training will be confronted by the specious problem of uniting in his person what appears to be an earlier un-Hobbesian classical scholar with the later Hobbesian philosopher.

Hobbes's contemporary critics, of which there were very many, never troubled themselves with the question of the compatibility of his interests. They were far more concerned about the compatibility of his materialism, his politics, and his theology with the Christian faith. He was, they said, manifestly an atheist. His ethics seemed to preclude an immutable and eternal morality, his materialism denied an incorporeal soul, and his metaphysics refused to grant reality to universals that were either antecedent to, or that subsisted in, particulars. Such essences or forms he regarded as the useless excrescences of the Schoolmen's illogic. The ironic consequence of this was that Hobbes, who was a man of both imagination and reason, and who had a Christian sense of duty, was reputed to be the author of that most unreasonable, un-Christian, and unimaginative doctrine which, with barbarian simplicity, holds that "might makes right."

Hobbes's political opinions, considered unpleasant to begin with, were made the more onerous because he conceived of them as doctrines to be put into practice, not mere academic theories: "For the inward glory and triumph of mind that a man may have for the mastering of some difficult and doubtful matter, or for the discovery of some hidden truth, is not worth so much pains as the study of Philosophy requires; . . . The end of knowledge is power."[19] Power is a far-reaching term in Hobbes for the means which allows us to achieve our ends: it is what one man holds over another when he is richer or more influential; it is what the local sheriff uses to apprehend criminals; and it is what a man with a club represents to a man without one. Coercive power is the least of its types, however. Power is also the power to build and civilize, the power to make nature yield the commodities requisite for a peaceful and secure life. Power is also what every man wants to protect himself against the things he fears and to ensure his future circumstances. It includes, finally, the political authority that a sovereign uses to make the state cohere. It was his opinions about this last kind of power, which his critics found either too great or too small according to their convictions, that made Hobbes spend many years first as a refugee and then as a polemicist.

While Hobbes professed to be a timid person, it was a strange kind of timidity that allowed him to broadcast his bold doctrines repeatedly, and the reputation he gained for them justifies Stephen's remark that "intellectual audacity combines awkwardly with personal timidity."[20] While courage is admired in Hobbes's writings, fear is not despised—it is the beginning of a necessary and cautious wisdom that served him well in turbulent times. Early in his career, he wrote of Anaxagoras that his "opinions, being a strain above the apprehension of the vulgar, procured him the estimation of an atheist . . . and in the end cost him his life."[21] Hobbes could not then have known with what relevance he was writing of himself, for he was to escape a similar fate only by virtue of his consistent preference for the counsels of prudence above the uncertain rewards of heroism.

I

The Education of
A Humanist

N apposition to Hobbes's name "humanist" may strike some as an irreverence to the names of More, Colet, Erasmus, and the others who established the standards of humanism in England; and so it would be if Hobbes represents only an attempt "to give, in terms of the 'new' philosophy, an exhaustive account of reality,"[1] in terms, that is, of contemporary mechanics. But to regard Hobbes as essentially an early herald of the English Enlightenment not only leads to insoluble difficulties in arriving at a feasible reconstruction of the development of his thought, it also deprives us of insights into the changes that took place between the late Elizabethan and late Stuart eras which Hobbes's long life offers us.

It is important for a correct perspective on Hobbes's life to recall that had he died before his forty-first year, he would probably be remembered today only as a rather minor representative of the last generation of Tudor humanists and translators who did so much to appropriate classical culture to the English language. This humanistic achievement of the Elizabethan period stood firmly grounded on the institution of its grammar schools; and Hobbes, like everyone else who attended them, acquired there a basic education in the learned languages, entailing in itself an introduction to classical thought and expression. The contemporary sources for biographical material on Hobbes[2] yield only enough information on his youth to fill a couple of pages; they certainly do not give detailed information about his early schooling, but the uniformity of Elizabethan grammar school education was such that one can speak with confidence about its general character. It was the first layer of traditional learning to be absorbed

25

by Hobbes, and his first step towards the goals of the Elizabethan educational processes, which were the cultivation of *ratio* and *oratio*, reasoned language.

Hobbes's early education was supported by Francis Hobbes, a glover, Malmesbury alderman, and brother of Thomas's absent and choleric father. Studying first at Westport, then at nearby Malmesbury, the eight-year-old Hobbes subsequently returned to Westport to be tutored by one Robert Latimer, a young Oxford man turned schoolmaster and reputedly the best Greek scholar to teach in the area since the Reformation. Latimer was pleased by his black-haired, hazel-eyed pupil (nicknamed "Crow"), and he took special pains to give further instruction to Thomas and a few other select students in the evenings.[3] The curriculum was naturally devoted chiefly to the principles of Latin and Greek grammar, syntax, and etymology. The exercises required numerous themes, translations, and re-translations, the latter being especially effective in sinking the texts of Tully, Caesar, Ovid, Vergil, and Prudentius deep into the student's bones. With grammar, which taught correctness in language and which included many parts of what is taught as literature today, went rhetoric, the art of speaking and writing well. First came the kinds of rhetoric, then the parts proper to each kind. This was followed by the divisions of the parts; the "places" of the divisions; and the figures and easier tropes, all learned by the application of the rules to classical texts and in the composition of themes. A good example of the depth and generality of this rhetorical and linguistic training in the Elizabethan schools can be seen in Edmund Hobbes, the philosopher's brother and schoolmate who became a glover, and who, despite the fact that he never pursued a scholarly career, could yet "make theme, and verse, and understood a little Greek to his dyeing day."[4]

Needless to say, the selected classical texts used by the schools were also intended to be the stuff of an ethical education. The precepts and examples of the ancients were learned thrice over in the course of a student's studies, and it was impressed upon him that persuasive speaking consisted in part of convincing his auditors of his honorable character. Every Renaissance student knew of Quintilian's insistence that the orator must be a *good* man, not only to impress the audience, but because speech is the reflection of a reasonable and ethical creature. Is not Caliban locked in his subhumanity and rudimentary speech by his lack of a moral nature?

> You taught me language; and my profit on't
> Is, I know how to curse. . . .
> (*The Tempest*, I, ii, 365–66)

Eloquence therefore, springs from the very fountain of understanding, or, in the phrase of Thomas Blount, "is chiefly grounded upon Wisdom."[5]

For six years Hobbes continued these studies, and there is nothing to indicate that he was in many respects an exceptional youth, other than the general approbation of his tutor. Edmund Hobbes reports that Thomas was playsome enough for his years as a boy, although even then he was given over to a "contemplative melancholiness."[6] At the least, however, he must have been endowed with very considerable powers of concentration since, at the age of fourteen, he repaid his tutor's labors by translating the Greek of Euripedes' *Medea* into Latin iambics. It was a substantial achievement, not diminished by the fact that it was accomplished in an era of marvellously learned children. This piece of juvenilia is lost, but it may be wondered how that play—full of Medea's fury and the passionate invocations to Zeus, Keeper of Oaths—sustained his attention to such an extent when his own adult writings display a logical movement so different. Perhaps this stray biographical detail is best regarded as a mark of Hobbes's linguistic progress and literary ability, as it always has been.[7] Yet, the theme of stern retribution for the unleashing of passions such as fragment the family and touch the state in *Medea* was later of consuming interest to Hobbes, and the tragedy unravelled in the play resembles the terrible vision of society's dissolution in his own works.[8]

Whatever the import of such speculations about images early impressed on Hobbes's mind, he had profited sufficiently from his studies by his fifteenth year to attend university, and his uncle, having profited sufficiently from the gloving business, continued to subsidize his education. He entered Magdalen Hall, Oxford, in 1603, and like so many eminent men of his time, he found little good to say of the universities in retrospect. The usual statutory curriculum continued grammar school studies by providing for two terms of grammar and four of rhetoric, during which one heard lectures on Linacre's *Rudiments* as well as some of the classical texts, and Aristotle's *Rhetoric* or Cicero's *Praeceptiones*.[9] The reforms of the humanists had succeeded in redressing the balance between logic and rhetorical studies in the universities, but dialectics or logic still retained a major place in the curriculum and Hobbes probably read and heard lectures on Aristotle and Porphyry for five terms, filling out his course of studies with several terms of arithmetic and music, based on the texts of Boethius. He tells us of having studied physics as well, i.e., natural philosophy, and of having struggled with the Aristotelian notions of 'species' that flew through the air, 'sympathy' and 'antipathy.'[10] These concepts were absorbed with difficulty, but if he already found them the bane of the university, he could not yet have found them the source of hilarity he was later to do since he was forced to learn them.

After his first year of residence, Hobbes most likely had to begin attending the disputations of upper classmen three times weekly for a year, and later take part in them himself as both respondent and opponent. At the end of his course work, he could petition for permission to take part in the Lenten exercises or "determinations"—the final public disputations requisite for admission to the bachelor or arts degree—which Hobbes did, earning the degree in February 1608. These requirements established the framework of the curriculum, but their rigidity was not unrelieved. There is good reason to believe that students, then as now, were not excessively diligent about attending lectures, and the statutes regarding declamations were not always strictly fulfilled; more modern texts were becoming available, and additional flexibility arose from the fact that discipline was not one of Oxford's strongest points.[11]

In the time Hobbes could spare from his academic obligations, he enjoyed dawdling at the local bookbinder's shop where he did "lye gaping on mappes" both terrestrial and astronomical, tracing in his mind the progress of the sun through the skies and the routes of Cavendish and Drake ("Filo Neptunum") over the seas.[12] Aside from such extracurricular work in astronomy and geography, Hobbes liked to lure jackdaws to strike at a bait of cheese parings attached to a limed pack-thread; and many years later in his study of optics, he still remembered this collegiate pastime, having wondered at the keen eyesight of the birds.[13] With respect to his studies, Hobbes says that although he thought himself a good disputant and well advanced in the philosophers, he preferred to return to the study of the classics, which he had learned only imperfectly before.[14]

There has been considerable speculation about what influence these years at Oxford had on Hobbes's later thought. His education is frequently described as having been primarily philosophical, scholastic, and logical in its coloring. Hobbes roughly confirms this impression, and the deductive methods of thinking associated with the schools undoubtedly found in him a kindred spirit. But while the education offered by the universities was scholastic in kind, scholasticism was not, after all, a specific content: it was an intellectual form that served to organize and communicate knowledge, and within which conflicting opinions could be analyzed and examined. It was an Aristotelian education, but of Aristotelianisms there were many, and which one Hobbes imbibed is not now known.

It is perhaps more important to remember the continuing force of rhetorical training in an age before the printed word became so ubiquitous. Besides the substantive representation of rhetorical studies gained through humanistic influences in the schools, the rhetorical element was strongly implicated in the dialectical pedagogy of the Schoolmen by the whole system of disputations, for where the student was not engaged in rigidly scientific demonstrations, debating constantly encouraged him to translate wordless thinking into suasive forms of language.[15] The two disciplines, dialectic and rhetoric, should not be kept too far separated in our minds when discussing seventeenth-century education since they could hardly be kept entirely distinct at the time; both were applicable to arguing topics based on opinion and arriving at probable truths, as opposed to the strictly formal truths derived from demonstrative syllogisms. Since Hobbes's later thought is so largely based on language analysis, the fluidity and interplay between these two forms require some emphasis: ever since the time of Plato, dialectic had a marked propensity to encroach on logic proper, while rhetoric, ever since the Sophists, had similarly tended to absorb literary and grammatical studies. But scholastic logicians had busied themselves with speculative grammar as well, and rhetoricians had traditionally taught the forms of logic proper to their art. Thus, dialectic was merged sometimes with logic and sometimes with rhetoric, showing in the organization of these academic disciplines that the languages of reason and passion, of science and poetry, were cut from whole cloth.

When Hobbes went to Oxford, then, he received a traditional education aimed at producing men who could speak correctly and eloquently, and whose ability to reason and persuade was cultivated through exercising the faculties of invention (*inventio*) and judgment (*iudicium*) in the basic disciplines of the *trivium*. The importance of the rhetorical tradition in Hobbes's work will be taken up later, but at this stage in his life it had the significance of being practical. It was intimately tied up with that fluency and ease in the learned languages and that copiousness of expression which never failed him and which qualified him to be a man of letters in a Latinate age. "Indeed," writes Foster Watson,

If there is one school subject which seems to have preeminently influenced the writers, statesmen and gentlemen of the 16th and 17th centuries, in their intellectual outfit in after life, probably the claim for this leading position may justly be made for Rhetoric and the Oration.[16]

When Hobbes received his degree, he was a tall, not very robust scholar of somewhat yellowish complexion. His origins were humble enough; he had little worldly experience, small means, and no reputation. The scholar still belonged to a rather amorphous class in society whose prospects for employment were uncertain, and for those who, like Hobbes, had not taken Holy Orders, the situation was even less promising. Through the good offices of John Wilkinson, the Calvinist Principal of Magdalen Hall, Hobbes was recommended to William Cavendish, Baron of Hardwick, who needed a tutor for his son, and Hobbes was retained for the position. Leaving behind him the Puritanism of the college, he moved into the royalist household of one of the great families of Stuart England, forming an affiliation with the Cavendishes that lasted the rest of his life.

Part tutor and part page to the Baron's son William, Hobbes waited on him as he made his calls in London, and accompanied him as he hunted and hawked in the country. With a pupil only two years his junior, Hobbes began a new way of life that must have taken time from his Latin studies, for we are told that he could be seen reading Caesar's *Commentaries* in antechambers and lobbies as he waited while William was visiting.[17] Minding his young master's privy purse was also part of his duties, but his charge was open-handed and Hobbes was perhaps not altogether successful as a financial manager, for he was sent up and down in search of creditors, which William was too ashamed to do himself. In the performance of this unpleasant chore, Aubrey reports that Hobbes was apt to drench his feet and take cold, adding inscrutably that the philosopher (what is most difficult to imagine) "trod both his shoes aside the same way." "Notwithstanding," we are assured, "he was well-beloved."[18]

In 1610, the Baron sent his son for that indispensable part of a seventeenth-century nobleman's education, the Grand Tour; Hobbes went along as an escort, though it was an adventure in which he was

William Cavendish, First Earl of Devonshire (1552–1626). Unknown artist. Devonshire Collection, Chatsworth. Reproduced by permission of the National Trust and the Courtauld Institute of Art.

as ignorant as his pupil. The journey receives scant notice in his writing, but since William was of gentle birth and high spirits, it is certain that the pair were well received and they probably sought out whatever novelties they could find. In addition, Hobbes acquired some knowledge of the French and Italian languages, equipping himself for the learning of the new age as his Latin and Greek had opened that of the past to him.

Without more specific information about the trip, one can only note that those were good years for an intelligent young man to be on the Continent. At the time, the Bands of Orion, though not loosened, were being subjected to Galileo's penetrating examination. His observations were published in the *Sidereus Nuncius* in March 1610, the volume greatly supporting the Copernican doctrine and reporting the discovery of the satellites of Jupiter. The following year, Kepler published his *Dioptrics;* Fabricius wrote on sunspots; Peiresc discovered the Great Nebula in Orion. In Paris, John Donne was writing his *Anniversaries,* and finding in the achievements of the New Philosophy an argument for impermanence, for men confess this world is spent

> When in the Planets, and the Firmament
> They seeke so many new, . . .

We know that this startling activity in science did not pass Hobbes by since he remarks in his autobiography that it was during this journey that he learned how widely the philosophy of the schools was held in contempt by the most advanced thinkers on the Continent.[19] But it is most difficult to determine exactly what impact this exposure to the critical new philosophy had on Hobbes, and what this *via moderna* among Renaissance philosophies represented for him. Hobbes tells us that when he returned to England, he intended to resume his humanistic studies rather than his scholastic ones, and this he appears to have done for the next quarter of a century or so. He pursued with particular diligence the development of his Latin style, "non ut floride, sed ut Latine posset scribere, et vim verborum cogitatis congruentem invenire; itaque verba disponere, ut lectio perspicua et facilis esset."[20] From the beginning, it was a perspicuous style he cultivated; clarity and the vigorous representation of ideas in suitable language, not floridity.

These remarks in his *Vita* tend to sustain the impression that his journey had, in fact, resulted in a disillusionment with the philosophic methods he had learned in Oxford, yet the *Vita* was written at the age of eighty-four and may reflect too much the wisdom of hindsight. Moreover, even if he was disillusioned enough to relinquish scholastic philosophy, we do not know if he considered his intellectual stake in that philosophy a significant one to give up; nor can it be said that he would have considered such a move tantamount to renouncing philosophy altogether, as is sometimes assumed.

Whatever stage his intellectual development had now reached, Hobbes was in an excellent position to satisfy his curiosity in the ample library at Chatsworth. He remained there in the Cavendish household long after his services as a tutor were needed, assuming some secretarial duties and spending his leisure time reading the histories and literature of antiquity, together with the best commentaries on them.[21] He even invested considerable time perusing "romances."[22] He enjoyed music, always approving of it as part of the worship of God as opposed to those who thought it too sportive, and he practiced the viol and flute.[23]

Hobbes was still enjoying this agreeable way of life in 1618, when Baron Hardwick received the title of first Earl of Devonshire, and he was still doing so eight years later when the Earl died and Hobbes's former pupil, William, succeeded his father to the title. It was sometime during this period that Hobbes took down notes from the dictation of Francis Bacon as they walked in the gardens of Gorhambury, and he helped the former chancellor translate some of his essays into Latin.[24] Retained by an eminent family, Hobbes could meet and talk with men who were accomplished not only in the arts and sciences, but who were also prominent in affairs of the state. He may have been too young to understand the political repercussions of the Queen's death in 1603, but the significance of Prince Henry's untimely death in 1612 would not have escaped him, nor could the ineffectiveness of James I and his Protestant allies in their command of the Thirty Years War. A letter to Hobbes from one Robert Mason tells us that Hobbes was keeping abreast of political events by 1622 at the latest. Mason's letter, a reply to a lost letter from Hobbes, is full of the news of who's in and who's out: Sir Horace Vere was out for giving up Mannheim, he says, and both Hobbes and his correspondent seem to follow public opinion in having favored the royal match with the Protestant Elector Palatine and in opposing one with Catholic Spain.[25]

Not much later, as a New Year's gift for his master, Hobbes described an excursion to the Derbyshire Peak near Chatsworth in a poem of more than five hundred Latin hexameters, aptly entitled *De*

Mirabilibus Pecci Carmen. The poem is of little interest here (Hobbes himself thought little of it later)[26] except that it shows Hobbes's continued delight in this classical form, and the way he chose to amuse himself during these obscure years. Much later, the philosopher looked back on this lengthy tenure with the Cavendish family as the happiest period in his life. It came to an end when the second Earl died in 1628, shortly after his father, and when his son was still a child too young for Hobbes's tutoring. Hobbes prepared to leave the family in whose service he had been for two decades; he was approaching the age of forty and he had not yet published one single word of all those works which today comprise the fifteen substantial volumes of the collected Molesworth edition. But he had not been idle, and a manuscript that had been completed some time before, but put aside, now found its way to a London printer. It was dedicated to the late Earl and addressed to his infant son, William. On November 6, 1628, Hobbes took care to submit the dedication to Lady Devonshire for her perusal and alteration with his customary deference, asking that she return it "as soon as conveniently may be, because the Press will shortly be ready for it."[27] Hobbes was a little anxious about the publication of his first book; it was an occasion of some moment for him, and he came to it with mixed feelings.

William Cavendish, Second Earl of Devonshire (1590–1628). Unknown artist. Hardwick Hall collection. Reproduced by permission of the National Trust and the Courtauld Institute of Art.

II

Thucydides Placuit

Sed mihi prae reliquis Thucydides placuit.
L.W., I, lxxxviii

RUTH and elocution are the soul and body of history, said Hobbes,[1] and Thucydides pleased him beyond all other historians by his excellence in both. Hobbes procrastinated for some time before committing his translation of the *History of the Peloponnesian War* to a publisher, partly because he had some reservations about the reception it would get. Even though the manuscript had gained the approbation of several of his literary friends, yet Hobbes felt that "there is something, I know not what, in the censure of a multitude, more terrible than any single judgment, how severe or exact soever."[2] The pains Hobbes had taken with his work made his hesitation unnecessary; his translation far surpassed that of his one English predecessor, Thomas Nichol, and Robertson refers to the work as "great."[3] Nichol's "crude"[4] version of the *History* in 1550 was based on the French of Claude de Seyssel (which, in turn, was based on the Latin of Laurentius Valla), whereas Hobbes worked directly from the Greek edition of Æmilius Porta,[5] further improving his text by illustrating it with maps. Such a work was the altogether appropriate result of half a lifetime spent mainly in the study of the ancient languages and authors. Emerging from the obscurity of his early years in this translation, Hobbes reveals a thoroughly humanistic mind, yet one can discern there the outlines of some of his later characteristics, as one can discern at great distances the already familiar features of a man, walking out of the darkness and carrying a small light.

The most readily and frequently observed characteristic of Hobbes's later thought which already appears in the *History* is his marked preference for monarchy.[6] He was goaded into the publication of the

History by the appearance of the Petition of Right in the previous year, finding in Thucydides an argument for the king. He notes that Thucydides distrusted both democracies and aristocracies, preferring a mixed or constitutional form of government, but approving, above all, of the form represented by Pericles' reign, which was a democracy in name, but a monarchy in fact.[7] He argues from the historian's text that the multitude is irresolute and easily swayed by demagogues, while the aristocracy is factious and full of seditious ambitions.

But contemporary politics was merely the occasion for Hobbes's publication of the *History;* his central concerns while writing it were of a somewhat different order. Aside from technical problems of translation posed by Thucydides' difficult prose, Hobbes faced two more general but related questions when he set to work on the *History.* As a teacher, he had to consider the pedagogic value of his translation and of history as a whole; as a humanist scholar, he was also concerned about the writing of history as a literary form. The prefatory materials to the Thucydides translation in which these questions are discussed have three parts: a short statement "to the Readers"; an uncommonly graceful dedicatory epistle addressed to William Cavendish, paying tribute to the integrity and "heroic virtue" of William's father, and suggesting that history teaches such virtue; and an essay entitled "On the Life and History of Thucydides." The last is the fullest, sketching Thucydides' life and setting forth Hobbes's own considerations on historiography, and it is the portion of most interest here.

Hobbes's prefatory essay is balanced and cleanly written, but it is nonetheless overlaid with a tissue of commonplaces current among historians of the time, many of them derived, directly or indirectly, from Cicero's application of rhetoric to history in *De Oratore,* which is cited a number of times. Many points that one would like to see as anticipations of Hobbes's later dispassionate approach to political behavior are exactly such traditional formulae. Hobbes, for instance, recommends Thucydides as an historian who never digressed to point a moral, never wrote to satisfy a grudge, and never hid the truth under an over-ornate prose.[8] His aim was to instruct by history, not primarily to delight "as if it were a song,"[9] he adds, thus echoing not only Thucydides' own words,[10] but also repeating what was a platitude among many Renaissance historians. If it seems appropriate that the future author of an authentic political science should pay tribute to the impartiality of the past creator of political history, yet exhortations to objectivity were usual among contemporary historians, even the most patently partial ("Indifferency and even dealing are the Glory of Historians,"[11] cried Edmund Bolton).[12] Thus, while Hobbes's appreciation of Thucydides' impartiality and objectivity may indeed have been a kind of salute from a kindred spirit, not much can be concluded from it: Milton, after all, praised Sallust (in many respects the Latin disciple of Thucydides) for much the same reasons as Hobbes applauded the Greek,[13] yet Milton never went on to develop a "science" of politics. In stressing the priority of truth above the delights of rhetoric or the utility of propaganda, both the poet and the philosopher were simply distinguishing the office proper to the historian from that of the rhetorician or politician, as Aristotle had done long before them.[14] But it is precisely among such commonplaces on the uses and nature of history that one must look for Hobbes's fundamental concerns, and it is among these surviving ideas from classical culture that one can find the beginnings of his own political thought.

The Basic Problem: History as Education

Hobbes's employment as a tutor would suffice, by itself, to explain his interest in history since history played an important role in the education of the English aristocracy, or as Cleland says, it "should be the chiefest study of a young Noble man, when he commeth to any perfection of speech and understanding."[15] It was particularly prized for inculcating practical judgment or prudence, for as Cicero noted, followed by most Renaissance historians, history is a storehouse of *exempla,* an artificial memory from which the student could accumulate experience quickly. Civic morality and political insight were the topics of central importance in training youths who would become servants of the state, and this was where history excelled: in history, said Hobbes, "actions of *honour* and *dishonour* do appear plainly and distinctly which are which," and a man could therefore learn from it to bear himself "prudently in the present and providently towards the future."[16]

The opinion was widely held that historical examples were more effective in teaching prudence and civic virtue than philosophic precepts, and Strauss rightly observes that "the opposition of philosophic precept and historical example . . . recurs again and again in the literature on the subject in the sixteenth century."[17] This opposition arose from the belief that the precepts of reason and philosophy may be true, but a student who sees the truth may not be moved to apply it; he is far more apt to do so if inspired by forceful examples that appeal to his emotions,[18] a form of argument proper to rhetoric, not philosophy. Strauss maintains that Hobbes turned to history because of this superiority of example over precept in the application of ethical norms,[19] and it is true, as will be seen, that Hobbes favors history *for the purposes of teaching*. But even here, Hobbes expresses some doubts, for just as politicians and rhetoricians wrote history for the wrong (partisan) reasons, so history was frequently read for the wrong reasons:

Men come to the reading of history with an affection like that of the people of Rome: who came to the spectacle of the gladiators with more delight to behold their blood, than their skill in fencing. For they be far more in number that love to read of great armies, bloody battles, and many thousands slain... than mind the art by which the affairs both of armies and cities be conducted to their ends.[20]

While Hobbes follows the convention of dismissing this problem as irrelevant to the "better sort of readers" for whom he wrote and who presumably read with more judgment, the issue was not to be so easily dismissed in his mind and it reappears in different forms throughout the essay. The distinction between two ways of reading—the one with judgment, the other with emotion—is like the earlier distinction between history and song: both are only special cases of the more general problem that is Hobbes's central concern, namely the conflict between reason and passion.

Hobbes's distinction between passions stirred instead of truths communicated, or wisdom versus eloquence, was of course numbered among the *loci communes* of the times; it is a question that underlies the opposition between example and precept, and when fully expanded, it becomes a conflict among the disciplines, reflected in different educational theories. If history was considered the favored road to the education of the citizen and the prince, it was also the battleground for these conflicting ideas on education. Around it was resuscitated the old debate about whether virtue—including civic virtue—was teachable to begin with, and if so, whether it was better taught by the dialectically established truths of the philosophers, by the moving examples of the rhetors, or by the delightful myths of the poets. Renaissance historians were few who did not allude to the conflict between Plato and Isocrates, or who did not note as Hobbes did, that the truths of precept are secure but fail to move the will, whereas eloquence alone presents only the picture of history and is therefore "unapt to instruct."[21] It was this issue, seen essentially as a pedagogic one, that occupied Hobbes in his translation, caught his imagination, and perhaps even initially directed it into a firmly political channel, as I shall try to show. At bottom, it was the question of the possibility of a moral education, of how a man may be moved to become a more virtuous member of the community through an appropriate method of argument.

Hobbes discusses these issues within a limited framework in the Thucydides essay, but with clear reference to the broader lines of argument found in the classical philosophers. Those lines of argument, though they can only be briefly recalled here, indicate the range of the issues and the relationships which Hobbes had in mind when he wrote. The Protagorean ideal of using rhetoric to link philosophy to life, theory to practice, was still alive in Hobbes's day, and it regarded rhetorical instruction as a political *techné* or art that shaped the virtuous citizen out of the raw materials of youth. Hobbes was also certainly aware of the view of the later Sophists who equated politics and rhetoric for all practical purposes and who therefore professed to give political instruction; yet they simultaneously denied that they taught ethics, asserting that virtuous conduct could not be taught. The inevitable consequence of this position was to regard rhetoric as a purely formal discipline, and politics was accordingly reduced to the manipulation of public opinion through eloquence.[22] Socrates therefore remarked with some disgust that rhetoric was a skill like that of the pastry chef whose sauces make food seem good that is otherwise unpalatable, and other schools joined in taking bitter issue with the Sophists.[23]

Plato, finding that education for the state begins with knowledge of the virtues, suggested that practical ethics could be taught effectively if guided by strict dialectic rather than resting on mere opinion, as rhetorical arguments did. Aristotle similarly opposed the Sophists when he began his analysis of politics with a discussion of the end of the *polis*—human welfare—and identified it with the *arché* of ethics as well, reuniting the two as complementary sciences.[24] Rhetoric he subsumes under dialectic since they are both universal arts and since persuasion, the goal of rhetoric, is a kind of demonstration, which is the goal of dialectic.[25] While he would like rhetoric to rely more on reasoning and less on emotional appeal, he concedes that the rhetor's art consists of finding all means of persuasion for any position, and he concludes rather ruefully that no separate names exist for the ethical and unethical orator.[26] Like Plato, he found the Sophists ethically irresponsible, and the rhetors did not escape blame for the inflammatory political debate and moral disintegration in Athens during the wars of which Thucydides wrote.

The ideal resolution of this many-cornered conflict stood behind the repeated efflorescence of the Ciceronian tradition, which dreamt of uniting wisdom with eloquence, ethical intelligence with the power to persuade and to rule. Hobbes's essay concentrates on the same conflict, his caveats on precept and example, reason and passion, standing squarely in the tradition of these ancient debates. To perceive the truth is a work of reason; to be moved to apply it requires the stirring of the passions. Hobbes grasped that there was an inherent contradiction between the means (rhetoric, eloquence) and the ends (truth, wisdom) stipulated by the humanist tradition for a civic education. When he begins his essay by defining history as "truth and elocution," relating them as soul and body, he is pointing to history as an area in which this contradiction might find its resolution. The whole of his discussion of historical writing is, in fact, an elaboration of this definition, particularly of elocution (style and method), as will be shown in the next section.

The point here is merely to stress the centrality of this old conflict in Hobbes's mind at the time, and to indicate in what light he viewed it. Much later in his life the same issue recurs, rephrased in terms of a psychological "contrariety":

Again, in all deliberation [they say], and in all pleadings, the faculty of solid reasoning is necessary: for without it, the resolutions of men are rash, and their sentences unjust: and yet, if there be not powerful eloquence, which procureth attention and consent, the effect of reason will be little. But these are contrary faculties: the former being grounded upon principles of truth; the other upon opinions . . . true or false; and upon the passions of men, which are different and mutable.[27]

In this passage, the "contrariety" of faculties is brought into relation with two of the three accepted types of rhetoric (the deliberative and forensic), whereas in the Thucydides essay he treats it in terms of the form of rhetoric proper for writing history such that it will instruct.

History in particular was caught up in this conflict because of its special relation with rhetoric: history deals with the rise and fall of states, and its roots therefore lie in deliberative rhetoric, as do its methods. But insofar as history is supposed to teach the causes of events, its aims are philosophic, and its worth rests on its truth. What Hobbes required to resolve these contradictions was a rhetoric that would convey the truths of political affairs even as it shaped the passions to conform with "heroic virtue."

While it is hardly a novel idea to suggest that the thinkers of Renaissance England were interested in the relationship between wisdom and eloquence, reason and passion, it is worth observing that Hobbes's approach to politics was by route of these ancient themes and the complex of ideas associated with them. The Thucydides translation is, after all, the first time we find Hobbes dealing with language as a political theme. He does so indirectly by allusion to the wisdom-eloquence conflict with its political ramifications, but also directly by remarking at some length on Thucydides' keen awareness of the psychological force of language as a means of social control. The Greek historian's version of the Peloponnesian War is largely the story of the fragmentation of Athens under the opposing influences of demagogues representing different factions and cultural views, and Hobbes notes that the wavering of the people's judgment when inflamed by rhetors was not only Thucydides' reason for distrusting democracies, it was also his reason for remaining aloof from politics himself.[28] The *History* is a case study of the failure of rhetoric to perform as an instrument of political deliberation and its transformation into an instrument of political instigation. In these terms, civil disruption can be described as a breakdown in the proper functions of language, and with it, the breakdown of the shared values of the community that language stabilizes. In Hobbes's later writings, the main social function of language is the communication of the law: through the sovereign's command, the common ethical norms of the community are expressed and established. Where there is no law, there is no society, only a mob, and there is no publicly acknowledged distinction between just and unjust. It is language, in short, that takes us out of the state of nature.

Thucydides was no Hobbesian, but Hobbes could have had no better source of inspiration or confirmation for his ideas on language than the Greek historian's description of the effect of demagogues on language and political passions. Hobbes's translation of the famous passage on the sedition of Corcyra is pungent:

War . . . is a most violent master, and conformeth most men's passions to the present occasion. . . . The received value of names imposed for signifi- cation of things, was changed into arbitrary. For inconsiderate boldness, was counted true-hearted manliness: provident deliberation, a handsome fear; modesty, the cloak of cowardice; to be wise in every thing, to be lazy in every thing. A furious suddenness was reputed a point of valour. . . . He that did insidiate, if it took, was a wise man; but he that could smell out a trap laid, a more dangerous man than he. But he that had been so provident as not to need to do the one or the other, was said to be a dissolver of society. In brief, he that could outstrip another in the doing of an evil act, or that could persuade another thereto that never meant it, was commended.[29]

Years later, in *Leviathan*, Hobbes's dour formulation of this way in which social norms hinge on customs of speech and decline concur- rently with them in violent times is striking: "Force, and fraud, are in war the two cardinal virtues."[30]

Thus the themes and conflicts which concern Hobbes in his essay as problems in the uses of rhetoric and history are reflected as political themes in Thucydides' text, and they would appear in Hobbes's later work as direct philosophical themes. It is suggested then, that Hobbes, through his very involvement in the spirit of classical culture and its legacy in the humanistic tradition, was led in a natural way to one of the most characteristic features of his later thought: his reflections on the linkings between the uses of speech and the powers and fate of the state.[31]

This line of thought concerning the relationship between rhetoric and politics may well have been supported by the fact that the condi- tions in Athens were mirrored to some extent in England: both de- manded of the successful politician a distinctive talent for rhetoric. Here the deepest roots of the humanistic rhetorical tradition, which lay close to the civic institutions of Greece and in the Roman *fora*, are approached. In classical times, as in Hobbes's, the statesman found the art of rhetoric essential for persuading the assembly of the wis- dom of his polity; the lawyer and barrister learned forensic from it to find the arguments best suited to pleading the justice of his cause; the public figure and pulpit preacher found in rhetoric the oratorical means for praising honor with eloquence and denigrating the base with instructive force. As an art then, rhetoric addressed itself to the very business of citizenship, giving its prominent place in seventeenth-century education a firmly practical basis.

In the context of this cluster of ideas, it is useful to look ahead and note the semantic or "legalistic" cast of Hobbes's later philosophy. It stemmed, in part, from his conviction that if the fundamental concepts of government—concepts like sovereign, law and right—were properly understood by the people, they would grasp the nature of their civic obligations more clearly and would be less susceptible to the manipulations of those who were rhetorically talented, but foolish or unprincipled. A generalization of geometry's axiomatic method later provided Hobbes with a means for elaborating his ideas, but the initial problem of fixing the meaning of words relating to public life and ethics goes back to the Thucydides period and his understanding at that time of the connection between language and communal stability.[32]

Truth and Elocution in History

Hobbes's definition of history as "truth and elocution" led him in the course of his essay to consider the notions of "method" and "evidence," ideas of undeniable importance in his later works. The formula itself, however, is derived from the usual five parts of rhetoric taught in the schools since antiquity. Two of the parts, *memoria* and *pronunciatio*, are irrelevant to written oratory and were, in all events, of no importance in Renaissance curricula, so they are excluded. *Elocutio*, which dealt with the elements of style, and *dispositio*, which dealt with the arrangement of material, are combined by Hobbes under "elocution." *Inventio*, the fifth part, dealt with gathering and investigating the material to discover arguments, and this is replaced by Hobbes with "truth." Hobbes's "truth" is like the usual *inventio* insofar as he discusses the collection of information under that heading, praising Thucydides for his diligence and thoroughness. It also includes for Hobbes the truthfulness of the historian, and he again finds Thucydides free of taint since he wrote without attempting to flatter either the authorities or the crowds.[33] But the scope given to *inventio* by both Aristotle and Cicero had been "true or *apparently* true arguments," and Hobbes's departure from these classical authorities seems intended to place historical rhetoric in a separate and more restricted class, such that its arguments can only be drawn from veracious facts and infer true conclusions.

In discussing the types of argument proper to rhetoric, it is useful to recall the overlapping of the disciplines already noted in Hobbes's education. Because men are not persuaded by eloquence alone, rhetoric also undertook to teach some parts of logic. The rhetorical example and enthymeme were ideal political instruments since they were quickly grasped and suited to speaking before mass audiences; they represented the forms of logic suited to rhetoric. History itself is a kind of teaching by example or a type of induction, while the enthymeme represented a variety of the syllogism.[34] Thus Aristotle said that rhetoric was not only an offshoot of politics (or ethics), but also of dialectic, for the end of rhetorical arguments is persuasion (*pistis*), which is a form of demonstration (*apodeixis*).[35] The effect of Hobbes's substitution of *inventio* by "truth" is therefore to prevent the arguments of history from falling under the domination of appeals to emotion of rhetorical trickery. In effect, he makes historical argumentation a separate branch of rhetoric by insisting that its dialectic be true; that is, that the facts be veracious and the reasoning sound.

The second part of Hobbes's definition of history—"elocution"—is composed of style and method or disposition, terms which Hobbes understands to be synonymous. Thucydides' style receives high praise from Hobbes for its purity of language, its grave and sinuous expression, and its sentences that run "thick with sense."[36] Hobbes's own translation is mostly remarkable for a compactness and forcefulness of style which tries to approximate the original. It exemplifies, moreover, the style recommended for historians by most rhetorical texts of the times, which required brevity, conciseness, aptness, and clarity.[37] Hobbes also defends Thucydides' style in some detail against the charges of Dionysius of Halicarnassus, who carped at his difficult use of some verb and noun forms, his use of antitheta, and other technical points, and everywhere Hobbes shows himself to be conscious and concerned about the propriety and efficacy of the language. There is no question therefore that Hobbes's objections to rhetorical garnishments were not directed against the art of rhetoric itself, but against its indecorous employment. Thucydides, on the contrary, is highly rated for the strength of his rhetoric; Dionysius is taxed for being a rhetorician in the crippling sense of continually sacrificing truth in favor of delight.[38]

Under the second part of "elocution"—method or disposition—Hobbes deals with the arrangement of materials, a crucial area since method determines how the sequence of cause and effect (the "truth" of the reasoning) is structured and also because the very word "method" was an increasingly loaded term, a nesting place for two concepts of unquestionable importance to the development of early modern science, evidence and demonstration. The questions of method that arise here concern such things as the over-all movement of the history (where it should begin and end), the disposition of events in time (Thucydides' use of winter and summer chronological divisions), the order of proofs of causality, and the extent to which all this may affect the selection of materials. Everywhere Hobbes's criterion for successful elocution is the same: the lucidity and force gained by truth when language is brought into its proper and adequate relation with the subject matter, so that "the narration itself doth secretly instruct the reader, and more effectually than can possibly be done by precept."[39] This happens when the "body" of history (elocution) is so shaped and colored that it vividly figures forth its "soul" (truth).

So far, Hobbes's idea of elocution (including both method and style) has more in common with the Renaissance literary-critical term "decorum" than it has with the Royal Society's later notion of a "plain" style, with its affinities to the concept of "method" in science and natural philosophy. This early concept of method as rhetorical disposition was entirely appropriate for a humanist translator who regarded historiography as a form of written oratory,[40] and whose critical vocabulary was largely derived from the ancients.

The meaning of Hobbes's terms becomes somewhat more complicated, however, when account is taken of the relation between "elocution" and his other critical concepts. Thucydides' method pleased him because of its lucidity, force, and judiciousness, but the word he repeats most in praise of both style and method is "perspicuity," a much-used literary term of the time. "Perspicuitas" was closely associated with "evidentia" and *enargeia* in contemporary rhetoric textbooks, accumulating several other related meanings in the course of its history of translation as well. Its meanings ranged from the basic and simple "clarity" to "vividness" or "illumination"; it was a quality of brightness or, when used to characterize the effects of various kinds of rhetorical description and word-painting, it implied a certain forwardness.[41] When employed as a rhetorical ornament in historical narrative, "perspicuity" is the evocation of the actuality of the past, an endowing of the past with palpability. Thus, testifying to the perspicuity of Thucydides' style, Hobbes cites Plutarch's laudatory remarks:

Thucydides aimeth always at this; to make his auditor a spectator, and to cast his reader into the same passions that they were in that were beholders. . . . [Scenes] are so described and so evidently set before our eyes that the mind of the reader is no less affected therewith than if he had been present in the action.[42]

By skillful description, the historian provokes the emotions of a spectator in the reader, and the events thereby become "evident"—a word that appears several times in the Hobbes essay and one that he uses more in the older meaning of the immediately manifest or "seen." While the events of the past are not open to present observation, yet the historian can present true images of them which the reader observes and thus becomes an indirect eyewitness to them.

Surely this is not what modern historians mean by "evidence," nor was Hobbes really satisfied to substitute belief engendered in the reader for a demonstration of historical causes and consequences. The nature of history, he said, is "merely narrative," and no style, no matter how vivid, could of itself make historical narrative instructive. This depended, in part, on having that "better sort of reader" mentioned before, a "man of understanding":

So that look how much a man of understanding might have added to his experience, if he had then lived a beholder of their proceedings, and familiar with the men and business of the time: so much almost may he profit now, by attentive reading of the same here written. He may from the narrations draw out lessons to himself, and of himself be able to trace the drifts and counsels of the actors to their seat.[43]

But it also depended on having the lessons embedded in the narrative so that they could be drawn out, and this was a matter of the second part of elocution, the method of the historian. Thucydides' method was perspicuous because, as was earlier remarked, "the narration itself doth secretly instruct," and the historian need not digress to point a moral, but lets it grow out of the sequence of events. Thucydides' major rhetorical device was the use of fictive speeches interspersed in the narration and put into the mouths of statesmen and generals. These deliberative orations (as Hobbes and the rhetoricians called them) showed what reasons the leaders gave to the public, and what means of persuasion they used, to garner support from the citizenry for their actions. These speeches, which give the immediate causes for actions, might admittedly represent only the pretexts of the orators, but Hobbes argues that "true and inward motives" are only conjectural, and not always "of that evidence, that a historiographer should be always bound to take notice of it."[44] Besides, even merely avowed motives fall within the field of historical causation since "without a pretext, no war follows."[45]

Deliberative orations are also used by Thucydides to deal with the underlying causes of war, however, and in them he treats of economic factors, opposing ideals, the clash of cultures, and the consequences of the alternative policies considered by statesmen.[46] In the Funeral Oration, for instance, Pericles depicts the Athenian image of itself as possessing a thriving, free, and highly developed culture that was the reward for its enterprise, ingenuity, and industry. But the Corinthian view, developed with considerable force in the Melian dialogue, sees Athenian prosperity as a threatening and aggressive expansionism. Both kinds of causation are presented in orations, but the underlying causes are abstracted historical concepts made concrete by rhetoric, while the immediate causes are themselves rhetorical motifs that form a part of the events in history. Hobbes calls the interweaving of the two and their sequential treatment "clear and natural";[47] it is a perspicuous technique because "the narrative itself doth secretly instruct the reader," the "lessons" emerging out of the flow of events themselves.

Hobbes's recognition of Thucydides' intentions in using a method of dialectically opposed fictive orations is clear in the fact that he finds no conflict between such reconstructed speeches and his requirements for "truth" in the historian. Indeed, he sees the coherence derived by an historical work from its method as itself part of historical perception: "In sum, if the truth of a history did ever appear by the manner of relating, it doth so in this history: so coherent, perspicuous and persuasive is the whole narration.[48]

The implications of this position are noteworthy, particularly since it is the first place we find Hobbes discussing causality. It is not so important that Hobbes objected to the biased digressions of previous historians, or that he was concerned about impartial documentation (in which he expressed only moderate interest), or that he rejected mere authority; it is rather much more important that he found in Thucydides a firm concept of causality arising out of the logic of events themselves. Such a concept, which also separates modern historiography from that of the seventeenth-century annals and universal histories, is necessary before significant historical periods and transitions can be marked off in accordance with major changes in principal causative factors.[49] Still more important, however, is that Hobbes's demands for impartiality and truth could accommodate the avowedly fictive orations as part of the flow of events. Hobbes was not, of course, alone in his time in permitting fictive orations to live alongside requirements for truth; such speeches were often considered allowable if they were "probable."[50] What is interesting here is that Hobbes's treatment of causality merges with his rhetorical treatment of methodology: Thucydides' method is perspicuous in its presentation of causal factors because it renders "probable" reconstructions of what would have been said under the circumstances and it concretizes true abstractions.

These are crucial terms to consider in view of Hobbes's later formulations about method. Inasmuch as his model for scientific knowledge would be drawn from geometry because its conclusions were demonstrable and necessary, history (both civil and natural) would be classified as indemonstrable knowledge of fact. Both kinds of history made a man prudent by adding to his experience; both were kinds of memory. It is important then that Hobbes, from the very beginning and before he had made any of his formulations about scientific knowledge, adhered to a method in history such that the phenomena he wishes to understand are allowed to dictate hypothetical constructions, irrespective of whether or not they were altogether fictional. This was precisely his later position on method in physics and other natural, indemonstrable sciences.[51] The most one can do in matters that deal with knowledge of fact (as opposed to the demonstrative sciences which deal with a knowledge of words) "is to have such opinions, as no certayne experience can confute, and from which can be deduced by lawfull argumentation, no absurdity," he wrote in an early (1636) letter on the subject.[52] It did not particularly matter to Hobbes that these hypothetical constructions might not be true as long as they made the phenomena to be understood intelligible. Profoundly skeptical of the evidence of the senses, he would hold that no *certain* knowledge of fact could ever be attained in any case. If good history could make these uncertain things seem evident to the reader, Hobbes nonetheless knew very well that everything evident is not necessarily true. He would become intrigued by the possibilities of geometrical methods precisely because they seemed to combine the evident with necessary truth, and they could be applied to moral philosophy.

If Hobbes's view of history is close to his later view of physical science, one can note an affinity between both and Aristotle's observations on poetry. Poetry, he said, was more philosophical than history because its fiction could make events more intelligible and could clarify the causes of things which history, being caught up in particular facts, could not. Historians who write in verse are not poets for that very reason, a position Hobbes would later repeat. According to this criterion, Thucydides would be a genuine poet in his speeches, though not in his narratives where he is held to fact, and it is hard to imagine that Hobbes, with his familiarity with Aristotle, was not aware of the affinity or failed to appreciate the function of the speeches in making Thucydides the most philosophic of historians.

In terms of his contemporaries' taste, Hobbes's choice of Thucydides was somewhat unusual since the English Renaissance was essentially Roman. Its model historians from antiquity were those who wrote in Latin; and Thucydides, in particular, was not popular in England even in comparison with the other Greeks who were read.[53] It has been remarked that England during that age "could not reach to the conceptions of large historical forces or extensive movements. Its ideals of rule were simple. . . . The personal and incidental view of history held by Plutarch was therefore the more acceptable. Thucydides and Tacitus were out of reach of the times."[54] This view was slowly beginning to shift when Hobbes wrote, but the history of imperial Rome and its emperors was still closer to the English, who never tired of pointing out the evils of rebellion against a monarch, than was the turbulent history of contending city-states. In this context, Hobbes's choice of Thucydides may indicate his propensity for looking for the larger causes and sifting to the grounds of civil disruption. It surely indicates that his outlook was already more secular than that of his contemporaries: his arguments for history are practical and pedagogical, Hobbes nowhere repeating the popular refrain that history supports religion by showing the hand of God in the events of men.

Having begun his career with the traditional relationships between logic, rhetoric, psychology, and politics and the conflicts inherent in what is loosely called the humanistic tradition, Hobbes arrived at a position that already had some bearing on his later thought.

Much of his orientation could have come from Aristotle at this point, especially the *Rhetoric* with its tough-minded approach to the psychology of the passions and its view of language as a civic and political instrument.[55] When he wrote the essay, Hobbes still thought that Aristotle retained his primacy in the field of philosophy,[56] and even after becoming a severe critic of Aristotle, Aubrey reports that Hobbes still found "his rhetorique and discourse of animals... rare."[57] It is also known that Hobbes was working heavily with the *Rhetoric*, using it as a text for his pupils and making a digest of it himself.

As noted before, the path that led from these humanistic studies to political and scientific concerns was a natural one for the seventeenth-century mind, just as it was natural then for a poet like Milton to write a textbook in logic as well as his poems. If it now seems odd that scientific philosophy should grow out of letters or logic out of poems, it was not considered a conspicuously unlikely mating of subjects in one mind by the contemporaries of either Milton or Hobbes.[58] The subject matter was congenial considering the close connections between rhetoric and politics and the cluster of ideas around them, and the problem of method was implicit in them all. In the light of Aristotle's probable influence on Hobbes at this point, it is worth quoting a passage from the *Rhetoric* at length which reflects the relations between the disciplines and which Hobbes must have been familiar with. Speaking of the concerns of the political orator, Aristotle remarks that

to enumerate and classify accurately the usual subjects of public business, and further to frame, as far as possible, true definitions of them, is a task which we must not attempt on the present occasion. For it does not belong to the art of rhetoric, but to a more instructive art and a more real branch of knowledge [i.e., politics]; ... But the more we try to make either dialectic or rhetoric not, what they really are, practical faculties, but sciences, the more we shall inadvertently be destroying them and shall be passing into the region of sciences dealing with definite subject matters rather than simply with words and forms of reasoning.[59]

The development of Hobbes's thought follows a course much like the one described above—a passing from the region of the practical faculty of rhetoric into the region of the theoretic science of politics, stopping on the way at the midpoint of history. As he paused at the definite subject of history and tried to define it according to the critical terms of rhetoric, he would complete his transition to political science by finding a method for framing "true definitions" on a geometrical model.

Even after Hobbes made politics a subject for science, there was no "break" in its relation to rhetoric as he saw it in his early years. When he raged against rhetoric and said that impudence was the "goddess of rhetoric," as he did in Behemoth, he was speaking of the confusion wrought by oratory in "democratical assemblies"[60]—a position he already took in the Thucydides essay. For the rest of his life, when Hobbes uses "rhetoric" in the pejorative sense (most of the time), he is thinking of the political oratory of democracies— "democracy is but the government of a few orators"[61]—whereas monarchy is associated with univocity, a single voice with a single meaning that will not split into factions and rebellions. But side by side with passages where he is critical of those who abuse rhetoric, one finds others where he reiterates his early conviction that rhetoric, properly employed, has its place in the moral sciences. Reverting to his original theme of the clash between reason and eloquence, he says in Leviathan, for instance, that if the two conflict in the natural sciences,

Yet, in the moral [sciences, they] may stand very well together. For wheresoever there is place for adorning and preferring of error, there is much more place for adorning and preferring of truth, if they have it to adorn.[62]

When Hobbes had seen the Thucydides through the press, he put aside political history and was not to return to it until the years after the Civil War with Behemoth. In the meanwhile, he was a man without an occupation, and he cast around for some employment. Since the Cavendish family had no need of his services, he soon took a position with one Sir Gervase Clifton of Nottinghamshire, who engaged him to accompany his son to the Continent. For a second time, Hobbes set out for Paris.

III

The Idea of Science

Cicero saith.. that there can be nothing so absurd, but may be found in
the books of philosophers. And the reason is manifest. For there is not one of
them that begins his ratiocinations from
the definitions... of the names they are
to use; which is a method that hath
been used only in geometry; whose
conclusions have thereby been made indisputable.

E.W., III, 33

The Method

O B B E S was punctilious in the performance of his duties
for Sir Gervase, writing to him from Paris that it was "a
necessity of good manners that obliges me as your servant to lett you knowe att all times where to find me."[1] Sandwiched
in between the elaborate expressions of respect usual in that age was
the information that he and young Clifton were preparing to move on
in about three weeks, hoping to be in Venice by October. It was
toward springtime, and the regular routes from Paris by way of Milan
were encumbered by French and Spanish troops then engaged in the
war of the Succession of Mantua.

The whole journey, which lasted over a year, included Orléans,
Geneva, and a return to Paris. Typically, the few letters surviving
from the tour are chiefly concerned with perfunctory business. Almost nothing of his impressions is communicated except for a very
occasional, brief and cryptically incomplete comment; for example,
"This towne [Orléans] is without newes, but for other passe-time
here is enough."[2] Sometimes he sent news of the war, and one Mr.
Aglionby sent him reports of the growing displeasure of the English

monarch with his Parliament.[3] The information is scanty, but a single momentous fact mentioned in Hobbes's autobiography tells us that during this trip, apparently while he was in Geneva, the philosopher first encountered Euclid's *Elements*.[4]

In Aubrey's inimitable version of this event, Hobbes happened on a copy of Euclid's work in a gentleman's library, where the book lay open at *Elements*, I, 47, which, barring a confused edition, was the Pythagorean Theorem. Hobbes read. "By G—," he exclaimed, "this is impossible." The demonstration of the proposition referred him to an earlier one, which in turn sent him back to still another one, *et sic deinceps*, until he was utterly convinced. This, concludes Aubrey, "made him in love with geometry."[5] To move, in one wave of thought, from incredulity to absolute conviction is a rare experience: for Hobbes, it had something of the force of a revelation.

The inspiration that philosophers have drawn from Euclid ever since classical antiquity needs little comment. Galileo's eulogies were only late additions to that long tradition celebrating the mysteries of the mathematical universe, and at least one earlier adherent is said to have willingly sacrificed a hecatomb in gratitude for the discovery of a new geometrical theorem. Speaking of himself, Hobbes explicitly said that it was not so much the substance of Euclidean geometry which he found so illuminating as it was the manner of ratiocination, the method. He was struck by the certitude of the reasoning, by the perspicacity of the demonstrations, and by its kind of logic which, if like the scholastic logic in its general deductive cast, was far superior in its precision and in its utility as an instrument for philosophic research. His reaction to Euclid's work was accordingly profound, and "diligentissime perlegit."[6]

If geometry seems remote from Hobbes's work on Thucydides and his involvement in rhetoric and history, yet it is close to his concern with method, and it was to provide him with a model for the art of reasoning proper to the creation of any science, political or other. The revelations of Euclid were thus logically as well as chronologically prior to Hobbes's writings in political science, and he intended to expound the bases of his method first and then proceed systematically to the other portions of his philosophy. But political events in England were to develop to such a crisis that Hobbes eventually felt obliged to publish his political work first, thereby disturbing for his biographers the chronological correspondence that usually exists between a man's publications and the development of his ideas. So while Hobbes eventually published his political works prior to his exposition of the method he wished to develop them by, it is more logical to follow him in the sequence of his learning and anticipate some of the results of his initiation into the venerable Thirteen Books.

Returning years later to his earliest and most enduring Thucydidean theme, Hobbes was to divide all learning into two kinds, the "mathematical" and the "dogmatical," which proceeded respectively from the two "principal parts of Nature, Reason and Passion":

The former is free from controversy and dispute, because it consisteth in comparing figure and motion only: in which things, truth, and the interest of men, oppose not each other; but in the other there is nothing indisputable, because it compareth men, and meddleth with their right and profit; in which, as oft as reason is against a man, so oft will a man be against reason.[7]

In proportion as mathematical learning was disinterested, while dogmatical learning in politics and ethics was not, the first had obviously made immense strides since antiquity, while the second had floundered among contradictions, promoting only disorder. Not until this period in history could some thinkers like Hobbes believe that science, because it was a product of reason, was capable of progress exempt from man's usual weaknesses and able to extricate him from the conflicts perpetrated by his passions. As geometry embodied the very spirit of analysis and mathematical learning, Hobbes invested it with the full force of this vision.

Science, for Hobbes, was a matter of the correct use of words, but all knowledge of whatever kind begins in the senses, and here we must reach rather far into his later thought to indicate the basis for his reasoning. Sense images, which Hobbes sometimes calls "original fancy" and which are always of particulars, are assigned "sensible marks" in the mind as mnemonic devices, enabling us to recall things we would otherwise lose. Similar signs are registered to stand for our thoughts and feelings, and these marks when used in speech are called names.[8] Universal names are *only* names: they stand for many particulars taken severally and bring to mind any one of them. If a series of images often occurs in the sense in the same order, so it is likely to occur in the same sequence in the imagination by association. The remembrance of such a succession of what was antecedent, what consequent, and what concomitant is called by Hobbes "experiment," irrespective of whether this observation of order in nature is done voluntarily (as in a scientific experiment) or involuntarily, "as when we remember a fair morning after a red evening."[9] Many experiments constitute "experience," the record of which is history. Experience may make a man prudent but not wise, for *"experience concludeth nothing universally."*[10] Experience of external effects is only conjectural: old men, having more experience, conjecture better and are therefore more prudent. By the same token, prophets are those men who guess best.[11]

Animals, however, also have a kind of prudence (which is only a *"presumption* of the *future,* contracted from the *experience* of time *past"*), so it is not prudence which distinguishes man from the beasts.[12] It is only through the invention of language that man has transformed himself and raised experience to the higher power of science:

> By the advantage of *names* it is that we are capable of *science,* which beasts, for want of them, are not; nor man without the use of them: for as a beast misseth nor one or two out of many her young ones, for want of those names of order, one, two, and three, and which we call *number;* so neither would a man, without repeating orally or mentally the words of number, know how many pieces of money or other things lie before him.[13]

Names allowed man to store up his experience and generalize inductive observations, making human prudence far superior to that of animals, but it still had the defect that empirical knowledge is uncertain. The kind of reasoning involved in prudence is a joining of words to form propositions as concepts are joined by association from experience, but in scientific reasoning we join words according to rules; science does not reason about the consequences of imagined things, but about the consequences of words.[14]

Reasoning is always a matter of adding and subtracting words to form propositions, and propositions to form syllogisms, and syllogisms to form demonstrations. The notions of true and false also come with language, for they are properties of words, not things, referring to correct or incorrect inferences. Thus truth is a matter of propositions in which one term comprehends the other, that is, an identity. But, Hobbes warns, if words have given us science, "as men abound in copiousness of language, so they become more wise, or more mad than ordinary."[15] For aside from true and false propositions, there is the third possibility of absurd propositions, "to which no living creature is subject, but only man,"[16] and which occurs when words are connected in a (literally) senseless way. A "round quadrangle" is such an absurdity, and it is matched, in Hobbes's view, by such scholastic terms as "incorporeal body," which he thought an impossible elocution.[17]

The right ordering of words, which is truth, is only part of knowledge, "for if words alone were sufficient, a *parrot* might be taught as well to know the truth, as to speak it."[18] What the parrot has not got is "understanding" or "evidence" of the truth. Evidence is present when there is a conception concomitant with the words; it stands to truth "as the sap to the tree, which, so far as it creepeth along with the body and branches, keepeth them alive; where it forsaketh them, they die; for this evidence, which is meaning with our words, is the life of truth."[19] A proposition may be true, but its truth will never be evident until we conceive the meaning of the words, and we cannot remember these conceptions without the image that caused the conceptions in our mind. With conception and perception thus linked into almost the same act, Hobbes defines science at one point as *"evidence of truth,* from some beginning or principle of *sense."*[20] To deliver oneself from equivocation by having a single idea or image for each word is therefore to have understanding; it is the beginning of science.

Given this theory, to which we will return in greater detail, it is clear why Hobbes came to choose geometry as his model for true knowledge. Words, which were originally arbitrary, are not equivocal in an axiomatic science, whereas in other fields they remain somewhat inconstant. In history, for example, the attribution of causes varied almost as much as the experience of men, and words are unstable: "for one man calleth *wisdom,* what another calleth *fear;* and one *cruelty,* what another *justice.* . . . And therefore such names can never be true grounds for any ratiocination. No more can metaphors, and tropes of speech, but these are less dangerous, because they profess their inconstancy; which the other do not."[21] Ultimately, our conviction that a history is accurate rests on the authority of one man or on our education.[22] "If Livy says the Gods made once a cow speak, and we believe it not; we distrust not God therein, but Livy."[23] Livy's assertions are not indisputable, being neither evident nor demonstrable, and if Hobbes was to contemplate a science of politics he would have to use terms that were more constant and teachable (demonstrable) than those of either history or poetry. Geometry, being wonderfully free of normative terms, was also wonderfully free of dispute.

A science composed of linked deductions from a few evident definitions, axioms, and postulates that have been agreed upon, its beauty is that all of its theorems are thus contained in its first definitions. To analyze the properties of the spatial figures it deals with, we need only combine these definitions and derive the correct inferences according to conventional rules.

In other words, geometry begins with a few primitive terms and undemonstrated propositions from which every subsequent proposition is logically derived and in respect to which every subsequent term is defined. Since the inferences are necessary, they meet Hobbes's requirement that they be indisputably true, but this is not the case with the initial definitions. For if the beauty of geometry is in its logical coherence, the bane of the science has always been the logical status of those initial definitions. For first principles are not themselves demonstrable; they must be agreed upon before, or accepted on trust.

"He therefore that proceedeth from untrue, or not understood definitions, is ignorant of that he goes about," said Hobbes, for if the principal terms of one's reasoning—the definition of a triangle or line in geometry, for instance—are vague, what becomes of the rest of the structure derived from them?[24] Ideally, these principles are evident definitions (although some of Euclid's are not) which succinctly state the intuitional properties of important concepts and general logical notions which make a further appeal to intuition unnecessary.[25] But what was "evident" to Hobbes as a definition was not, unfortunately, "evident" to other geometers, and their first definitions differed accordingly. Even non-mathematicians will see that behind this apparently technical problem issues of deeper import lie concealed, and Hobbes was later to find it worth his while to spill much ink defending his position. Among others, the question of universals is ultimately at issue here, and Hobbes debated it in terms of geometrical notions with mathematicians of the caliber of Descartes and John Wallis, Savillian Professor of Geometry at Oxford.

Among Euclid's primitive terms, for example, are those of a point and a line, the former being defined as that which has not parts, and the latter as length without breadth. Most geometers were content to deal with just such ideal points and lines, for they considered the definitions to be evident and true. The definition of a line was proper, they said, for it captured the very essence of a line, namely its length alone. Hobbes, on the other hand, was always distrustful of abstrac-

tions that were too sharply removed from their concrete manifestations since he had observed that they tended to turn into mere empty
words. He therefore insisted that lines did indeed have breadth and
Euclid had only meant that for the purposes of calculation, the
breadth need not be taken into consideration.[26] Was not a line without breadth an absurdity, after all? Was it not meaningless, an impossible concept because it was literally inconceivable? Because no image
could be formed of such a line, it lacked "evidence." Like the errors of
the Schoolmen who, carried away by their phrases, argued about
self-contradictory things like "incorporeal bodies," these misguided
geometers were proposing a definition that was only a special case of
the same thing with their "lines without breadth." Geometry, it
seems, was not wholly free of dispute.

   Abstractions were undoubtedly most necessary instruments of
reason, but on no account could Hobbes tolerate confusing them with
assertions about reality. In accordance with his nominalist approach
to language, essences, forms, determinate natures, or whatever else
general ideas are called, are only the names of concepts which arise
from the observation of similar qualities in many particulars; they are
not the names of really existent things. It was only a step from speaking of a triangle whose lines had no breadth simply because we can
imagine it without considering the breadth, to speaking of an independently existent triangleness. It was, he said, a great abuse of language and a great self-deception to register in words what can never
be conceived. Looking ahead to 1641, Descartes was in fact to speak of
having an innate idea of the nature of a triangle in his *Meditationes,*
and Hobbes objected emphatically.[27] The idea of triangularity originated in triangles we have actually beheld and is a name for the
qualities they have in common; while we can recall the image of a
triangle and let it stand for all triangles, we cannot imagine a "triangularity." Now if every triangle in the world disappeared, neither the
triangle nor the determinate nature of a triangle would remain, but
only the mere name. For himself, Hobbes opined, if the triangle
existed *nowhere,* he could not see how it could have a nature at all.
"Essentia absque existentia est commentum nostrum."[28]

   To explore the mathematical controversies of the period is thus
to relate them to issues of more general philosophic concern when the
points in dispute are questions of principle. The principles in this case
were to preoccupy Hobbes all his life, for he carried on an indefatiga-
ble campaign, in geometry as in politics, against any kind of reifica-

tions, innate ideas, or separate essences. He was convinced that close attention to words and an understanding of their nature would resolve this confusion, which was at the root of philosophic error. He therefore insisted that the premises of demonstration embody a particular, material cause, and his definition of lines had to include a notion of breadth if they were to be "known" causes and not mere names. It is clear from this that his warfare with the Schoolmen was not directed against their deductive logic; on the contrary, their favored weapon, the demonstrative syllogism, was essential for his notion of a true science whose inferences were necessary. His whole treatment of language is heavily colored by the Ockhamite tradition, moreover, though he fails to mention the Franciscan philosopher.[29] He has the further likeness with Ockham that, both in his time and through the subsequent history of philosophy, his position has called upon him the indignation of thinkers who wish to preserve any kind of realm of the *a priori* or real universals. "We can never teach him through external experience what does not belong to external experience," said a later distinguished critic with typical exasperation. "We cannot show him a point without extension and a line without breadth. . . . He shuts himself off from every non-empirical perception."[30]

To say that Hobbes's intuitions of things like lines, points, and triangles differed from those of other geometers is thus a way of saying that he intuited a rather different disposition in the universe; his world, so to speak, carried its accent mark on another syllable. Certain facets of the world he found much more impressive than others, and intuitions are expressions of what we find most noteworthy in the environment. His metaphysical proclivities thus account for the fact that Hobbes found *his* intuition of a line as a material thing a necessary part of a geometrical demonstration, while others considered *their* intuitions of the essence of a line undeniably more evident if no mention of breadth whatsoever were made in its definition. As Hobbes well knew, since primary definitions embody such basic intuitions and cannot be demonstrated, they lie outside of geometry proper and in the realm of metaphysics, or *philosophia prima* as he called it.[31] Fortunately, geometry does not stand or fall according to the resolution of this issue of the definition of a line and a point,[32] but if it was to serve as a model science that contained only necessary inferences *ex firmis principiis,* Hobbes was obliged to examine the modes of definition yielding such principles.

Ultimately, it seemed that the intuitions embodied in basic definitions could only claim the support of private conviction since they are prior to logic, frequently appearing to the mind as completely evident truths. Hobbes had already observed in his Thucydides that everything evident is not necessarily true, but here, even in geometry, he was once more thrust back upon the divisive element of mere belief and private opinion. Since private opinion in matters that involve the self-interest of men (as politics does) is the source of controversy and its arguments the slaves of passion, it remained for Hobbes to find initial principles that were as necessarily believed as logical deductions were; he required, as he bluntly put it, primary definitions such that we would have to believe them whether we wanted to or not ("volentes nolentes credimus"). Thus, when Descartes rested an argument on intuitive certainty or "mental illumination" in his *Meditationes*, Hobbes took him severely to task. Anyone who is free of a feeling of doubt will claim a like illumination, said Hobbes, and his belief will be just as firm when he is wrong as when he is right. Such a conviction may be the cause of his tenacious defense of his opinion, but it is certainly not the cause of his knowledge of whether it is right or wrong.[33]

If even the foundations of geometry were subject to such controversy, how much more difficult it would be to transform politics into a perfect science, bearing as it did an additional burden of subjective factors. Hobbes could hope, however, that if he untied this knot in geometry, he might also untie it in politics. The question of private judgment in both areas was, after all, analogous: it was no less difficult to persuade Descartes of the possible unreliability of his "mental illuminations" than it was to persuade the Protestant sectarians that what they variously experienced as the dictates of conscience was not necessarily a direct sign of the will of God. But while Descartes harmed no man with his philosophic tenets, the latter were setting "all England . . . ablaze with inner lights"[34] as they pitted their conflicting opinions against each other and against the established Church.

Among the initial propositions of Euclid there are some that, strictly speaking, are not definitions, but are nonetheless essential for the demonstrations; these are the postulates. "It shall be possible to draw a straight line joining any two points," for instance, adds nothing to the substance of the theorems, being rather a principle of operation that gives the rules for generating the subject matter of geometry itself, to wit, the figures.[35] Hobbes concluded from this that our own motion, moving according to these fixed rules or postulates, is the cause of the figures. He was therefore dissatisfied when conventional geometers simply pointed to the general properties of a figure as the cause of geometrical conclusions, for example, the right-angleness of a triangle. These formal causes were not causes at all; they were descriptions of sense perceptions of the figure. Alternatively, to say that the conclusion was caused by the premises was a passable elocution, but it did not go far enough. For while our understanding of the words of the premises (their "evidence") is the cause of subsequent understanding, a premise by itself is just a "speech" and "speech is not the cause of speech."[36] However, if the geometrical figure is broken down and analyzed into its parts—the triangle into lines, and lines into points—and if the postulates are then applied to these parts to synthesize them and generate the figure once more, who could deny then, that his own motion working on matter was the efficient cause of the demonstration? The geometer, Hobbes concludes triumphantly, need only deduce the consequences of his own operations.[37]

Science rests on the knowledge of causes, according to Hobbes, and no other science held for him such a firm principle of causality. In no other science did cause and effect so closely approximate the formal logical relationship of antecedent and consequent. While Hobbes began with intuitive or arbitrary definitions which, since they could not be proven, had to be accepted to start with, yet by basing such primary concepts on the inferential process of analysis, he insisted that the formulation of these intuitions partakes of a logical status and does not remain arbitrary. By showing that these first principles were established through analysis of the figure in geometry, he could assert that they were thus inferences themselves.[38]

To know something in this sense is to construct it oneself; the science of any subject is then "derived from a precognition of the causes, generation, and construction of the same; and consequently where the causes are known, there is place for demonstration, but not where the causes are to seek for."[39] We do not construct natural bodies ourselves; hence their causes cannot be perfectly known. In geometry, however, only wholly "artificial" bodies are involved and the reasoning is entirely according to conventional rules.

Geometry is therefore demonstrable, for the lines and figures from which we reason are drawn and described by ourselves. . . . But because of natural bodies we know not the construction, but seek it from the effects, there lies no demonstration. . . . Therefore where there is place for demonstration, if the first principles, that is to say, the definitions contain not the generation of the subject, there can be nothing demonstrated as it ought to be.[40]

Geometry need not be regarded as a constructive science to be useful,[41] but for Hobbes the method of genetic definition had the advantage of collapsing the scholastic formal cause into the efficient cause of things, and it brought to the fore the constructive, active element in knowledge.[42] The method, which he called "analytic-synthetic" or "resolutive-compositive," was set firmly against the categorical logic of the Schoolmen and against all appeals to separate essences said to exist independently of material embodiment, which Hobbes thought had rendered philosophy static and erroneous. As Ernst Cassirer remarks:

A genuine genetic definition permits us to understand the structure of a complex whole; it does not, however, stop with this structure as such, but goes back to its foundations. Hobbes is the first modern logician to grasp this significance of the "causal definition." He does not look upon his discovery simply as a logical reform; he sees nothing less than a transformation of the ideal of philosophical knowledge itself. His charge against scholasticism is that it thought it could understand being, while in reality it considered being merely as a passive something with static properties and characteristics.[43]

A philosopher once remarked that the man who starts his philosophizing by developing a method is like the poet who composes his verse according to some given aesthetic. Method was logically prior with Hobbes, but he did not start his philosophizing with it. He began, as we have seen, with a series of observations and questions about the role played by reason, passions, and words in knowledge, and how they related to the concept of causality. These he voiced in his essay on Thucydides, and the intermediate steps he took toward an idea of science lie in his development of a method yielding necessary conclusions and based on the undeniable "evidence" of certain concepts. The difference between the possibilities of a political history like the Thucydides and political science like *Leviathan* rests precisely on an idea of method concerning what constitutes "perspicuous words". In the Thucydides, it had been a narrative which made both the immediate and deeper causes of war "evident" even if these were hypothetical causes in fact; in science, perspicuous words also make causes "evident," but these words are "by exact definitions first snuffed, and purged from ambiguity,"[44] and the causes were demonstrable. Finally, while both rhetorical disposition in history and axiomatic procedure in geometry could be used effectively to cast material into a teachable form, the latter method also proved to be eminently useful as a tool for philosophic analysis and "discovery."[45] To use the older term, it provided a method of *inventio*, of finding arguments—the very thing which, in the Thucydides, Hobbes had replaced by "truth" in his formula. In short, Hobbes's new method opened up new possibilities for research for him: his subject remained the actions and words of men in political society, but in the Thucydides, truth had to be argued on circumstantial grounds because it could not be proven, while his new method now allowed him to find out analytical truths, if only his definitions were granted. The method, moreover, would allow him to take politics out of the realm of "dogmatical" learning, where it was governed by rhetorical manipulation and subject to unstable passions, and to transfer it to the realm of science, where intellectual necessity rules.

The transition from political history to political science came when Hobbes asserted that the state could be regarded as a wholly artificial body, analogous to a geometrical figure. We, the citizens, are surely the constituent matter of the state, and surely our adherence to the laws is the cause of the state's generation and existence, as our adherence to geometrical rules generates the figures. Was not the state in this sense an artificial body created by our art? And since we ourselves construct the state, could we not understand the properties and implications of civic institutions simply by deducing the consequences of our own voluntary motions? If it was a failure to understand first definitions which caused dispute in geometry, was not political conflict similarly caused by a failure to understand the fundamental concepts of the state and such primitive terms as "sovereign"? After all, how could one think correctly about one's obligations to the state if one did not grasp the meaning of the terms involved? In politics, however, the primitive terms involved were not "point" and "line" but "just" and "unjust"; misapprehensions did not issue in philosophic controversy, but in sedition and civil war.

Hobbes's methodological outlook has a certain resemblance to that of the Italian Aristotelians of the period,[46] but it departs from the Schoolmen's Aristotle (except the Ockhamite tradition) in precluding

formal causes. Hobbes would break with Aristotle again on the question of the origins of the state. The works of Aristotle had taught for
centuries that the state was prior to the individual; that man created
or realized the larger community "by nature." Christianity, on the
other hand, tended to regard the state as God's instrument, and its
creation as the fulfillment of a divinely fore-ordained destiny. Hobbes's
concept of the artificial state created by man, in imitation of the art
of God in nature, through a contract, would stand in clear opposition to both views.

Much remained to be done before Hobbes filled in this new ideal
for philosophic knowledge, but it was only the beginning of his long
enchantment with Euclid. Biographically speaking, he had not yet
developed the theory of knowledge which has been briefly described
here and its theory of signs, and he had yet to work out a psychology.
Most importantly, he had still to develop a theory of perception and
to discover the implications of his own primary term, motion. When
we left him, he had written his Thucydides and he had just found
Euclid; everything else remarked upon here was anticipatory. But the
Euclidean romance was to endure, and after twenty years acquaintance his passion did not flag, for he still spoke of geometry with
continual praise as "the only science that it hath pleased God hitherto
to bestow on mankind."[47]

The amplification of his ideas would wait for many years, but the
seeds of his system were already planted in the problems posed by
the Thucydides and in the possibility of their solution by the Euclid
discovery. For the next years, Hobbes plunged further into science
and philosophy, and his aim can be summarized in his own words,
partly quoted before:

To conclude, the light of human minds is perspicuous words, but by exact
definitions first snuffed, and purged from ambiguity; *reason* is the *pace;* increase of *science,* the way; and the benefit of mankind, the *end.*

He adds, with cavalier disregard for his own precept:

And, on the contrary, metaphors, and senseless and ambiguous words,
are like *ignes fatui;* and reasoning upon them is wandering amongst in-
numerable absurdities; and their end, contention and sedition, or contempt.[48]

If Hobbes's practice belies his preaching even as he speaks, yet he had
always said that eloquence stands well with reason where the truth is

being adorned and advanced. And with his method, Hobbes was sure that he had the truth to adorn.

The Intellectual Milieu
and the Doctrine of Motion

Hobbes published nothing for a dozen years following his translation of Thucydides and his discovery of Euclid except for a short digest of Aristotle's *Rhetoric*, but it was an important period of growth for him, partly because of the intellectual milieu in which he lived, and partly because of his further exposure to Continental thought on a third voyage there. To this period too, belong his original thoughts on the nature of motion, an idea which held the same compelling fascination for him that geometrical method did.

We also begin to get a fuller picture of his life in these years, and it seems that as he went into a new time of flourishing intellectually, his physical appearance changed as well. The somewhat sickly scholar of his Oxford years belatedly developed into a tall, brisk man of ruddier complexion and an ample forehead. Describing him in the summer of 1634, when Hobbes paid what was to be his last, brief visit to his home country of North Wiltshire, Aubrey says that the mallet-shaped head was still topped by a crop of black hair, but now it contrasted to yellowish-red whiskers that grew with a natural turn upward—a turn then considered a sure sign of inborn wit. A tip of a beard worn beneath the lip completes a not unfashionable picture of this vigorous figure at the age of forty-six.[49] It was on this visit, when Hobbes dropped in to pay his respects to his old teacher Mr. Latimer, that he was introduced to one of the eight-year-old students—how surprised he would have been had he known that little John Aubrey would one day be both a devoted admirer and his most enthusiastic biographer.

Hobbes was again employed by the Cavendish family in 1631, this time as tutor to the young third Earl of Devonshire, and his experience in this position provides a lesson about the role of the patron in seventeenth-century English intellectual life. As a man who could not participate in the learned world through either the church or the university, Hobbes's opportunities for finding a stimulating intellectual environment rested wholly with his patron—he needed a good library, financial support, contacts with educated men, and access to new ideas. In his post, Hobbes got exactly that. He was quickly brought into contact with William Cavendish, Earl and later Duke of Newcastle, and his circle of friends at Welbeck Abbey, a circle that included Ben Jonson, John Dryden, and William Davenant. Cavendish himself, aside from being in the political thick of things, was a horseman of some accomplishment, a writer of verses, and a collaborator in some of the plays of his famous and irrepressible wife, Margaret. In this atmosphere, Hobbes was so far from being wholly occupied with his new method and with becoming a full-time philosopher that Aubrey reports him to have been full of the talk of Ben Jonson and Robert Ayton (or Aytoun, the Scottish poet),[50] both of whom he had consulted about his Thucydides translation before.[51]

Yet, aside from the literary business, the new philosophy was very much in the air at Welbeck Abbey and Hobbes was not untouched. The Earl of Newcastle asked Hobbes to procure a copy of Galileo's *Dialogues* on a visit to London in January 1633/34, for instance, and even as Hobbes was searching for the scarce volume, another member of the Cavendish household, one Dr. Webbe, was busy translating it.[52] Still more important for Hobbes, perhaps, was the Earl's brother, Sir Charles Cavendish. This scholarly gentleman was born in 1591, went abroad for his Grand Tour with Sir Henry Wotton, and returned to become eventually one of the most energetic and intelligent patrons of learning in the period. It was on his urging that William Oughtred published his work, so influential in the history of algebraic notation, the *Clavis Mathematicae,* and it was probably through Cavendish that Hobbes came to meet the English mathematician John Pell.

Cavendish also had extensive contacts with Continental scientists, being in communication with the well-known intellectual friar, Marin Mersenne, not later than 1636,[53] and corresponding with the eminent French mathematician Mydorge, as early as 1631.[54] Hobbes eventually met both. A network of scientific correspondence began to form when Cavendish, together with John Payne (a friend of Hobbes's and apparently Cavendish's chaplain),[55] embarked on an exchange of letters with the accomplished English scientist Walter Warner. Both Hobbes and Dr. Webbe became involved when Cavendish circulated through letters or manuscipts Warner's speculations on magnifying lenses and burning glasses,[56] and a treatise dealing with the place of the image on concave and convex lenses.[57] Hobbes offered his own opinions on these matters and made his own experiments;[58] he and the others also consulted Mydorge on the question of refractions.[59] Altogether, the whole group seemed to be deeply involved with the possibilities of optics, until finally the Earl of Newcastle wrote that "Mr. Warner would make us believe miracles by a glass he can make"; but he adds, "I doubt he will prove Ben's Doctor Subtle."[60]

In this way, Hobbes's contact with various scientists in England and on the Continent continued to grow, largely due to his association with the Cavendishes.[61] By being intelligently curious and by serving as a center for communications, the Cavendish family helped to expand the orbit of information available to Hobbes; they functioned for his own personal intellectual world in much the same way as Mersenne functioned for the scientific world at large in Paris, as Fabri de Peiresc did at Montpellier, and as Henry Oldenburg would do at the Royal Society of London.[62] Such postal communications networks were essential in the days before the organization of science and the publication of professional journals. The patron partly fulfilled the role of the journal and also the role, of course, of the grant-giving research institution. To Hobbes, the Cavendishes were always liberal (his salary was £50 a year, excluding gifts); and while William Cavendish became a patron of both Descartes and Gassendi, Charles Cavendish solicited the king's attentions for Descartes and Mydorge, attempting to bring them to England under his patronage.[63]

Hobbes's association with the Continental scientific world did not remain wholly epistolary. He made a third trip abroad with his pupil, and this time he met the revered Galileo, who won his unending respect for having opened "the gate of natural philosophy universal, which is the knowledge of the nature of motion."[64] When Hobbes met the great scientist in Florence in 1636, Galileo was ageing and had only shortly before endured the humiliation of the Inquisition. There is no record of what passed between these two extraordinary men, but it is a question of great speculative interest since it is not known how far Hobbes had by then developed his own doctrine of motion and hence what Galileo's influence might have been.[65]

Hobbes's doctrine of motion was, from the first, closely related to his analysis of sense perception. It was either on this voyage, or more probably sometime before, that he met with some learned gentlemen and sense perception was mentioned, whereupon one of the company asked, "What is sense?" Brooding over this offhand question and wondering how a person could pride himself on being a savant without even understanding the nature of his own senses, Hobbes "luckily" ("forte fortuna") hit upon the idea that the cause of all things resides in the diversity of motion ("Causam omnium rerum quaerendam esse in diversitate motuum").[66] All natural knowledge begins with sense perception, he reasoned, and all that we perceive about things are changeable qualities or accidents such as shape, position, color, and sound. Hobbes did not doubt that there is an underlying stratum of independently existent substance or body, the chief property of which is extension—in fact, he believed it to be the only really existent thing. What we perceive of it, however, is only an appearance, its changeable qualities, and where there is change there is motion. If all things were in uniform motion or uniformly at rest, there would be no perceptible difference between them—that is, no sense. Accidents are consequently not things at all; they are not *in* a body, but neither are they imaginable apart from a particular body. An accident is rather *"the manner by which any body is conceived."*[67] Body needs only magnitude to exist, but we need its accidents to know that it exists. They are our epistemological liaisons with external reality, so to speak, causing "phantasms" or concepts in our minds of material existence.

This idea is, as Hobbes well knew, indemonstrable; it is a principle or starting point which must be known "by nature."[68] In particular, if bodies are not subject to direct observation, but are known to exist only through their accidents, their reality can only be a kind of desperate inference: there must be something out there, independent of mind, for us to be able to have experiences at all, and that something is what Hobbes calls body.

Hobbes was further obliged to offer an hypothesis to explain precisely how this matter in motion gives rise to sense perception. Everything, he said, is moved by the push or pull of other objects that impart some of their own motion to the internal parts of man and thence to the heart (or brain),[69] where it meets resistance or a counter-pressure. Because this counter-pressure is an outward motion, we experience our phantasms as if they were external objects. "This *seeming* or *fancy*," he said, "is that which men call *sense.*"[70] Since thinking is also a kind of activity, it too, is motion, and is accordingly classed with sense as part of the inner "tumult"[71] that is our experiential world.

Using sound as an example of sense perception, Hobbes wrote:

Nothing can make any thing which is not in itself: the *clapper* hath no *sound* in it, but motion, and maketh motion in the internal parts of the bell; so the *bell* hath motion, and not sound, that imparteth *motion* to the *air;* and the *air* hath motion, and not sound, the *air* imparteth motion by the *ear* and *nerve* unto the *brain;* and the brain hath motion but not sound; from the *brain,* it reboundeth back unto the nerves *outward,* and thence it becometh an *apparition without,* which we call *sound.*[72]

The motion in the medium (air) is not sound, but the *cause* of sound, or rather of that inner phantasm which we call sound.[73] Where Galileo had wittily ridiculed the notion of a feather possessing a "tickling faculty," Hobbes remarked to the same point that *"our* heat is *pleasure* or *pain,* according as it is *great* or *moderate;* but in the *coal* there is no such thing."[74] Hobbes would take the idea one step further, following it to its bitter conclusion by characterizing both time and space itself (the impression of withoutness that adheres to mental images) as equally phantasms.[75] Everything is matter in motion—and since we know matter only through accidents generated by motion, even it tends to be reduced to the idea of motion. This conclusion led him back to geometry, which studies simple motion, and to Galilean mechanics. While it is not clear just how far Hobbes had developed this concept by the time of his third voyage to the Continent and his meeting with Galileo, the idea had certainly taken hold by then—he may well have conceived of it as much as six years before—and he tells us that wherever he went and whatever he was doing in this period, he was thinking about motion.

Sometime during this span of 1630–36 Hobbes began to make initial formulations of his ideas in papers which remained unpublished in his lifetime, most notably in his *Short Tract on First Principles.* These served as first drafts for his *De Corpore* of 1655, in which his philosophy of science was expressed in its maturest and fullest form. While Hobbes was later to assert that he had verbally espoused his doctrine of the subjectivity of secondary qualities as early as 1630,[76] the *Short Tract,* whenever precisely it was written,[77] already propounds an early refutation of the Aristotelian theories of sense perception and of species travelling through a medium. Secondary qualities are represented as being neither wholly subjective nor wholly objective, but are conceived as residing in motion itself, and the act of illumination is conceived as an act of emanation consisting of particles. Both sense perception and the higher functions are already derived from local motion in this remarkable little tract, sufficient causes are collapsed into necessary causes, and the whole presentation is cast in a semi-geometrical mode of definitions, conclusions, proofs, and corollaries. It is an early, somewhat primitive coalescence of his thoughts, not yet mastered at this point, but its approach is already marked by one of the most prominent characteristics of Hobbes's philosophic impulse: the drive toward discovering and building on the simplest, most basic elements of reality, and reasoning about them with such force and directness that his explanations seem to become almost intellectually *coercive*.

That Hobbes's earliest work thus approaches science partly through an analysis of sense experience, partly through optics and geometry, was not, of course, accidental. They were interrelated not only through his "lucky" idea about motion, which was his own individual hypothesis, but also through the very nature of the subject matter of optics and its position in early seventeenth-century science. Optics then held an important place among the sciences since theoretical progress could find a direct application in solving technical problems of instrument construction. Most importantly, the geometrical nature of the operations required in optical calculations made it possible to conceive of light and color in purely quantitative terms rather than qualitative ones: "For that reason, optics became an excellent standpoint for a distinction between those accidents which are inherent in matter and those which had only a subjective existence."[78]

It is important that Hobbes's various scientific interests—the geometry, the optics, the study of motion and mechanics—gelled around this very idea of the subjectivity of secondary qualities. The concept was, of course, a milestone in early modern science since it allowed natural phenomena to be reduced to quantitative problems, and for Hobbes it provided a basis for his more general mechanical view of nature. Galileo first introduced the idea in 1623; Hobbes may have arrived at his version independently some years later; Descartes followed the same line of thought, and there were others. Hobbes was well aware of its significance, so that when some years later he was accused of complaining of the backwardness of the schools that still taught Aristotelian physics, he replied: "This is a little mistaken. For I do glory, not complain, that whereas all the Universities of Europe hold sensation to proceed from species, I hold it to be a perception of motion in the organ."[79] Precisely because the importance of the idea was recognized by leading thinkers, a controversy was to grow up as to whether he or Descartes (who had preceded him in publishing his idea) had arrived at the concept first, despite Galileo's preceding them both. The development of this dispute will be taken up later, however, where it can be best understood in the light of Hobbes's rising reputation among the French scientific intelligentsia and his warm relationship with Mersenne, in particular.

The doctrine of subjective secondary qualities has a further significance for Hobbes's philosophy, reaching back into its theories of truth and language, and throwing his concepts of causality and "evidence" into a special light. As remarked before, in empirical thinking we perform mental calculations with concrete images (all images being of particulars), but there is no notion of predicability involved in those images; there is no basis for universals or for connections between particulars either psychologically or in nature. Empirical observation can therefore yield knowledge, but not true science, which deals with known causes: in empirical observation, the concept of causality arises merely as a reflection of the association of ideas, of the temporal before-after sequence, but in science a cause is defined by Hobbes as the aggregate of all accidents in the agent and patient which, when present, must instantly and *necessarily* produce the effect.[80] All abstract ideas and universals come into existence only with language, not with sense perception alone. They have a purely logical or linguistic existence, and Hobbes might have said with Ockham that "their being is their being understood."[81] Language allows us to perform the analyses impossible to simple experience but essential to science: it permits us to separate bodies from accidents to form propositions in which they serve as subject and object respectively, joined by the verb "is." The predicates define the subject, or are the causes for the subject's name, and these causes are the same as the causes of our concepts, namely accidents.[82]

Here we come to the heart of Hobbes's theory of knowledge. Since accidents are only appearances and experientially without connection, those propositions which make up science (the causes of which are ultimately accidents) threaten to lose their reference to anything beyond the phantasms that they signify.[83] With the connection to the ontological realm thus almost wholly cut off as a source of truth, Hobbes's interest is thrust back onto the realm of words themselves. This is why Hobbes's epistemology centers on the relationship between concepts and the signification of words, and why science must be essentially a matter of the formally correct use of language. Hobbes's notion of "evidence" or understanding—the possession of an image correlative to words—still provided a hypothetical link between words and the non-linguistic universe since those images were supposed to be related ultimately to an external material reality, and he was thereby rescued from lapsing into a total subjectivism. But in the late *De Corpore,* even this notion of evidence, which had stayed with Hobbes since the Thucydides, does not appear and becomes more implicit than explicit.[84]

From this vantage point, on the brink of solipsism, Hobbes draws for us a forceful image of the philosopher at work. Asking us to suppose that the whole world has been annihilated, he tells us that any man remaining would still remember and imagine all the things he had seen while the world existed, and that they would appear to him as if they were external objects. He would reason about them just as we do now:

Nay, if we do but observe diligently what it is we do when we consider and reason, we shall find that though all things be still remaining in the world, yet we compute nothing but our own phantasms. For when we calculate the magnitude and motions of heaven or earth, we do not ascend into heaven that we may divide it into parts, or measure the motions thereof, but we do it sitting still in our closets or in the dark.[85]

It is clear that those motions which act on us from external sources, whether in the form of original sense perception or recalled as imagination, are not *mere* phantasms. On the contrary, they supply us with our sole link to the outside world, and the most marvellous thing about sense to Hobbes is that they appear at all.

The importance of these phantasms goes further and completes Hobbes's assimilation of the human universe to the mechanical one. He held that motion is always propagated to infinity, and those motions which act on our senses and appear to us as phantasms continue to travel inward, where they are experienced as feelings—pleasure or pain, depending on whether or not they act beneficially on our vital motions. The tendency we have in reaction to move toward or away from the external sources of these feelings Hobbes calls "endeavor," and it is the beginning of all of man's voluntary motions.[86] Endeavor is conceived as an infinitely small, instantaneous motion or tendency toward motion, a concept Hobbes can apply equally to mankind and inanimate objects. (He uses it, for instance, to explain weight and the tendency of objects to fall when not supported.)[87] The world is to be understood as thronged with such miniscule motions, wherever there is matter. Insofar as many external stimuli strike us at any moment, the inner world of man must also contain a multitude of these tiny vectors of force, the resultant appearing when we walk, talk, or otherwise perform physical activities. As Hobbes frequently works on two levels of diction, he tells us that endeavor, (called *conatus* in mechanics) is "appetite" or "aversion" in men, depending on whether the endeavor is toward or away from an object. Those two passions will form the basic building blocks for Hobbes's description of human nature, and will also serve as the final terms in the chain of reasoning which connects his mechanics to his psychology.

When Hobbes travelled back to Paris from Italy and Galileo, his thoughts on science were given further impetus by his introduction to some of the most prominent scientific thinkers in France. He could participate in the discussions of these men—Roberval, Beaugrande, Mydorge, Gassendi, and others—who customarily gathered in Mersenne's cell in the Place Royale. This group, held together by the Franciscan philosopher's personality and stimulated by his pertinent questions, was then thrashing out and reformulating some of the most interesting problems of the day in mathematics. The method of "indivisibles" was being developed toward the integral calculus; there was progress made toward the solution of problems of maxima and minima; there were advances made in the theory of equations and number theory.[88] Aside from these special problems, various questions in physics were under discussion and general problems in natural philosophy were examined. If becoming "professional" means to receive the acknowledgment of men accomplished in their field, it was here that Hobbes became a professional philosopher of science, for he was held in some esteem by this scientific coterie. In the eight months that he remained in Paris before returning to England, he enjoyed their company and began, as he put it, to be "numbered among the philosophers."[89]

When Hobbes returned to England, Charles I was rapidly provoking national resentment to the point of civil war. The philosopher was back in time to witness the great Hampden case of 1638, and Bishop Laud's subsequent mismanagement in Scotland, precipitating the First Bishop's War. Hobbes's mind, however, was also on his philosophy; and when he landed in Byfleet, he wrote to the Earl of Newcastle begging to be free on his service to Lord and Lady Devonshire in order to devote himself to his work. In this letter, which is largely concerned with the question of light, he wrote:

For though my Lady and my Lord do both accept so wel of my service as I could almost engage my self to serve them as a domestique all my life, yet the extream pleasure I take in study overcomes in me all other appetites. I am not willing to leave my Lord so, as not to do him any service that he thinkes may not so well be done by another; but I must not deny my selfe the content to study in the way I have begun, and that I cannot conceave I shall do any where so well as at Welbecke, and therefore I meane if your Lordship forbid me not, to come thither as soone as I can, and stay as long as I can without inconvenience of your Lorship.[90]

His request granted, Hobbes went to Welbeck.[91]

The studies he so urgently desired to continue were undoubtedly partly scientific and partly political in character. Despite his deep involvement with scientific subjects, Hobbes had also kept up with political events and had not neglected the development of his political and moral philosophy. In 1636, for instance, he was writing to the Earl of Newcastle about Selden's *Mare Clausum*,[92] and corresponding with Payne about Lord Herbert's *De Veritate*.[93] Sir Kenelm Digby, who had praised Hobbes's "sweet and learned conversation,"[94] kept him informed on French political news after his return to England, and they carried on a philosophical correspondence ranging from general questions to some more esoteric ones about the nature of human foreknowledge.[95] It was probably at this time, on his return from his third journey abroad, that Hobbes became part of Lord Falkland's circle at Great Tew, and there was no coterie in England that gave more earnest or serious thought to the political pressures of the times or to their religious and moral implications. Since the circle included eminent clergymen, in particular Chillingworth and Sheldon, it may be speculated that Hobbes was first encouraged in this environment to study the bearing of biblical literature on politics, an area in which he would display enormous learning in his later works.

The political turmoil in England demanded Hobbes's attention and he tells us that he completed a "little treatise" in 1640, defending as the sovereign's those parts of the royal prerogative then being challenged by Short Parliament. It was perhaps not altogether accidental that the period between the Thucydides translation and this "little treatise" coincided more or less exactly with the eleven years in which Charles I had not called Parliament into session. This treatise, which was not to appear in an English version for ten years, received circulation in manuscript form, of which "many gentlemen had copies" and "which occasioned much talk of the author."[96] Aubrey reports that Bishop Manwaring was then preaching Hobbes's doctrine of absolute monarchy (to be taken up later) at St. David's (as was Robert Sibthorpe, vicar of Brackley), and that when Short Parliament put Manwaring in the Tower for his opinions, the philosopher thought it might be time to leave the country.[97] Long Parliament convened in November 1640, and Hobbes feared it no less—he promptly left for Paris, later boasting that he had been the first of all that fled.[98] The treatise itself contained little direct commentary on English political events, being more theoretical in nature, but its relevance to the situation was clear. In this light, Hobbes certainly thought his flight to Paris an act of prudence, although Sir Leslie Stephen suggests that it was probably unnecessary: "Hobbes surely might have given credit to members of parliament for sufficient stupidity to overlook logical implications."[99]

Hobbes and Descartes

In France, where Hobbes was to remain for the next eleven years, he was again welcomed into Mersenne's philosophic circle. Since his reputation there was already established, it was entirely natural when, in 1641, the Minorite monk sent him a copy of Descartes' yet unpublished *Meditationes,* which the author had asked Mersenne to distribute in manuscript form for criticism from various viewpoints. Hobbes was already familiar with Descartes' work, Sir Kenelm Digby having sent him a copy of *The Discourse on Method* while Hobbes was still in England in 1637. The volume had arrived with the strong recommendation that Mydorge thought well of Descartes and that Digby himself regarded him as having "a most vigorous and strong braine."[100] The exchange of "objections" and "responses" between these two philosophers, with Mersenne acting as postal intermediary, captures in one vignette the most powerful trends in seventeenth-century philosophic thought.

The controversy centered around Descartes' notion of an "idea" and the separation of *res cogitans* from *res extensae.* To Descartes' "Cogito ergo sum," Hobbes could not but agree that the knowledge of the proposition "I exist" depended on the other, "I think"; something that thinks could not be nothing. But for Hobbes, knowledge of the proposition "I think" devolved from the fact that we can conceive of no activity apart from its subject; we cannot, for example, imagine the act of thinking apart from something thinking any more than we can conceive of the act of leaping apart from something leaping. Moreover, we can only conceive of this subject of an activity as corporeal or in material guise. Thus, while Descartes would derive from his statement a certainty of the existence of his soul, Hobbes concluded to the contrary that that which thinks is corporeal.[101] Descartes replied somewhat impatiently by reminding Hobbes that everyone distinguished between corporeal and incorporeal substances, and mind was obviously of the latter type. This was not in the least bit obvious to Hobbes, for whom mind was simply a name given to the aggregate motions of the brain. And he replied:

But if M. Descartes shows that he who understands and the understanding are identical we shall lapse back into the scholastic mode of speaking. The understanding understands, the vision sees, will wills, and by exact analogy, walking, or at least the faculty of walking will walk. Now all this is obscure, incorrect, and quite unworthy of M. Descartes' wonted clearness.[102]

The controversy continued at length along these lines, and through the points already touched upon in the last chapter. Just as geometers would insist that points and lines had some kind of ideal or independent existence and Hobbes would insist on a specific material cause for everything, so in this argument Descartes sturdily defended his dualistic universe, while Hobbes implacably went about absorbing *res cogitans* into a scheme of matter in motion. Reasoning, Hobbes reiterated, yields conclusions not about things, but about the terms that designate things. Reasoning, then, depends on names, "names on the imagination, and imagination, perchance, as I think, on the motion of the corporeal organs. Thus mind will be nothing but the motions in certain parts of an organic body."[103] Confronted with an assertion which so audaciously annihilates the immaterial nature of mind, it is hardly to be wondered at that Descartes and Cartesians subsequently seem to regard Hobbes with a mixture of pity, anger, and contempt. Hobbes closes the Cartesian hiatus between mind and body here, but he also draws up the lines of battle which divided philosophers throughout the rest of the century. Atomists like Gassendi followed a materialistic line which tended to support Hobbes, and they pointed out the difficulties arising from the fact that Descartes excluded by definition any contact between mind and body. Cartesians, like the early Henry More, on the other hand, became

Hobbes's most outspoken enemies, and they asserted that Hobbes could give no satisfactory explanation of the way in which organic motions are transformed into mental images.

The rather sharp and exasperated tone in which the Hobbes-Descartes debate was carried on testifies perhaps to the unbridgeable distance separating the two philosophers' temperaments as well as their metaphysics. When Mersenne sent Descartes another set of objections to other of his works from an unidentified English friend, the same impatience and irritation colors his responses, despite the fact that he did not know his critic to be Hobbes. The two had not yet met personally, but as Pell wrote to Sir Charles Cavendish, he did not expect "that the Genius either of Gassendus or of Mr Hobbes should ever close with that of Des Cartes though you seeme to hope that Des Cartes & Mr Hobbes will grow acquainted in Paris."[104] On the other hand, there is probably some truth in Brandt's thesis that the dispute, which engendered an enduring coolness between the philosophers, was at least in part founded on the things they held in common, for both were among the first to espouse a purely mechanical conception of nature.[105] Descartes did, in fact, privately write to Mersenne that he suspected the Englishman's good faith.[106] He then dismissed Hobbes's asserted priority in arriving at a theory of the subjectivity of secondary qualities as childish and ridiculous ("puerile et digne de risée"),[107] and he finally broke off any further communication.[108] Fifteen years later, Hobbes's detractors still clung to this issue in an attempt to discredit him, claiming priority for Digby and Gassendi as well as Descartes in working out an explanation of sense by principles of motion. Hobbes took the opportunity to point out that their doctrines were not, after all, alike. Digby and Gassendi (both good friends of his) shared the opinions of Epicurus, which were not like his,[109] whereas Descartes "attributeth no motion at all to the object of sense, but an inclination to action, which inclination no man can imagine what it meaneth."[110] And there the matter rested.

Hobbes and Descartes did eventually meet, an event recorded by Cavendish in a letter to Pell. He wrote from Rotterdam, August 2, 1648:

Mr de Cartes & Mr Hobbes have met & as they agree in some opinions so they extreamlie differ in others, as in the nature of hardness. Mr Hobbes conceiving the cause of it to be extream quicke motion of the atomes or minute partes of a bodie which hinders an other bodie from entring & Mr

de Cartes conceives it a close joining of the partes at rest, which appears
to me more reasonable.[111]

There is no evidence that the two philosophers ever met again, or that
they desired to do so.

Hobbes's thinking now advanced along many fronts at once toward a synthesis of his system. Part of the "little treatise" that had
circulated in England had been reshaped and grown into a Latin
volume, and this first published account of his political theory was
published in Paris in 1642 under the title *De Cive*.[112] Hobbes was then
fifty-four years old, and on the verge of the most productive period in
his life. This volume, which already contained the core of his political
teachings and which had been completed in its earlier form well before the outbreak of the Civil War in England, added considerably to
the esteem in which he was already held in France, and even Descartes read it with grudging admiration.[113]

Aubrey writes that after Hobbes became involved in political
problems, for ten years "his thoughts were much, or chiefly intent on
his *De Cive*, and after that on his *Leviathan:* which was a great putt-
back to his mathematicall improvement. . . . for in ten yeares' (or better)
discontinuance of that study (especially) one's mathematiques will
become very rusty."[114] This appears to be a piece of Aubrey's habitual
extravagance, for in view of the extensive activities Hobbes had engaged in during this period, mathematics or the other sciences never
seemed far from his mind. In the course of the next few years, although he did not publish much, he was still very much engrossed in
adding to and refining his education in the sciences. For instance,
when William Petty, the anatomist, pioneer in comparative statistics
and later Fellow of the Royal Society, came to France, he bore with
him a letter of introduction to Hobbes from Pell, and together they
read Vesalius and did some dissecting.[115] It was Petty who drew the
diagrams for Hobbes's brief work, the *Tractatus opticus*, which Mersenne included with a collection of scientific papers and published in
1644 under the title *Cogitata physico-mathematica*. In the same year,
Mersenne again performed Hobbes a service by publishing another of
his short papers, this one on the doctrine of motion, in his own
Ballistica. The following year, Sir Charles Cavendish (who had fled to
Paris with the Earl of Newcastle after the battle of Marston Moor)
wrote to Pell (who, in turn, took a professorial post in Amsterdam) of
Hobbes's current studies. These included recent works on as-

tronomy[116] and "Reietas booke," which Hobbes did not care for because it recommended "hyperbolick glasses above sphaericall, for perpectives."[117] Meanwhile, Pell himself was in a bitter dispute with the Dane, Longomantanus, over the quadrature of the circle, and Hobbes was called upon to submit a mathematical demonstration in Pell's favor along with such notable Continental scientists as Carcavi, Mersenne, Descartes, Roberval, and Cavalieri. He was probably even then also preparing his *Minute or First Draught of the Optiques*, the manuscript of which is dated 1646.

These papers by Hobbes and this list of activities are significant here only insofar as they attest Hobbes's continued ambition in scientific areas and the esteem in which he was held by the scientific community. Through Cavendish and Pell, as well as through his French acquaintances, Hobbes's sources of information and communications now spread to virtually every important capital of scientific work. In view of the later course of his reputation, which has been overwhelmingly concerned with his political thought, it is important to note that he was then regarded as a practicing mathematician and natural philosopher of considerable ability.

Hobbes's fourth voyage to the Continent, which was really an exile, thus began by setting him in very much the same intellectual milieu as that of his third trip, but with the important difference that his reputation was rapidly reaching a high point. Moreover, his range of command over a variety of kinds of subject matter had expanded substantially, and he had embarked on his career as a political figure with the publication of *De Cive*. Soon to be added to his roles as mathematician, natural philosopher, and political theorist would be that of a servant to the royal household, a role which he undertook in a minimal way when the English court began its exile in France.

It would be a mistake to suppose that the philosopher of Malmesbury had by this time become a mechanical philosopher who would simply systematize the calculus of political behavior with Olympian disinterest, or alternatively, with a purely royalist interest which made of his works mere propaganda tracts. His greatest passion was really for the philosophic endeavor itself, and the gusto which he brought to it was of Elizabethan proportions. When he was already aged, he could still speak of philosophy with a certain sensuous Elizabethan enthusiasm, as a pursuit that even voluptuous men neglect not, "but only because they know not how great a pleasure it is to the mind of man to be ravished in the vigorous and perpetual embraces of the most beauteous world."[118]

IV

The Politics

The Paris Exile

$\mathcal{H}$ O B B E S had sojourned in France for six years before the somewhat makeshift English court came to Paris, shortly preceded by Sir Charles Cavendish and his brother the Earl of Newcastle, and shortly followed by a stream of the other English nobility.[1] Hobbes was once again thrown into an English royalist milieu. He had just been planning to retire to Montauban as a guest of one of his French friends, and translator, François Du Verdus, where he hoped to complete his work, when he was employed as mathematical tutor to the Prince of Wales and had to stay in Paris. The appointment certainly reflected no disapproval of his *De Cive,* and in the light of some remarks by Sir Charles Cavendish, it might even have been intended as a reward by the exiled faction: "My Lord Jerman [i.e., Henry Jermyn, lord St. Albans, and possibly the husband of Henrietta Maria] did (I beleeve) doe him that favoure & honor," wrote Cavendish to Pell, "for his friends heer I am confident had no hand in it."[2] Hobbes was even then preparing to have a second and larger edition of *De Cive* published in Amsterdam by the Elzevir press, a task which was completed by another French friend and admirer, Samuel Sorbière, the Historiographer Royal, in 1647. Sorbière was not a man to overlook the possibilities of good advertising, and he therefore proposed to describe Hobbes as tutor to the Prince of Wales on the title page of the new edition, despite Hobbes's objection, "Doceo enim Mathematicam, non Politicam."[3] In a long letter, Hobbes makes it clear to Sorbière that such an inscription under his name might reflect poorly on the Prince as adopting his principles; furthermore, he did not want to appear vain. Besides that, he was thinking about returning to England, and being known as the Prince's preceptor would not be prudent and was, in any case, not

81

true since he did not belong to the royal household.[4] The astonishing thing about this letter was that Hobbes could, in 1647, conceive of political developments in England taking a course that would eventually permit him to return safely—despite the writing of De Cive, and despite the anticipated publication of Leviathan, which he had even then begun to write. Whether his thinking on this point was based on utterly naive or remarkably astute reasons is not now known, but he *did* return safely within a few years.

To this period too, must belong Edmund Waller's offer to translate De Cive, a book with which he was much taken. Hobbes willingly agreed and himself translated some pages as a specimen from which Waller could work. After the poet saw them, he "would not meddle with it"; asserting that no one could do the job as well as Hobbes, he sagaciously withdrew the offer.[5] No doubt Hobbes would have been happy to see his volume in English, for he seemed dissatisfied at this point in his career to continue restricting his audience to the learned classes by writing in Latin. The Leviathan was being written in English, and he would himself translate the De Cive. But now both his literary tasks and his employment at court were interrupted for some six months by a serious illness which, it was said, was very nearly fatal. Its nature is unknown, but Aubrey reports that before 1650 Hobbes had developed a palsy that grew progressively worse as he aged, and this illness may have been related.[6]

The question raised by this episode is that of how history would have evaluated Hobbes had he indeed died then at the age of fifty-nine, having authored only the De Cive, the Thucydides, some small scientific tracts, a couple of unpublished papers, and nothing else. What had he accomplished that was of substance in philosophy? The answer, as far as Hobbes himself was concerned, was that he had by that time created nothing less than political science. He was not too modest to assert, in his uniquely contentious way, that civil philosophy was "no older (I say it provoked, and that my detractors may know how little they have wrought upon me) than my own book De Cive."

But what? were there no philosophers natural nor civil among the ancient Greeks? There were men so called; . . . But it follows not that there was philosophy. There walked in old Greece a certain phantasm, for superficial gravity, though full within of fraud and filth, a little like philosophy; which unwary men, thinking to be it, adhered to the professors of it, some to one, some to another. . . .[7]

This passage, written in the most pungent later style of Hobbes, was set down years later, even after *Leviathan,* which he must certainly have considered his *magnum opus.* There are indications that he was by no means entirely content with his position on every issue in *De Cive,* and he made modifications in the material when it was incorporated into *Leviathan.*[8] Nonetheless, without contending that political science or "civil philosophy" had received its definitive formulation in *De Cive,* he simply maintained that it was no older than *De Cive,* and that the work was prior to the greater *Leviathan* in this respect. He was fully aware that, however imperfect, the volume had succeeded in achieving something that neither the Greeks nor the political theorists of the Middle Ages had done. Inasmuch as his preferred exposition was in *Leviathan,* the discussion of his political theory here must be drawn largely from that more comprehensive work. But his claim was first staked out in *De Cive;* it was that he had found a way of rationalizing inquiry into political behavior and that he had thereby created a new science.

It was probably because of this special place won by *De Cive,* and because it was the book that had given Hobbes his reputation in Europe, that he went ahead with the second edition, even though he knew it would be superseded by *Leviathan.* As if to announce that he was preparing a volume of such importance, Hobbes now allowed the original "little treatise" of 1640, the *Elements of Law,* to be issued, splitting it up into two volumes which appeared in 1650, *Human Nature, or the Elements of Policy,* and *De Corpore Politico, or the Elements of Law, Moral and Politic.*[9] Having gotten well into *Leviathan,* he then began working simultaneously on his translation of *De Cive,* and it seems that the more demands made upon him by his literary labors, the more prodigious became his powers. Despite another illness in the summer of 1650, he completed *Leviathan* by the fall.[10] His translation of *De Cive,* entitled *Philosophical Rudiments concerning Government and Society,* was finished at around the same time, with Hobbes probably working under pressure in an attempt to forestall a pirated translation.[11] Hobbes was certainly aware that his work had alienated some (but by no means all) of the clergy, and perhaps he reasoned that his arguments were so clear and evident in *Leviathan* that they would exonerate him from the charges of disloyalty or atheism already being brought against *De Cive.*[12] But he was apparently oblivious of the reverse possibility that *Leviathan* would instead have the effect of making his relationship with the exiled court untenable. With touching good faith, therefore, he straightway presented a beautiful vellum manuscript copy to Charles, who had just returned from his last defeat at Worcester. Robertson justly remarks of this gesture that Hobbes "was so little conscious of disloyalty that he was forward" to make the gift,[13] for Hobbes had neither the personal physical courage nor the inclination toward subtle ambition and vanity which distinguishes the martyr. Yet he had been warned by friends of his among the English clergy, who both liked him and feared to provoke him against the Anglican Church,[14] that his views would be taken amiss. Robert Payne wrote to Gilbert Sheldon, later Archbishop of Canterbury, even before the publication of *Leviathan*, that he was trying to restrain Hobbes. Payne had not met with much luck:

I have written to my friend [Hobbes] abroad again & again, since I wrote to you last, & heard from him. He assures me, he hath no particular quarrel to [sic] that tribe: Only this position he shall set down and confirm, that the Civil Sovereign (whether one or more) is chief pastor, & may settle what kind of Church Government he shall think fit for the people's Salvation. Which will be enough to justify those, who have cashiered Bps., & may tempt others, who have not, to follow their Example.

The truth is, I fear he is engaged too far already to retreat, & therefor I have small hopes to prevail. Yet in my last I commended this consideration to him, that all truths are not fit to be told at all times: ... But all this is said to you in your Ear: & if our Tribe have got so sharp an Adversary, you may guess whom we may thank for it.[15]

Payne was evidently of the opinion that Hobbes was determined to write whatever the logic of his sytem required him to write, and that arguments would not prevail with him if they were inconsistent with it. Hobbes, however, did not find his position to be intrinsically hostile to Anglican politics and always protested that he was a true son of the Church, though its response to his book was no less than alarming. The general secularism of his approach was tantamount to atheism in the eyes of the Anglican clergy advising the king, and the French authorities resented its attack on the Roman Catholic Church and on the papacy, which Hobbes had comically depicted as "the ghost of the Roman empire sitting crowned upon the grave thereof."[16] Bearing in mind the fates of the murdered anti-royalist envoys Dorislaus and Ascham, Hobbes made haste and secretly fled to London in the middle of the winter, though he was no longer young and still somewhat infirm. Saddened by the death of his friend Mersenne in 1648, and deprived of the company of Gassendi, who had left Paris for reasons of health, Hobbes was probably just as glad to return

William Cavendish, Third Earl of Devonshire (1617–1684) by Van Dyck. Devonshire Collection, Chatsworth. Reproduced by permission of the Trustees of the Chatsworth Settlement.

to his companions at home where, by submitting to Parliament, he was permitted to work undisturbed.

Reestablishing contact with the third Earl, who had already returned but who had retired to the country until the Restoration, Hobbes chose to settle in intellectually livelier London. While he eventually rejoined the Earl's household (with a raise—the account books at Chatsworth show his salary was increased to £80), it is doubtful that his service was active. When the Earl sent his son William, the future fourth Earl and first Duke of Devonshire, on his Grand Tour, he would not be escorted by the philosopher, now in his mid-sixties, but by the younger Dr. Killigrew.

Hobbes had never tried to climb the winding stair to great place, but neither had he ever been averse to fame. Now that one book had followed close upon the heels of the next in the short span of 1650–51, books which combined novelty with forcefulness of expression, Hobbes was no longer merely a scholar of considerable reputation among the very learned. He was now both famous and formidable, though his fame was largely of the kind accorded to those who are extremely obnoxious, but too cogent to ignore. His claim that political science was no older than his own *De Cive* was carried through in *Leviathan*, and he was catapulted into notoriety as a result. No sooner was he back in London than the gossip began: "Hobbes is caressed at London," wrote one loyal servant of the king, "for his traitorous and rebellious tenets."[17]

The Causes and Generation of the State

Ironically, Hobbes's "traitorous and rebellious tenets" grew out of a near-Utopian vision of the possibility of establishing a permanent peace among men. Everything, he wrote in *De Cive*, by which "this present age doth differ from the rude simpleness of antiquity" was a debt owed to geometry. Had moral philosophers arrived at an understanding of human actions comparable to our understanding of quantity as given to us by geometry, Hobbes holds out the promise that then "the strength of *avarice* and *ambition*, which is sustained by the erroneous opinions of the vulgar as touching the nature of *right* and *wrong*, would presently faint and languish; and mankind should enjoy such an immortal peace, that . . . there should hardly be left any pretence for war."[18] In the dedication to *De Cive*, Hobbes asserts that he has surpassed the ancients because he found an "idoneous principle of tractation" or apt way of approaching his subject. In a some-what neglected passage, he sets forth his own analytic process of discovery:

There is a certain clue of reason, whose beginning is in the dark: but by the benefit of whose conduct, we are led as it were by the hand into the clearest light. So that the principle of tractation is to be taken from that darkness; and then the light to be carried thither for irradiating the doubts. . . . From this it was, that when I applied my thoughts to the investigation of natural justice, I was presently advertised from the very word *justice*, (which signifies a steady will of giving every one his *own*), that my first enquiry was to be, from whence it preceded that any man should call anything rather his *own*, than *another man's*.[19]

He found the answer not in nature, but in agreement, which led him to ask why men do, in fact, "think it fitting that every man should have his enclosure." This, in turn, led him to the basic questions about human nature.

Following his analytic-synthetic method, Hobbes therefore began his study of civil government by investigating its very matter, man, and then went on to its generation and form. For everything is best understood by its constitutive causes:

For as in a watch, or some such small engine, the matter, figures, and motion of the wheels cannot well be known, except it be taken insunder and viewed in parts; so to make a more curious search into the rights of states and the duties of subjects, it is necessary, I say, not to take them insunder, but yet that they be so considered as if they were dissolved. . . ."[20]

The mechanical analogy, rather than the older traditional one of the state as an organic unit, was perhaps inevitable, for civic trouble was actually taking the state "insunder" and demonstrating that the sanctions which had held it together were not eternal or "natural." By an act of the imagination, Hobbes proposes that we can conceive of man existing outside of the state, without the form of law or even the moral cohesiveness of the clan; and this conception is man in the state of nature. It is an ideal conception which Hobbes knew could not be observed empirically, and which had sprung from a radical application of his method.[21] It is man regarded as the basic "matter" of the state, stripped of his "secondary" qualities—all of his acquired social characteristics. Man's will, as determined by his reason and his passions, is the "beginning of motion" that generates the state. To consider man "by *himself*, without *relation to others*,"[22] was therefore to investigate the permanent qualities in his make-up which would condition every social relationship into which entered.

Hobbes set it down as a principle "by experience known to all men"[23] that the primary characteristic of man is that he has passions, and that it is toward the fulfillment of his desires and the avoidance of pain (in the last instance, death) that man bends all his physical and mental powers. He also hungers for "glory" or precedence over his fellow man and will compete for it wherever he can. In this sense, men are substantially equally endowed, all of them continually aspiring to these general ends, and none so superior to the others that he can for long supersede them by himself. Since men will invariably interfere with one another in the course of pursuing the different objects of their passions, and since there exists no law in the state of nature to arbitrate their conflicts, Hobbes calls this condition a state of war of all against all.[24]

While man in the state of nature could never be observed empirically and was, in fact, a conceptual instrument of analysis created by Hobbes, he can and does appeal to each individual to confirm his observations by introspection.[25] But here a problem arises since Hobbes had affirmed that his science of politics and the study of human nature should be derived from "the first part of philosophy, geometry and physics."[26] Because his political writings now preceded his scientific ones, he asks instead that his principles regarding the essential characteristics of human nature be confirmed by every man consulting himself. Moreover, he continues, his principles can be confirmed simply by observing other men, for in their actions "they publicly profess their mutual fear and diffidence."[27] Even in times of general peace, the basic psychological factors pre-eminent in the state of war can be observed; they are merely attenuated when men live under the regulation of the state. Elsewhere, Hobbes asserts that this kind of psychological principle can be arrived at in either way— through a deduction from his basic sciences (although he never did it) or from introspection. It is knowledge that can be attained either analytically or synthetically, to use his terms.[28]

At stake, of course, is the much vexed question of the relationship between Hobbes's psychology and politics, and the mechanical laws of motion upon which his idea of science is based. Hobbes seems to have remained convinced that the rules of psychology could eventually be derived in a demonstrable fashion from geometry and physics, but that introspection yielded sufficiently evident knowledge of them.[29] The fact that not everyone found his principles evident, however, is well attested by his many critics.

Amicable relations are obviously difficult to establish in the state of nature where man indulges in an unabated egoism, and where he is chiefly ruled by the fear of death and the desire for self-aggrandizement. It was of course traditional to think that man was by nature a social animal and that he created civil society to achieve some benefit which a rational soul would find "good." It was the peculiarity of Hobbesian man in the state of nature that he did not share with his fellows a common set of moral values which are scaled up to some commonly acknowledged "good." Each man is essentially solitary, and what he denominates in his mind as desirable may never coincide with any one else's idea of the good. Indeed, the very idea of goodness arises out of individual appetites, the object of which for any man is what he calls good, and the object of his aversion being "evil" to him. All of man's values can be derived from these fundamental appetites and all motivation is ultimately rooted in them. While they are basically responses to external stimuli, yet they are closely associated in Hobbes's mind with life itself since they are the sources of our motion.

Building on these basic appetites, Hobbes sets out definition after definition, showing how the other passions are derived from them and are given different names when considered differently:

> For *appetite,* with an opinion of attaining, is called HOPE.
> The same, without such opinion, DESPAIR.
> *Aversion,* with opinion of HURT from the object, FEAR.
> The same, with hope of avoiding that hurt by resistance, COURAGE.
> Sudden *courage,* ANGER.[30]

Laughter, said Hobbes with an astonishing flash of insight, is "sudden glory,"[31] and in the same pithy fashion, felicity, which we associate with a philosophical contentment, Hobbes defined as "continual success in obtaining those things which a man from time to time desireth. . . . For there is no such thing as perpetual tranquility of mind, while we live here; because life itself is but motion, and can never be without desire, nor without fear."[32] Hobbes's treatment of moral values and normative judgments is thus altogether analogous to his subjective, relativistic treatment of secondary qualities. In the state of nature where man cannot guide himself by conventional rules of morality, neither can he appeal to any objective, absolute ethical norms—they simply do not exist.

It was perhaps this vision of man as a singularly egoistic species that Hobbes's contemporaries would find most offensive, and men of all creeds and backgrounds would band together in a mutual abhorrence of it. How different, and how much more acceptable, was John Locke's amiable vision in his famous attempt to overthrow Hobbesian principles: "Man, living together according to reason, without a common superior on earth, without authority to judge between them, is properly the state of nature."[33] As we shall see, the opposition to Hobbes's version gave him good cause to say a few years later, "I know, by experience, how much greater thanks will be due than paid me, for telling men the truth of what men are."[34]

While other thinkers universally agreed that men were inherently benevolent or gregarious in some sense, it cannot be too strongly emphasized that Hobbes never said that men were essentially wicked. It is precisely because moral standards are inoperative in the warlike state of nature that man cannot be called wicked—wickedness having no more of a functional existence than goodness does outside of a social context. In the state of nature, man cannot be called naturally wicked—a position Hobbes considers impious—but only naturally passionate.[35] His behavior is regulated by his appetites or by expedience in an environment that offers no security:

For the affections of the mind, which arise only from the lower parts of the soul, are not wicked themselves; but the actions thence proceeding may be so sometimes, as when they are either offensive or against duty.[36]

A judgment of "wickedness" thus presupposes a society which defines the conventions of behavior and duties, on the one hand, and a mind that can grasp the extent of these conventions and duties, on the other. When the second factor—a reasonable mind—is lacking, as in children and the insane, society no longer holds them accountable for their behavior and the judgment of "wickedness" is set aside. So Hobbes says,

A wicked man is almost the same thing with a child grown strong and sturdy, or a man of a childish disposition; and malice the same with a defect of reason in that age when nature ought to be better governed through good education and experience.[37]

Given this view of human nature and morality, Hobbes's first concern was to explain why man does in fact form society, or rather why he finds it expedient to do so, and to develop a hypothesis about how he might go about it. Hobbes also thought that man *ought* to act morally, subjecting himself to the authority of the state at the cost of some of his liberty, but this question was held distinct from the question of how men in the state of nature could be induced to do so. That is to say, Hobbes had to deal with the separate questions of the nature of political obligations and of psychological motivation. These, in turn, are bound up with his notion of natural rights and natural laws, which require some exploration.

Since Hobbes understands self-preservation to be an absolutely fundamental right of nature ("the liberty each man hath, to use his own power, as he will himself, for the preservation of his own nature"), and since the state of nature is a perilous place, a man may find anything (even another's body) of use to his own survival.[38] It is a basic characteristic of the state of nature, therefore, that everyman has a right to everything, where "right" is defined as the liberty to do or to forbear as one chooses. In this sense, "right" is not to be understood as an entitlement such as the right to property or the right to vote, as Warrender points out. Hobbes means that in the state of nature man cannot be *obliged* to renounce anything.[39] Seeking his security, a man is under no obligation to relinquish anything whatever which he feels may enhance his chances of survival, while every other man may, with equal right, deprive him of everything.

In this parlous condition, no man can be secure, and reason advises him that his fears may be best averted and his desires best fulfilled in a more peaceful situation. It is this hint from reason in the service of his passions that leads him to consider entering into an agreement with his fellows. (Indeed, if reason did not serve the passions well, what possible function could it have at all?) For if competition, diffidence, and the urge for glory make men quarrel, the overriding passions of mutual fear—ultimately, the fear of violent death—lend weight to the counsels of reason:[40] "Reason suggesteth convenient articles of peace, upon which men may be drawn to agreement. These articles are they, which otherwise are called the Laws of Nature."[41] The basic framework here is the interplay between the demands of passion and those of reason, much as it was in Hobbes's Thucydides. But whereas in the art of history the two are reconciled through the agency of a "perspicuous" rhetoric which teaches civic prudence, in the state of nature the two merge in an enlightened self-interest that teaches man a kind of pre-civic prudence—that of entering into an agreement with his fellows—and it moves him toward the great task of founding the state.

The first and most fundamental of these natural laws, which are described by Hobbes as "theorems" or "general precepts" of reason, bids man defend himself by all possible means. It also tells him that he "ought to endeavor peace, as far as he has hope of obtaining it."[42] From this first natural law, a second is derived: that a man be willing (as far as it is consistent with self-defense) to lay down his right to all things if his fellows are prepared to do the same thing, and to suffer this constraint of his liberty for the sake of peace.[43]

Hobbes's prescriptive language in describing the first law (men "ought" to endeavor peace) and in a number of other passages has led some commentators to argue that natural laws impose moral obligations on us, and the search for peace is then construed as a *duty*. But, as others have pointed out, natural law also dictates self-defense, and the preservation of our nature is a natural *right*, and thus cannot be a duty.[44] Besides, if natural laws were obligatory, failure to fulfill them would mark a man as unjust or bad, but in the state of nature, goodness is determined by each man's appetite and just or unjust does not exist, as Hobbes repeatedly said:

Justice, and injustice are none of the faculties neither of the body, nor mind. If they were, they might be in a man that were alone in the world, as well as his senses, and passions. They are qualities, that relate to men in society, not in solitude.[45]

Hobbes describes the laws of nature as "dictates of reason... or theorems" conducing to self-defense and conservation. Their fulfillment may therefore characterize the rational man, but does not define the just or good man, for Hobbes nowhere equates rationality with morality.

The laws of nature are thus general maxims which every man respects because rational self-interest tells him to and his motivation is prudential, but they lack the distinctive characteristic of true laws—they do not oblige him to obey and he has in no way relinquished his right to do exactly as he thinks fit. It would be an offense against natural law, for instance, to rob or injure another man when such aggressive behavior were unnecessary for self-preservation since that would expose the offender to greater risks. Since each man in the state of nature must determine for himself whether theft or injury is required for his security, an incorrect calculation breaches natural law in the sense that it is irrational to endanger oneself: such behavior is misconceived, not immoral. Natural laws may thus be said to bind, loosely speaking, in that it would be folly not to heed them by seeking peace, but they cannot be said to oblige as laws, properly speaking, oblige.[46] As we shall see, that would require the relinquishing of some rights:

These dictates of reason, men used to call by the names of laws, but improperly: for they are but conclusions, or theorems... whereas law, properly, is the word of him, that by right hath command over others.[47]

The single but very important exception to the nonobligatory status of natural laws is the case of the man who understands them to be the commands of God. He is then truly obliged to obey them by seeking peace (though never by acts that endanger his security) for he construes them as the word of one who "by right" can command all things. Should a man be devoid of religious belief, prudence takes its place and dictates adherence to the same rules of conduct. The major function of civil society, when established, is to make the laws of nature fully operative for the generality of men by interpreting them in enforceable, positive legal codes, for "what is to be called *theft* ... what *injury* in a citizen, that is not to be determined by the natural, but by civil law."[48]

The escape route by which humanity may leave the state of nature and enter civil society is suggested by the second law of nature, bidding man lay down his right to all things if his fellows are prepared to do the same thing. Rights may be simply renounced or they may be transferred to another person. When two or more people mutually agree to transfer some right, they are said to make a contract, and from this obligations first arise:

And when a man hath... abandoned, or granted away his right; then he is said to be OBLIGED, or BOUND, not to hinder those, to whom such right is granted, or abandoned, from the benefit of it.[49]

A covenant between individuals which transfers their right to govern themselves (their right to be free of obligation) to a single sovereign authority is what makes the establishment of civil society possible.

This transition into civil society through covenants is by no means easy to accomplish because of the uncertain durability of contracts in the state of nature, and therefore of obligations. Primarily, the difficulty arises from the fact that no contracting party can be guaranteed that the other fellow will uphold his end of the bargain, and Hobbes holds that if a man feels a "reasonable suspicion" that the other party means to endanger his security by acting in bad faith, the contract is nullified and all obligation ends. In instances where both parties perform instantly, this is no problem, but where future performance is required and where there is no common power set over both parties to compel performance, each man must judge for himself the likelihood of his betrayal by the other. Hobbes is specific in saying that where one party has already upheld his part of the bargain, the second performer is firmly obliged and ought to do his part. Nonetheless, in the case of the first performer, it seems that covenants must remain contingent upon trust and, perhaps, hope.[50] Thus men move toward building society in cautious steps, taking upon themselves obligations of uncertain durability, and endeavoring to heed natural laws the effectiveness of which must recede whenever self-preservation is threatened.

As obligations spring from covenants, so do the notions of just and unjust. From the natural law which bids us endeavor peace, another follows which dictates that we keep our covenants. Not to do so is what unjust *means*, according to Hobbes, for without covenants every man still has a right to everything, and no action can be unjust.[51] Covenants are therefore the "original of justice," yet Hobbes says there can be no "injustice actually" in the state of nature for the same reason that covenants themselves are conditional: the fear of non-performance by the other party which makes covenants of mutual trust invalid. Such fear cannot be removed in man's natural warlike condition, but only in a commonwealth:

So that the nature of justice, consisteth in keeping of valid covenants: but the validity of covenants begins not but with the constitution of civil power, sufficient to compel men to keep them.[52]

Civil society is consolidated when a common authority can by right (and force, if necessary) compel the performance of obligations to a large extent, thus sharply narrowing the range in which reasonable suspicion can exist between contracting parties. Insofar as our original covenant entails relinquishing our liberty to do as we please, the sovereign power governs by the authority we gave him—we are the authors of his acts. His laws, according to Hobbes, are therefore commands which *by right* (authority) suffice to make us do something. Disobeying the command of an authority one has covenanted to accept as the representative of one's will belongs to the category of unjust actions—that is, it is a breach of contract or a crime.[53]

The purpose of this original covenant is defense and safety, and from it springs the effectiveness of every subsequent contract by virtue of the new common authority over everyone. That authority provides a certain guarantee or "sufficient security" which makes durable contracts a feasible aim. In sum, it may be said that we are *motivated* to enter covenants and build society by fear in the state of nature; we are *guided* by natural laws in this, but we are *obliged* to maintain peace and obey the common authority because we promised to do so in covenants and *ought* to keep our word. Finally, we are *able to* endeavor peace without risk to our self-preservation and thus keep our covenants because the sovereign authority provides secure circumstances that preserve the effectiveness of those covenants.

The transference of rights to a single common authority is by no means total. Clearly the right to defend one's life when it is threatened by violence is inalienable, for a man cannot lay down his right to self-defense in society when the very purpose of covenanting is security.[54] Thus a man may, without offense, fight tooth and nail as he is being led to his execution, notwithstanding the fact that it was ordered by the authority whom he is covenanted to obey. It also appears that thoughts remain in the state of nature since Hobbes gives as a condition of valid covenants that their performance be possible.[55] A man cannot promise to do, or be obliged to do, the impossible, and it is not possible for a man to control his thoughts entirely. Besides, the degree to which thoughts may or may not conform to some covenanted standard is unobservable, hence unenforceable, until expressed in words or deeds. Thoughts of criminal deeds are called "sins" by Hobbes only when they are accompanied by intentions, for intentions indicate a wish or disposition to breach the laws and express contempt for the legislator, which is against natural law, but they are not crimes, which involve a *perceivable* breach of obligations. Thoughts by themselves, without intent, never seem to be blameable no matter how unsavory: "For to be pleased in the fiction of that, which would please a man if it were real, is a passion so adherent to the nature both of man, and every other living creature, as to make it a sin, were to make sin of being a man."[56]

Much has been made of the fact that Hobbes, by finding the origins of society in a contract, makes it an entirely "artificial" body; and his famous introductory passage to *Leviathan* is often quoted, where he speaks of the commonwealth as an "artificial man" and the original covenant as analogous to God's *fiat* pronounced at the Creation. Indeed, were it not for this artificiality, a science of politics would not be possible since we can only know the causes of things we make ourselves. Yet it must be equally stressed that the state *is* "natural" in the sense that "natural" instincts for self-preservation and the directives of "natural" law combine to motivate men to bind themselves into communities. The state is certainly not "natural" in the Aristotelian sense of men uniting to seek the best way of life "by nature"—that turn toward final causes or purposes is quite absent in Hobbes. The state is "natural" more in the sense of the Marsilian tradition, which linked its creation to the biological instincts of each man to seek a sufficient life, though Hobbes perceives nature itself in a more mechanical manner than Marsilius of Padua did.[57] Man's motivation in creating the state is natural, but his creation is a work of art. He brings into existence an artificial construct that runs according to its own rules and that is not found in nature. Art and Nature (those favored twin topics of the Renaissance writers) are sharply distinguished in Hobbes, but they function complementarily, not separately.

In this brief outline of the way in which Hobbes conceived that civil associations might come about, it has been noted that the idea of a state of nature is analytical: it breaks down society into its simplest parts in the same way as one dissolves a triangle into its lines and its lines into points in order to define its material cause. Hobbes's observations on human psychology, on the other hand, are empirical: each of us can observe the traits he attributes to man in the state of nature in ourselves and others because civil society merely creates new circumstances, it does not change human nature. Hobbes's theory of the rights and duties of the subject and the sovereign authority, finally, were to be deductively derived from what it means to be obliged by a covenant since neither the name "subject" nor the name "sovereign authority" exists outside of covenants. As in geometry, he thought, once the definitions of these names are accepted, all of the inferences which follow must also be accepted by any reasonable person, and in politics the consequences of the covenant must be taught and recognized. Where the state is perceived as wholly artificial in its form like a geometrical figure, citizenship becomes a matter of rules and not, as Hobbes says, like tennis, a matter of practice.[58]

Hobbes's position has evident connections with the natural-law tradition that regarded reason as embodying universal moral concepts, apprehended by all men, though in Hobbes's system only Christians are bound by them as the commands of God. But, as noted, Hobbes did not think society could be built on each man's apprehension of natural laws construed as having a specific content relating to what is just and unjust. The concept was too antinomian, the results for society too chaotic. The content of the laws—to keep one's word, endeavor to establish peace, and so on—is not moral but procedural in that these laws are aimed at establishing some kind of order from which security can be derived,[59] and their motive is prudential. The obligations they impose are moral only for Christians both in and out of the state of nature since breaches are punishable by God. Had Hobbes not considered natural laws binding on Christians, he would have had little use for the term in his system. He could have been content, then, to discard the concept altogether as a superfluity and conceive of the state as founded on expedience and prudence alone.

Thus, government and society are to be derived from both an enlightened self-interest and, on the other hand, from a Christian obedience to the commands of God, but his detractors have often seen this scheme as a system of "selfishness in equilibrium."[60] They found it particularly offensive that Hobbes linked reason itself to such primitive physical roots as the instinct for self-preservation and that he traced man's noblest emotions—benevolence, patriotism, and civic conscience—back to less laudable and less magnanimous beginnings. Because actions prompted by self-interest cannot be easily distinguished in Hobbes from actions prompted by moral obligations, Richard Cumberland, Bishop of Peterborough, berated the philosopher for having "assign'd no larger bounds to . . . the Laws of Nature, than the Preservation of this frail life; as if men, like Swine, had Souls given them only, instead of Salt, to preserve the Body from Putrefaction."[61] The indignant, sarcastic tone was everywhere in Hobbes criticism of the period: Common Decency, when she is outraged, will grow satiric.

The Theory of Sovereignty

In the eyes of his critics, Hobbes not only brought the laws of nature down to the level of mere self-preservation, he also seemed to be destroying the transcendent sources of ideas of right and wrong, making them merely a function of the sovereign's will. Few covenants can remain effective for long in the conditions of the state of nature, said Hobbes, and if they are not effective they cannot be broken and an injustice committed. This was understood by John Eachard, a witty clergyman and a popular critic of Hobbes, as meaning that there was a "supposed time, in which it was just and lawful for every man to hang, draw and quarter whom he pleased and after what manner he pleased."[62] After all, had not Hobbes asserted that there was no such thing as just and unjust except by the sovereign's command? In fact, Hobbes had never said that the sovereign creates moral distinctions, although he was widely read that way. The sovereign only creates the circumstances for lasting valid covenants and thereby creates the conditions necessary for significant moral situations.[63] It is a notion of justice that is neither empirical nor analytic, but a deduction from what it means to be obliged by a covenant.[64] This dichotomy between the ideas of morality and justice, together with Hobbes's dictum that the sovereign could do no injury to a subject, gave him the reputation of defending the thesis that "might makes right."[65] The only instance in which this is true is the case of irresistible might—the might of God—and Hobbes nowhere implies that the sovereign cannot be judged as having acted immorally.[66] He deduces rather, that since the sovereign authority is a necessary condition for durable covenants, the very ground of legal order, it is logically absurd to say that he has broken a covenant and committed an injustice. The sovereign is always in the state of nature, bound only by natural laws that make him accountable to God alone. A subject, on the contrary, lets natural law be his sole guide only where the civil law is silent. He is always bound by natural law only in the sense that civil law is an interpretation of natural law, and he is obliged to obey them in the name of peace.

Moral issues aside for the moment, it is not difficult to understand why a monarchist of Hobbes's stamp eventually received his worst political criticism from the Cavaliers, once the logic of his position is grasped. Every essential element in his political theory stems from two fundamental aspects of the sovereign's position. First,

Hobbes affirmed that the foundations for every form of government are democratic since society itself springs from the covenant between individuals that subjects them to a common authority. The pact is composed of words the meanings of which are imposed by will (words being arbitrary), the agreement in words thereby signifying the agreement of wills, which is thereafter represented by the sovereign will. This arrangement provides another reason why the sovereign can do no injustice to a subject: he cannot both represent the will of the subject and at the same time do him an injury. By virtue of that initial pact, every act of the sovereign is authorized by the subjects. This part of Hobbes's theory leads to its first distinctive characteristic, the unaccountability of the sovereign.

Secondly, Hobbes made it very clear that while his sovereign is legally and theoretically absolute, yet if he is not also efficient in actual practice, his claims to sovereign authority will avail him but little. The citizenry contracted themselves into society to escape the perilous conditions of the state of nature, and if the sovereign authority cannot provide them with that protection, their contract is void. Thus, the second distinctive characteristic of Hobbes's theory is the lack of any sanction for an established government other than the covenant, together with the good faith of the subjects who obey the law of nature which tells them that self-interest is best served by observing their obligations and remaining acceptably docile.

The first characteristic of Hobbes's sovereign, his unaccountability, makes the state absolute and has led some traditional commentators to conclude that Hobbes's sovereign may arbitrarily declare what is right by virtue of his might. In fact, the sovereign can only declare what is law, and this he does by right of the authority invested in him. The second element, the lack of sanctions, demonstrates the radical weakness of the sovereign authority, although he is paradoxically absolute in theory. The state is built on a contract that bespeaks the will of the people, but that pact is not an historical document and it is no more immutable than "just" and "unjust." "The end of obedience," said Hobbes, "is protection," and only the individual's own judgment can tell him whether he feels sufficiently protected to remain covenanted. The state's coherence therefore requires the continual reaffirmation of the good faith of the people. It has been justly pointed out that had Hobbes really thought might makes right, he could simply have stipulated an adequate standing army to maintain the government. The introduction of a covenant concept, the insistence on the democratic basis of the state, and the deduction of the subject's obligations with respect to it would have been wholly unnecessary. But even then, some means would have to be devised—by covenant or otherwise—to ensure the obedience of the army. The problem would have been merely transferred to a new setting. Indeed, the essential meaning of Hobbes's covenant theory is to point out that the basis of political power is ultimately *authority*, not might.

To Roundhead interests during the Civil War, the strength of Hobbes's sovereign was objectionable for the obvious reason that his unaccountability seemed to absolve him from his responsibilities to the people. Hobbes appeared to be reverting to the theory of James I, that the king was the most responsible public servant, but responsible to God alone, not to parliament or the courts. To royalist interests, however, the weakness of Hobbes's sovereign did not recommend itself because it seemed to court rebellion. Surely, said the Earl of Clarendon, the royal prerogative is "founded upon a better title than such an accidental convention" as Hobbes's mythical covenant, notwithstanding Hobbes's insistence that adherence to the covenant was a strict duty.[67]

Hobbes's thought is further distinguished from the political ideas current in his time by its concern with the nature of government in the abstract rather than any particular form of government, though his personal preference for a monarchy is very marked. Theories of the divine right of kings, like theories of popular representation, devised hypotheses about the foundations of the state that would support arguments in favor of some particular religious sect or some special relationship between the branches of government. Hobbes, on the contrary, was intent on creating a true theoretical science; he was concerned with basic principles rather than changing institutions. His Leviathan was therefore a political creature without a face: the rise and fall of republics, monarchies, or democracies was simply a change of mask. His theories applied to them all, and the sovereign authority was still a sovereign authority for him whether it happened to reside in a king or a parliament.

This abstract interest in investigating the causes of the foundation and dissolution of political authority was liable to dangerous misreading in turbulent political times. The Hobbesian sovereign power, since it might reside in parliament or the king, might as well have been Charles II or Cromwell's parliament, and Hobbes had argued that English subjects were justified in changing their allegiance to a new, conquering sovereign when to do otherwise would endanger their lives or contradict rational self-interest. Royalists naturally read this as more useful as a justification for those who had capitulated to Cromwell's *de facto* government than for the restoration of their rightful but deposed king. Hence the Earl of Clarendon's bitter accusation that Hobbes had shown a "very officious care that Cromwell should not fall from his greatness."[68] Those interested in securing the throne for Charles "might well feel that Hobbes's friendship was as dangerous as Cromwell's enmity,"[69] and it was no wonder that Hobbes fled France under a cloud of rumored betrayal of the royalist cause after the publication of *Leviathan*.

The monarchical principle was itself never the key issue in English politics of the period, but rather the nature of the king's prerogatives and of the sovereign power, and these were sometimes derived from the monarchical principle.[70] Thus, for instance, Sir Robert Filmer, a staunch royalist, asserted that since the "Kingly Power is by the Law of God, so it hath no inferiour law to limit it," from which he concluded that Parliament could not infringe upon the prerogative.[71] Hobbes was only too happy to grant the monarch powers not subject to any other law of the land, but his reasons were utterly different. Hobbes argued that there was an authority in every state beyond which one could not go and that it was called the sovereign power. If the sovereign happened to be a king, his power was unrestricted simply because he was sovereign; that is, by definition. By definition, his authority was the basis of law, and not subject to it. Both the sanction of hereditary right to the throne and divine will were stripped from the monarch, and he, like every other sovereign, was merely a representative of the people's will. Hobbes's royalist enemies were therefore quick to accuse him of trimming his sails to catch the Commonwealth winds in *Leviathan*. But that was hardly fair, for the doctrine espoused in *Leviathan* in 1651 was no different from the one he embraced in *De Cive* in 1642, when monarchists had found it very agreeable and it had brought him into royal favor. It was scarcely Hobbes's fault that circumstances now made the very same doctrine repulsive to the king's supporters, while the parliamentarians from whom he had fled now found it more acceptable. The powers that he had accorded to the sovereign had shifted through historical caprice from Charles to Cromwell, and the fact that Hobbes could return to England safely was at least tacit recognition that the parliamentarians, if they did not openly avow his ideas, at any rate found them compatible with the new order.[72]

As the sovereign's power was indivisible, according to Hobbes, and not subject to any law other than the law of nature, so it extended over ecclesiastical institutions and excluded any of the "mixed" forms of government advocated by constitutionalists of both the royalist and parliamentarian varieties. Every form of constitutionalism limits the power of the sovereign in some way, either through the review of the judiciary or through a legislative power of parliament or some other representative body. But Hobbes had argued that it was a necessary condition of sovereignty that there be some power outside of the civil law which is the ultimate source of the law. It was logically inevitable: for "whosoever thinking sovereign power too great, will seek to make it less, must subject himself, to the power, that can limit it; that is to say, to a greater."[73] That greater power would of course be the true sovereign.

In disallowing any constraint whatever on the sovereign power, Hobbes virtually stood alone. He went against the entire trend of English constitutionalism as it was to develop in the Restoration, and whose function it was to reconcile the notion of a monarch who was absolute in dignities and title with the notion of a monarch who was restrained in some ways and therefore not really entirely absolute or sovereign. Thus John Bramhall, Bishop of Derry and robust monarchist, argued that while all civil powers are indeed exercised by the king's authority, yet he restrains his own authority by his coronation oath and by his great charters, and the parliament participates in legislation by a kind of "preparative power."[74] Sir Matthew Hale, Chief Justice, also inquired into what kind of authority Parliament wielded that could be reconciled with the royal prerogative. Hale called the assent of the Houses a "necessary solemnitie" that was prerequisite to the institution of laws; others vaguely referred to Parliament's "receptive" power.

Sir Robert Filmer came closest to Hobbes's position in placing the king above the regulation of either common law or statute law. Like Hobbes, he held that it was a verbal confusion to speak of a divided sovereign, and yet, he added, though the king be above the law, still he will act through the law.[75] The Earl of Clarendon acknowledged the king to be the sole legislator and it was only the king's stamp and "Royal consent, and that alone, that gives life, and being, and title of laws, to that which was before but counsel."[76] But having once consented to follow parliamentary forms, he added, the king must abide by his word and may not breach the trust of the people. While all of these representatives of English constitutionalism varied in their formulations and the degree of constraint put upon the monarch, they had one thing in common.[77] They insisted that although he is not accountable as a subject is, yet he must or ought to act through the laws. The difficulty with this position was clear in the constitutionalism of the Stuart era: it failed to provide any means of enforcing penalties on the recalcitrant prince who in theory "must" or "ought" to act through the laws, but who in fact failed to do so.[78]

Constitutionalists thus struggled with the evident contradiction of attempting to place legal obligations upon the prince whom they simultaneously held to be above the law and the very fountain of legal obligations. It was Hobbes who pointed out this confusion when he asserted the existence of an undivided power that created a law beyond which one could not go, and that this law was the sovereign's law. The obligations which the constitutionalists attempted to place on the sovereign could therefore have no more force than that of an ethical injunction, for the sovereign always remains in the "state of nature," that is, outside of civil law. The sanctions of custom, privilege, and natural justice which parliamentarians upheld as limitations on the monarch, like the sanctions of divine hereditary right which the royalists upheld to emphasize the independence of the monarch, were equally meaningless within the Hobbesian scheme.

The first fruit of Hobbes's application of his method to political behavior was thus conflict, and Hobbes had to defend the self-same *Leviathan* against the diametrically opposed views of both royalist and parliamentarian. The issues became increasingly complex, however, since the questions of sanctions and of the respective powers of parliament and the monarch were theoretically contested by political thinkers, but practically worked out in the courts of law (if not on the fields of battle). A further ingredient was added by antinomian thinkers, who appealed to laws beyond the reach of parliament, court, or king. Here, therefore, we must investigate further the manner in which "law" operates in Hobbes's vocabulary. It was one of his most important words, but also one of the most difficult to use univocally in the seventeenth century.

The Law

Nowhere is the centrality of language for Hobbes more evident than in his discussion of law. Speech is the great gift which Hobbes thought had raised man's ability to think above that of the animal world; sociologically, it was also speech which had allowed humanity to transcend a bestial condition by establishing covenants and communicating the law. Law lays down the rules according to which society functions; it introduces the public norms of right and wrong. Words, particularly the verbal formulations of civil law, in fact play the same role in Hobbes's scheme as "reason" does in more traditional philosophies, and it was typical of him that he should thus dignify the more external principle rather than the more internal subjective one. Justice has a Janus face which looks outward toward obedience to the letter of the law, on the one hand, and toward inner harmony, on the other. It was necessary for Hobbes to emphasize the public side if he was to shape a unified science where there had only been a mass of individual opinion before. Internal harmony is not a *political* consideration nor can it be regulated by law; actions directly affect society, however, and are liable to the power of the sword when they are criminal. It is for this reason that men of the law know Hobbes more as the progenitor of the science of jurisprudence than as the mechanistic philosopher who heralded the English Enlightenment.

For the seventeenth-century mind, the laws governing the physical universe are only obscurely differentiated from the laws which instill the principles of moral conduct in the political universe. Science and ethics were connected by laws which, if they functioned differently and in different spheres, had yet the same divine source. The term "law" was no less than protean: there were human laws and divine laws, statute laws and laws of reason, laws which were fundamental and laws which were not, civil laws and ecclesiastical laws, canon laws and common laws. Each use of the word had its burden of connotations pertaining to the way it operated in a particular art or field of learning. The meeting ground for all of them was in the no-man's-land of the natural-law tradition and in the old faculty psychology, for reason or experience sought out the laws peculiar to any particular subject matter. Hence, when Hobbes wrote of law or of reason with regard to some specific field, repercussions inevitably carried over to other fields by a multiple process of association, and his distinction between the way the moral and civil law operate would have been quite sufficient by itself to arouse the interest of barristers. As it was, he did much more.

According to Hobbes, the single most important cause of the

Civil War was, as already noted, the public confusion over the nature of the sovereign authority, and the notion that it could be divided or held accountable to some other power. Aside from the infringements on the sovereign power which had issued from the Church and Parliament, there had been trespasses by the courts of law, and they did not escape Hobbes's rebuke in *Leviathan*. He was nettled by the inherent constitutionalism of the common-law tradition in England, and in later years he advanced a full-scale attack against it in his *Dialogue between a Philosopher and a Student of the Common Laws of England,* which, however, remained unfinished. The whole complex of ideas centering around the relationship between civil law, moral law, the rights and duties of Parliament, and the sovereign had now to be worked out within the province of the courts themselves.

To watch an intelligent jurist in the constitutional tradition like Sir Matthew Hale confront the rigorous formulation of the nature of law by Hobbes is an engrossing spectacle, repeated in many other fields in which Hobbes was opposed. It not only illuminates his relationship to the age, but it also shows Hobbes's critics being forced to grapple with the fundamentals of their beliefs, being forced to clarify them, sometimes angrily, in order to defend themselves against his aggressive spirit of modernity.

The mutual confidence between ruler and ruled is a "Golden Knott," wrote Sir Matthew Hale, and the principle behind a peaceful commonwealth. Referring to Hobbes, the Lord Chief Justice affirmed that there was no better way to breach this confidence than "to tell the world that the Prince is bound to keepe none of the Laws that he or his Ancestors have by the advice of his greate Councill Established. . . . Such a Man that teacheth such a doctrine as this as much weakens the Sovereigne Power as is imaginable and betrayes it with a Kisse."[79] For Sir Matthew, to free the sovereign from obligations is to invite rebellion, but for Hobbes, who put the source of the law squarely in the hands of the sovereign, it was meant to check rebellion by avoiding confusion about where and to whom the subject owed his primary allegiance. Clearly, if people did not understand where the sovereign power was, they would not understand their duties to the highest law in the land. Was the unenlightened citizen to obey the "higher law" espoused by the Stuarts, for instance, the law upon which the royal family based their claim to kingship and to the succession? Or was the highest law the "fundamental law" of the parliamentarians to which they appealed in defense of such privileges as freedom of speech in the House? Perhaps the "fundamental law" of the Levellers was more fundamental still? And what of the common law of a Coke, Selden, or Hakewill, that intricate concept of law which negotiated the interlegal relationship between common-law rules and statutes? Finally, where did the natural-law tradition that England had inherited from the Middle Ages fit in, a tradition which regarded the general rules of right conduct as evident to all men as rational beings, even in their fallen state, and that were disobeyed not from ignorance but from prideful rebellion of the will?

What should the subject decide when one or another of these manifold laws was appealed to against the "arbitrary" law of a duly constituted government, which is precisely what the Petition of Right had done? Law, in the abstract, said Hooker, "is a directive unto goodness of operation";[80] in particular, it is the soul of the body politic which inclines the commonwealth toward peace and prosperity. But what if a subject finds this or that specific law to be unjust, or to be in conflict with those natural laws which all men are supposed to understand? To what other authority could he bring his appeal? These were questions, left unresolved by England's classical and medieval legal heritage, that Hobbes's theory was designed to confront.

The opinion that a sovereign king could injure his subjects by breaking a law (natural or civil) and that a statute could be unjust had cost Charles I his head. The king's trial implied that his person was separable from his office and that he could be held personally accountable for acts of injury or illegality. Hobbes, on the other hand, maintained that a sovereign cannot be held accountable no matter how arbitrary his rule, nor can arbitrary rule be equated with tyranny. Since all governmental forms differ only in the location of the sovereign power, they are all equally arbitrary. In the words of Sir Robert Filmer, "there never was, nor ever can be any people govern'd without a Power of making Law, and every Power of making Laws must be Arbitrary"; it is precisely "the Compulsory Power of Laws . . . which properly make[s] Laws to be Laws."[81]

According to this kind of analysis, therefore, Parliament had risen up against the arbitrary rule of the king only to confer it upon themselves. It followed from Hobbes's argument that "the legislator in all commonwealths, is only the sovereign, be he one man, as in a monarchy, or one assembly of men, as in a democracy, or aristocracy. For the legislator, is he that maketh the law."[82] To be sure, Hobbes had begun on the democratic note that the commonwealth is itself the legislator since it alone can prescribe the observation of the law, but upon this idea he built the absolute state. The commonwealth, he notes, is no person with a will except through its representation in the sovereign, and the sovereign is therefore the sole legislator. While the foundation of government is the good faith of the people, the people have no distinct personality apart from the state (they are the atomic pieces of a personality, so to speak), and once their allegiance is covenanted, they cannot retract their promise to obey the sovereign on the grounds of natural rights still inherent in that nonexistent original personality called society. With this argument, Hobbes completely obliterated one of the radical features in contract theory by destroying the distinction between society and government, a distinction which also fell victim to Ockham's razor. One of the mainstays of earlier liberal political philosophers had been exactly this idea that men, by virtue of their natural inclination to be sociable, had existed as an entity prior to the state, and that they therefore preserved inherent rights which were inviolable, even within the superstructure of the state.[83]

Law, said Hobbes, is the command of the sovereign. It locates and bespeaks his authority.[84] As for the "fundamental law," it is the natural law which bids us keep the peace and our word by obeying the sovereign's civil laws. That is essentially the meaning of his famous dictum that the civil law and the natural law are of equal extent and contain one another.[85] Since there can be no conflict between the two kinds of law in this formulation, there can also be no excuse for a subject's disobedience on the grounds that the sovereign's laws do not conform to natural law—a line of argument that constituted one of Parliament's strongest grounds for attack against the king.[86] The theoretical significance of Hobbes's contention, however, is to point out that any theory resting the foundations of the state on natural law must inevitably run aground on the shoals of subjectivity if the interpretation of natural law is ultimately allowed to become a multitude of private judgments, for no civil code coincides entirely with everyone's notion of the content of natural law.[87]

Common-law jurists of the time espoused legal theories, on the other hand, which in various ways made the administration of law a good deal more independent of the crown than Hobbes did, and in this they represented a legal version of the opposition to him that has already been seen in the political arena. The formulation of their ideas was expressed within the framework of a dualistic theory of the nature of sovereign power, in which comtemporary jurists usually distinguished *jus privatum*, or common law, from absolute law. The former was subject to determination by the courts and the law of the land, while the latter concerned the indisputable prerogatives of the crown, such as the power to set the value of coin in the realm. All of the purely constitutional issues of the seventeenth century were concerned with determining the boundary which divided the two, *qubernaculum* from *jurisdictio*.[88] For the common-law barrister, it was a problem of providing law with sanctions sufficient to protect it from the invasions of government power; for the king, it was a matter of preserving government from the trespasses of parliament and the courts, and from their threats against the liberty of the crown. The famous and crucial constitutional cases of first part of the century all employed the dual theory of sovereign power,[89] leaving the determination of the boundary between government and adjudication largely to the king's discretion.[90] The important *Case of Ship-Money* (1638) is an example, the Justice of the King's Bench, Sir Robert Berkeley, arguing that the law is the channel through which the royal prerogative flows, but that it is not designed to yoke the fundamental powers inherent in the crown, which included the power to command provision in the event of emergencies without the consent of parliament. The royal power was consequently absolute in some spheres and in some circumstances, but those spheres and circumstances were defined by the law of the land to protect the liberties of the subject, and it had a "directive" force with regard to the king.

The way in which this medieval distinction between the directive and coercive power of the law was to develop is exemplified by Sir Matthew Hale's treatise. There he accepts the division of law into *Potestas Coerciva*, which does not extend to the king but only to the subject, and *Potestas Directiva*, which obliges the king to observe the "greate Charter and those other Laws and Statutes that Concerne the Liberties of his Subjects"; but he adds to this division *Potestas Irritans*, remarking that here "the Laws also in many cases bindes the Kinges Actes, and makes them void if they are against Law."[91] Hale, a man of moderate political convictions and unimpeachable integrity, thus takes the traditional constitutional position that the king's person cannot be coerced, that he is obliged to act through the law though he is above the law, that he is obliged to respect the liberties of the people, but also, in a newer vein, that the rule of law can override the rule of the monarch's will. The opinion that a subject may rebel against laws contradicting the law of nature was a familiar theory, but Hale's statement of the constitutional relationship between king and parliament, each having separate functions and powers, was one which emerged especially in the Restoration.[92]

Nothing, of course, could have been more alien to Hobbes's thinking than the constitutional limitation of the sovereign, and here the issue of ship-money was very pertinent, for Hobbes dwelt on it frequently as a pivotal example and Hale clearly had it in mind while writing his treatise. Nothing could be more illogical to Hobbes than the subsequent Act Declaring the Illegality of Ship-Money (August 7, 1641), where it was claimed that the writs for the imposition were "contrary to and against the laws and statutes of this realm, the right of property, the liberty of the subjects, former resolutions in Parliament, and the Petition of Right." How, in Hobbes's scheme, could the king's impositions be illegal, if legality is only a function of his will? As for the liberty of the subject, that is merely the natural liberty to do or forbear in the performance of any act which remains after the constraints of law are declared.[93] More ineffectual still, to Hobbes, were the contentions of common-law jurists who held that there was no precedent for the impositions, for the philosopher never wearied of asserting that they were confusing the sanctions of custom and precedent with the sanctions of law properly so-called. Precedent does not make law, and if custom or precedent obtains the force of law, it is only because the silence of the sovereign implies his tacit consent.[94] Moreover, there was a practical point to consider: as most people agreed, government's prime purpose was the defense of the people, and upon such occasions as sudden invasion or rebellion the prince should be freed from the letter of the law and allowed to raise supplies without consent of parliament lest the kingdom be overrun and the subjects lose the benefit of protection because of a legal punctilio. Constitutionalists like Hale, on the other hand, always reverted to the plaint, "Itt is better to be Governed by certaine Laws tho' they bringe some Inconvenience att Some time then under Arbitrary Government."[95]

Part of the constitutionalism of the common-law jurists was the idea that English common law was unique and indigenous, embodying in custom the wisdom of time beyond recall. Special training and long study were the only means by which one could become qualified to unravel its mysteries. Sir Edward Coke was simply the most emphatic spokesman of this view when he defined law as an artificial perfection of reason. All lawyers agreed that the law was grounded on reason, but it was held that law developed according to its own peculiar principles and its own special reason. The administration of justice was therefore a closely guarded profession that even the king could not participate in since he lacked the requisite study, although this generated still another paradox concerning the sovereign, since the king was simultaneously held to be the highest judge in the land.[96] Now Hobbes stood for reason in the law in quite a contrary sense, in the sense of logical operations of the mind which all men could understand. Coke's artificial perfection of reason was altogether too much like some kind of private reason for Hobbes.

On this issue, Lord Chief Justice Hale is again enlightening. Antecedent to human understanding there is a reasonableness displayed in the "Decorum, Congruitie and Conseqution" of things and motions, and the reasonableness of law participated in that more general reason which governed the ordered universe. The institution of laws is an "artificial system of morals," but the agreement between it and natural morality is analogous to the agreement between mathematics and natural manifestations of quantity. Law and moral judgments, however, are not as open to demonstration as mathematics because of the great diversity of possible cases:

And therefore it is not possible for men to come to the Same Certainty... as may be expected in Mathematicall Sciences, and they that please themselves with a perswasion that they can... make out an unerring Systeme of Laws... equally applicable to all States and Occasions, as Euclide demonstrates his Conclusions, deceive themselves with Notions which prove in effectual, when they come to particular application.[97]

Experience is the great teacher of jurists, not the abstract notions of philosophers or mathematicians. Common law must be flexible to make general rules of equity conform to particulars, said Hale, and this constitutes a special kind of logic, whereas Hobbes held that the ordinary man should be able to give as good an opinion about the application of a law as the jurist could, if he would but use common logic and if the laws were properly written.[98] Nor was Hobbes's criticism of English common law entirely abstract: he is quick to note laws which are not administered uniformly but which are based on precedent and which in particular cases have the practical consequence of often being neither expedient nor just. As an instance, he points to

Coke's defense of such outdated rules as one which prescribed the forfeiture of the goods of someone who, having fled from prosecution for a felony, is subsequently acquitted.[99] Hale's reply is that though certain determinate rules produce their mischief, yet, he repeats, they are preferable to "that Arbitrary and uncertaine rule which men miscall the Law of Reason."[100]

The two positions are difficult to reconcile, if not impossible. What are the sources of the law? Is natural law the description of some existent system, or an ideal which ought to exist? Hobbes insisted that judges made the law because the sovereign gave them the power and authority to do so. The courts, however, were reluctant to admit that they did in fact make the law. Instead, they held that they only discovered or declared the law, and precedent was evidence of pre-existing law. To cite Sir Matthew once more:

The decisions of courts and justice . . . do not make a law properly so called (for that only the king and Parliament can do); yet they have a great weight and authority in expounding, declaring and publishing what the law of this kingdom is. . . . And though such decisions are less than a law, yet they are greater evidence thereof, than the opinion of any private person, as such, whatsoever.[101]

Professor John C. Gray puts the issue aptly when he says that this conflict rests on a confusion between law and the sources of the law.[102] Hale, Coke, and the common-law jurists generally agreed that the sources of the law, namely universal ethical precepts and moral dictates, sanctioned particular rules and that it was the purpose of law to conform to these normative standards. Hobbes, on the contrary, said that laws are sanctioned and made law only by the sovereign power, whether or not they are good laws. The legal status of commands is not to be confounded with their ethical content.[103] In the end, it seems that the opposition of the common-law jurists was not at bottom very different from that of Eachard, Cumberland, the churchmen, or the constitutionalists. They would all have joined Bishop Bramhall in his lament: "God help us! Into what times are we fallen! When the immutable laws of God and nature are made to depend upon the mutable laws of mortal men; just as if one should go about to control the sun by authority of the clock."[104]

The philosopher was subjected to this opprobrium simply because he asserted that, in the strict sense of the word, natural laws were not laws until interpreted by statutes, and that civil law must therefore have priority over the individual's interpretation of natural law if there was to be a just and stable society. The definition of the sovereign power and its relationship to these various laws could well go undelineated in the period of Elizabeth, when a harmony of interests existed between the needs of parliament and those of the sovereign. In the Stuart era, however, no such mutuality existed, and it was perhaps among Hobbes's contributions that he recognized the inadequacy of the traditional, rather vague concept of government as a harmony between organically united interests when it came to dealing with internal crises. Thus his insistence that there be some absolutely unfettered authority which binds the state, if it is to remain a state, when its internal machinery cannot be brought to act in unison. It is a theory which takes into account the extreme situation and which looks for minimum grounds of agreement from which to build. On another level, Hobbes thought of it as really a logical problem, for if people used words properly and clearly understood what "sovereign" means, they would not try to meddle with its jurisdiction as both Parliament and the courts of law had done.

V

Hobbes, The Churchmen, and the Moral Philosophers

> Considering how different this doctrine
> is, from the practice of the greatest part
> of the world . . . I am at the point of be-
> living this my labour, as useless, as the
> commonwealth of Plato.
>
> *E.W.*, III, 357

CRITICISM of Hobbes was by no means limited to the kind already noted, and the philosopher spent much of his later years in defending his moral and theological position. *Leviathan*—not least those sections dealing with religion in a Christian commonwealth, which will be taken up here—provoked a storm of criticism which would not be equalled until perhaps the Darwinian controversies of the nineteenth century, the anti-Hobbes literature reflecting voluminously the many winds of doctrine then sweeping across seventeenth-century England.[1] For his own time, publicity of these proportions, both among the general reading public and intellectual circles, was virtually unprecedented.

Controversy of that magnitude reflected not only the fact that Hobbes's work was found by many to be singularly unpalatable, but also certain specific historical circumstances into which he happened to be born. The English civil wars "mark the first appearance of public opinion as an important factor in politics,"[2] thus making it obligatory for anti-Hobbists to work at winning the public ear and disparaging the "traitorous" tenets of *Leviathan*, which ran through three editions in its first year of publication. For persons with public authority, Hobbes was a public-relations problem, a troublesome status which may not have been so acute in an age before the literate public had expanded into an important consideration. It was in this period too, that the essential features of modern journalism were developed, the staples of the Elizabethan printers becoming replaced by political pamphlets,[3] and this growth of printed material in circulation among the general reading public contributed early to the popularization of the Hobbes controversy, as it would later contribute toward the feasibility of making a living as a professional writer, as Dryden did.

Since seventeenth-century political thought developed in close accord with religious objectives, it was virtually impossible for Hobbes to participate in the first without discussing the second, and it is not surprising that the political and legal criticism directed against him was extended to the religious sphere with unbroken continuity. Heresy, after all, had been made over into treason, and political theory would not be liberated from theology until the religious controversies of the period had subsided and permitted the secularization of the issues with which politics must deal. In England, Hobbes marked the beginning of this process, for although he was a religious man and fully one-third of *Leviathan* is given over to religious or theological discussion, his approach to the relationship between church and state, Christianity and other faiths, was more logical than emotional. His contemporary critics said that he was manifestly an atheist, while his modern commentators have often suggested that prudence led him to cloak his opinions in theology,[4] or they have suspected him of the worse sin of merely hypocritical observance of religious requirements. Hobbes was certainly aware that some opinions had to be expressed with delicacy in his time, and that other opinions could not be expressed at all with impunity, but there is no reason to doubt his sincerity unless it be to disparage him, and it is certainly philosophically perilous to assume that he did not mean what he said.[5] His contemporaries did him the honor of taking him seriously, so seriously in fact that popular opinion reportedly blamed him for bringing down the wrath of God and causing the Plague of London in 1665, as well as the subsequent Great Fire. Aubrey remarks that Hobbes and Galileo shared "a Consimilitie of Fate, to be hated and persecuted by the Ecclesiastiques," and shortly after the Restoration, some of the bishops made a motion to have Hobbes burned for heresy.[6]

Religious opinion was so far fractured in the period that it was difficult to hold a belief that somebody would not find heretical, but Hobbes was accused of being everything from a Mohammedan to a

Socinian, sometimes by the same person in the same breath. Alexander Ross, an eccentric but popular publicist, listed Hobbes's heresies:

in holding life eternal to be only on earth, he is a Corinthian and a Mahumetan; in giving God corporeity he is an Anthropomophit; a Manichean, a Tertullianist and an Andean; in holding the Three Persons to be distinct names and essences ... he is a Sabellian, a Montanist, an Aetian, and a Priscillianist.... in making the soul to rest with the body till the resurrection, he is an Arabian; in making the soul of man corporal he is a Luciferian, by putting a period to Hell he is an Origenist; ... and in making our natural reason the word of God he is a Socinian.[7]

And this is only *part* of Ross's list. Specific theological points were the stuff for endless debate and for the kind of elaborate name-calling seen in Ross; the more central and important of the points seized upon by Hobbes's critics will be taken up at appropriate places. But the fact that Hobbes's religious position is well integrated and articulated throughout his works is itself an argument against the notion that his Erastianism was simply a response to the times and that his religious doctrine was primarily political in motive, although he would be the last to deny that it had important political consequences.

Hobbes's treatment of religion in *Leviathan* is divided into two sections, the first (Chapter 12) growing out of and continuing his discussion of human nature and the manners of men. In it, Hobbes discusses religion itself or superstition as something proper to man alone, and traces it back, as he does other attributes, to fear and curiosity. The natural seeds of religion are ignorance of second causes; the inference of a first cause which, since unknown, is feared; fear of invisible powers (ghosts) and superstitions which led men to think of gods or a god, and to worship them as a sign of reverence. The diversity of religions and their ceremonies is attributed to the diversity of cultures and judgments among men in a purely naturalistic manner. If such fear bred false religion among primitive people who trembled before false gods, yet it was also the beginning of wisdom among Jews and Christians, who fear the true God. While Hobbes does remark several times on the difference between Christianity and other religions here, he is fundamentally interested in religion as a part of human psychology which is employed by governments to encourage obedience and which, as such, is part of human politics. It is amenable to philosophic discussion because it is observable and can be reasoned about. The reasons for change in religion are handled in a similarly aloof manner (though Hobbes cannot forebear a brief assault on Roman Catholicism), Hobbes attributing the loss of faith in people to the ignorance, fraudulent intentions, or corruption of the clergy in every case, including that of the Reformed churches.

It is only in the third part of *Leviathan*, after showing how man in the state of nature could generate a commonwealth guided by the laws of nature, that he turns his full attention toward those people who acknowledge their obligations to obey the laws of God and to the special case of the Christian commonwealth, which depends not only on reason, but also on revelation. A law is a command which exacts our obedience *by right*, and in the case of God, his natural right is derived from his *irresistible power*. In the state of nature, where men are substantially equal, no one had such power to obtain his right to rule by force, so that it was in the interest of men to relinquish their right to govern themselves and to establish a common authority for their own self-preservation. God's right was never taken away, nor can it be. He rules naturally "not as Creator, and gracious, but as omnipotent."[8] Job is Hobbes's appropriate text here. God proclaims his laws either by the dictates of natural reason, by revelation or through faith, but it is only the first that concerns us immediately. The divine laws declared through reason are, of course, the natural laws discussed before, and they embrace all of the moral virtues including equity, justice, mercy and, in general, the Golden Rule. Natural reason tells us also to express our understanding of God's power and goodness through worship, such as prayers, gifts, oblations, and sacrifices, which are marks of honour proceeding from our duty and performed from fear, hope, and thankfulness.

This whole line of reasoning, reconstructing the beginning of religious feeling in fear and following it through to the worship of God as dictated by reason was, in the words of Bishop Bramhall, "brim full of prodigious impiety." "What is now become of that dictate or precept of reason," he inquired, "concerning 'prayers, thanksgivings, oblations, sacrifices,' if uncertain opinions, ignorance, fear, mistakes, the conscience of our own weakness, and the admiration of natural events, be the only seeds of religion?"[9] But Hobbes could find nothing to be faulted in his position: "What prodigious impiety is here?" he innocently asked, "I said superstition was fear without reason. Is not the fear of a false God, or fancied demon, contrary to right reason?"[10]

More vexatious were Hobbes's inferences about what may be known about God by natural reason. The principles of natural science, which can tell us nothing about our own nature, are certainly of no use in telling us about God's—it is a subject that falls outside of philosophic discourse and dispute, for "it is by all Christians confessed, that God is 'incomprehensible,' . . . there is no idea of him; he is like nothing we can think on." He can therefore be described only by negatives or by indefinite terms and superlatives.[11] Bounded by our finite intelligence, the only attribute that we can properly ascribe to him is existence. But existence for Hobbes meant material existence, so that God must be corporeal, and so also must the human soul be corporeal. Hobbes did not deny the existence of spirit, he only affirmed that it was the name of a corporeal substance, though a very subtle one to be sure.[12] He certainly did not equate such a belief with atheism, though his critics did, and the mere thought of a material soul made them gasp. "God only knows what becomes of man's spirit, when he expireth" in an Hobbesian universe, protested Bramhall.[13]

If natural reason dictates that we worship God by every mark of honor, what constitutes honor varies from culture to culture, and natural reason does not specify more particularly the forms of worship. Who is to interpret these natural dictates into concrete forms of devotion, for instance? Who is to evaluate the canons of reasons as they pertain to questions of establishing a religion? Moreover, while God speaks to us through natural reason, he also declares himself through the Holy Scriptures, and a similar problem arises; for the Scriptures, which lay down the rules of Christian life, also require interpretation. In an era of religious factionalism, this was a problem of the most pressing urgency. Every parish priest preached another concept of what was right, supported another authority in religion, or gave a divergent reading of God's word in the Scriptures. Ever since the translation of the Bible, said Hobbes, "every Man, nay every Boy and Wench that could read English, thought they spoke with God almighty, and understood what he said."[14] The rampant sectarianism in the religious sphere, the fragmentation of a central religious authority, seemed exactly analogous with the social disintegration in other areas that had led to the Civil War—England's religious development had reverted to the stage of a war of every man against every man.

The resolution of these conflicts involved for Hobbes an extension of the same kind of duality which he had held to exist between the subjective, egoistic state of nature and the artificial, political state. He drew a strict distinction between private, subjective belief and the conventional rules of public religious observance. He argues, in the case of the Scriptures, that we cannot *know* they are God's words unless God reveals that to a man supernaturally, so that the Scriptures are not, properly speaking, a question of knowledge. Nor are they a question of belief, for men believe for diverse reasons and no general answer can be given. "The question truly stated is, *by what authority they are made law.*"[15] Insofar as the Scriptures do not differ from the laws of nature, they may be said to oblige in the same fashion—binding on those who acknowledge God's commands, but not to those who do not, at least not until declared by the sovereign authority, who has the legislative power. To put it historically, the New Testament was not canonical until the time of Constantine; though earlier converts may have accepted it as the true faith and felt it binding within themselves, yet it was not law properly speaking. Should the sovereign condone forms of worship unpleasing to a subject, Hobbes held that he was nonetheless obliged to conform to them, nor should he rebel on the grounds of a violation of conscience.[16] Bearing in mind the dictates of natural law to keep the peace and to preserve oneself from destruction, it is almost never in error or against conscience to be obedient. "It seemeth," quipped Bishop Bramhall of this view, that "T.H. thinketh there is no Divine worship but [that which is] internal."[17] And Cudworth indignantly objected that, in Hobbes's view, "the Diety must of necessity be removed and displaced, to make room for the Leviathan to spread himself in."[18]

If Hobbes could not countenance the "inner lights" of the various sects, neither could he allow the political power sought by the Anglican clergy, for the prince, in order to be truly sovereign, must also be able to determine the form of worship. He must be sovereign over every corporate body or organized group within the kingdom, not excluding the church. What is a church, after all, Hobbes reasoned, but a synthesis of its members (the "matter") and the power of convocation (the beginning of motion)? And has not the prince the legal power of convocation, and were not the members his subjects? In fact, the state is a church. The prince, therefore, may appoint his ministers of religion in much the same manner as he appoints his magistrates, and ordinations are but "commemorations."[19] If this were true, observed the astute Bramhall, "a Cardinal's red hat or a sergeant-at-arms his mace, may be called Sacraments as well as Baptism or the Holy Eucharist."[20] The designation of the prince as chief pastor and his absolute supremacy over the church "doth quite overthrow all the authority of General Councils," Bramhall added, quite aside from completely usurping the power of the bishoprics.[21]

Essentially, Hobbes's position was that while the state cannot and need not make a window into men's souls, yet where religion enters public life it is a matter of law and not of philosophy, social reform, or even pure emotion. Public forms of religious devotion are simply conventions, and officially designated religions need not be the same in all countries, though the religion in each must be indisputable for the sake of peace. Needless to say, perhaps, such external controls over the forms of worship struck many Protestant reformers as a denial of the spirit and as a blow to their conception of the church as a voluntary association of believers. Anglicans of Bramhall's stamp were no less indignant, for to invest such spiritual authority in the prince was to deny it to the ecclesiastics. The "right reason" which made dissenters obey their consciences in order to achieve salvation had become, in Hobbes's scheme, a command to obey the state as the path to salvation.* Similarly, the alliance between church and state which the Anglicans supported in return for the crown's favors for Episcopacy had become, for Hobbes, an alliance in which the church supported the monarch only to have Episcopacy absorbed by the state.

*Hobbes had a *Christian* state in mind when he defined the state as a church; the prince is then accountable to God and obliged to consider the salvation of his subjects. But he runs into difficulties where the state is not Christian: the Christian subject's covenant to obey the prince remains in force for temporal matters, but what of spiritual ones? In *De Cive*, Hobbes made the hard ruling that resistance was "contrary to our civil convenant," so the Christian subject was left no alternative other than martyrdom. In *Leviathan*, however, Hobbes revises his position, allowing the subject to deny his faith outwardly so long as it remained strong in his heart. This holds only for lay Christians; a pastor with a calling to preach the gospel should still opt for martyrdom. As W. B. Glover points out, Hobbes's revisions do not therefore change his position "in any essential way, but merely reduce the number of cases in which the practical problem would arise." "God and Thomas Hobbes," in *Hobbes Studies*, ed. Brown, pp. 156–57.

Many of the points in Hobbes's treatment of the Christian commonwealth in *Leviathan* are argued from Scripture, a form of argument clearly inappropriate to the first two parts of the book, which are grounded on human nature and reason alone. He nowhere indicates a knowledge of the Bible as essential to salvation—again seeking minimal grounds for agreement in a mass of diverse opinion, he stipulates only obedience and a faith in Christ—but since it comprehends the rules which Christians should observe in their relations to other men and reveals their duties to God, he works from Scripture. The mysteries of the faith cannot be comprehended by reason, but divine politics can be found out by careful interpretation. Doubtlessly it was exceedingly galling to those who found Hobbes atheistic to see him advance his arguments in the form of long strings of citations from the Scriptures, and he may be accused of inconsistency since, by his own principles, the interpretation of Scripture belongs in the hands of the sovereign. Hobbes later argued that when he wrote *Leviathan*, in 1651, there was no established doctrine and each man was free to speak what he chose, so he had committed no fault.[22] It was a small excuse for a large section of his book—a section that was very likely the most crucial for his contemporaries in terms of its application to the events then taking place.

The Cambridge Platonists

If clergymen felt that Hobbes had placed religion in the hands of the prince, the moral philosophers were more perturbed by what they regarded as his ethical skepticism. Primarily they objected to his idea that private appetite is the measure of good in the state of nature, and they took strenuous exception to the apparent ability of the sovereign to determine moral values. Had not Hobbes written that "what the legislator commands, must be held for *good*, and what he forbids for *evil?*"[23]

While Hobbes was frankly dubious about the force moral ideas can exert over men when their interests are threatened, he did not deny a moral basis for human associations in as total a sense as his contemporary critics feared and alleged. It is true that private appetite defines "good" in the state of nature, but such individual appetites may still agree on certain things. Most importantly, all men (though each finds his own survival the greatest good) agree that peace is good because it makes self-preservation more likely. If men then endeavor peace, as the law of nature suggests, because it is good, so Hobbes holds that the means of peace is good: *"justice, gratitude, modesty, equity, mercy,* and the rest of the laws of nature, are good; that is to say; *moral virtues."*[24] In or out of the state of nature, moral virtues are always good, but fear must limit their sphere of operation in the natural condition of war.

As for the commands or laws of the legislator, they must indeed be held for good, even if they are bad laws, because they put an end to the anarchy of private judgments and because obedience to the law is always consistent with right. This does not mean that the laws become the best that could be devised for a given situation, but only that they must "be held for good" to preserve peace. Another indication of Hobbes's moral feeling is in his frequent asides and passing comments which praise the rare man who has a "generous nature," a "relish of justice" that leads him to act righteously, or of gallant and noble men.[25] But such men are exceptional, and Hobbes's system is meant to deal with the generality of humanity in whom, Hobbes said, fear is the passion to be reckoned with. In short, as A. E. Taylor said, anyone who did not obey the Golden Rule was a *Nichtswürdiger* in Hobbes's eyes,[26] but his emphasis must always be more on prudential motivations than the elaboration of moral values.

The most substantial philosophic opposition to Hobbes came from a small but diverse group of schoolmen and clergymen, the Cambridge Platonists. Together with Richard Cumberland, who was sympathetic to their outlook, they represented a liberal intellectual segment of the community whose aim was not unlike that of such popular authors as Eachard and Ross, namely to uphold Christian ethics and an immutable and eternal morality against Hobbes's dangerous Leviathan. The Platonists, however, were almost forced to ground their teachings on the *lex naturalis* rather than traditional theological dogma since they, like Hobbes himself, were aware of the instability of religious doctrine in England. They, no less than he, wished to avoid grafting ethics onto too narrow a religious doctrine when the condition of religion was such an explosive, fluctuating quantity in English society. They consequently found themselves in a position of attempting to demonstrate the ungodly and destructive character of Hobbism and to defend orthodox Christian ethics, while yet being unwilling to base their demonstrations upon theology in any orthodox sense. Thus we see Cumberland expounding a kind of natural morality of reason, affirming benevolence and the common good as the true law of nature, while Cudworth pursued an undogmatic Christian theism. This emancipation of ethical theory from theology by precisely those thinkers who were most concerned with defending religion from Hobbes's alleged atheism is one of the most interesting aspects of these seventeenth-century debates. Much of this latitudinarian thought and the development of religious tolerance was a reaction against both excessive "enthusiasm" and a Laudian kind of sacerdotalism in the Church, but much of it also found expression as a reaction against Hobbes.

Cumberland's philosophy is difficult to rescue from its verbosity, but insofar as it was intended as a refutation of Hobbes, it consisted chiefly of affirming with equal vigor the opposite of everything propounded by Hobbes. There are, he declared, "prepositions of unchangeable Truth which direct our voluntary actions, about choosing Good and refusing Evil, and impose an obligation to external actions even without Civil Law."[27] These immutable notions arise in the mind with experience, and they depend only upon the will for their execution. It is Cumberland's major contention that in observing the voluntary actions of men and the design of the world, one cannot but perceive something tending toward "the more flourishing condition of others" which imprints "upon us the notion of a Good common to many."[28] The specific classification of the virtues is not carried through in Cumberland, his concept of natural laws tending to be utilitarian. He sees both man's altruistic and egoistic inclinations as equally basic, but merging in the higher principle of the common good: "The greatest benevolence of every rational Agent towards all, forms the happiest State of every, and of all the Benevolent, as far as is in their Power; and is necessarily requisite to the happiest State which they can attain, and therefore the Common Good is the Supreme Law."[29] Every man, said Cumberland, is involved in the commonweal since the whole is the sum of its parts, and the very general principle of the common good he held to be a law of God, having the full sanction and force of law.

Now while Hobbes also conceived of the individual's welfare as an integral part of the commonweal and therefore urged obedience to the civil authority, he meant it in a wholly different sense than Cumberland did, underlining the gap between his ideas and more common philosophic precepts of his time. For Hobbes, a citizen's perception of his involvement with the good of his fellow man is an insight gained by rational self-interest; in Cumberland, on the contrary, it is a direct provision of God expressed in rational benevolent inclinations common to all men. An effective morality was therefore in no way contingent upon society as it was in Hobbes, but was a demand of natural reason.

Ralph Cudworth, who represents the thinking of the Cambridge group at its best, was like Cumberland in his concern with establishing an objective standard of right and wrong prior to civil law.[30] As a Platonist, he was naturally not disposed to identifying the real with that which is perceived by the senses, contending instead that there were principles native to the soul which actively take notice of essences, in distinction to the senses which note only external contingencies. With this metaphysical groundwork laid down, Cudworth did not so much refute as ignore Hobbes's argument that men can have no idea of God, and he could assert the existence of an ideal moral rectitude which the mind perceives as such in the course of its normal development. Thus, while it was true that people may err in their private judgments, as Hobbes contended they did, yet it did not necessarily follow that the state should therefore decide matters of conscience. "The rule by which conscience judges is not private. . . . The rule of conscience is the eternal law of God and his revealed purpose."[31]

Although his insistence on an innate criterion of justice and morality in man was Cudworth's hallmark, as it was that of all the Platonists, his first purpose was the refutation of atheism. To men of his persuasion, Hobbes's mechanical conception of man and nature seemed to embody the atheistic possibilities of the new science. His work seemed to comprise an attempt to dethrone the deity by explaining the world's phenomena without the assistance of God, nothwithstanding Hobbes's insistence that the new knowledge could restore peace to the world, bringing it closer to its prelapsarian order.

The foundations of contemporary atheism, said Cudsworth, were a revivial of the "Democritic Fate," a philosophic atomism involving the material necessity of all things. Yet Cudworth's position here was not an easy one: he himself accepted as "unquestionably true" the essentials of atomism, while simultaneously trying to stem the atheism which so many believed to be its necessary consequence. He subscribed to the hypothesis that the only principles of body were magnitude, figure, motion, and rest, and approved the concept of primary and secondary qualities current among scientists. But he asserted that atomism need not have an irreligious implication if it were united with some kind of dualism which allowed for spiritual existence. On the contrary, "this Atomic physiology, rightly understood, is so far from being either the mother or nurse of Atheism or any ways favorable therunto (as is vulgarly supposed) that it is indeed the most directly opposite to it of any, and the greatest defense against the same."[32] Cudworth contended that life and mind are not explained by inert body because they are not contained in it, nor can the mechanisms of the body be explained by body itself, the true understanding of them requiring active cogitation. The very concept of body therefore must give rise to the affirmation of a substance distinct from it, the incorporeal. He concludes that whoever admits the atomic physiology "and rightly understands it, must need acknowledge incorporeal substance; which is the absolute overthrow of atheism."[33]

Cudworth's dualism is not of the Cartesian kind since, in his system, everything incorporeal is not necessarily mental, and not everything mental is conscious. It is rather a dualism between the activity of the "intellectual system" of the universe, and the passivity of the physical system. The soul is conceived of as a whole, not compartmentalized into faculties, and life is regarded as a dynamic struggle between the possessive animal passions and the creative force of divine love.[34] Necessarily, Cudworth's identification of all things that have life and activity with spirit led him to regard a great part of the universe as spiritual in character. From this arose a curious situation, for in a system such as Cudworth's where spirit and intentions in nature are not necessarily intelligent or deliberated about, incorporeality is not a direct proof of immortality—a position of dubious theological orthodoxy. Thus Cudworth, the zealous defender of faith against the "atheism" of Hobbes, was rewarded in the end by sharing with him the stigma of heresy.[35]

Diverse as were the arguments employed by Hobbes's opponents, they were unified in the principles they sought to establish. Ethical relativism and egoistic psychology could be combated by an appeal to common sense or to feelings of fundamental human sympathy, as in the writings of Eachard and the more popular critics, or it could be fought by evocations of the Scriptures, as in the work of some theological writers and in Filmer's book. Cumberland and the Cambridge Platonists, however, strove to transcend the faults of common sense by raising the level of their argument to Hobbes's and by confronting first principles in a more methodical fashion. They also strove to overcome the failings of the theologians by making ethics independent of religious dogma, though in neither endeavor were they altogether successful. In their attempt to unite reason and religion in a generally tolerant attitude, the Platonists did contribute to modern ethical theory by heavily emphasizing the psychological aspects of their theories, as Hobbes himself did, rather than religious dogma. But one unintentional consequence of this procedure was the further secularization of moral attitudes, while their motives had rather been the refutation of atheism. Shaftesbury, in his *Sermons*, recognized this when he commented that the Platonist emphasis on psychological qualities in society—such as an innate "goodness" in man or a principle of benevolence—had led some to fear "the apparent need of a sacred revelation . . . should be in some measure taken away" from the notion of ethical obligations.[36] The same was said, usually less politely, of Hobbes, of course,[37] so that no matter how much Hobbes and his opponents disliked each others' theories, yet they sometimes inadvertently worked toward the same end as if by some perverse "cunning" of history.

Liberty or Necessity

Another fundamental philosophic issue which the Platonists, and more prominently Bishop Bramhall, fought out with Hobbes was freedom of the will. The history of Hobbes's controversies on this point properly goes back to the publication of *De Cive* in 1642, and his formulation of a determinist viewpoint there. In 1645, when Hobbes was in Paris, one of the refugees to go into exile in France was John Bramhall, Bishop of Derry and Laud's lieutenant during the reign of Charles I, and one whose Arminian convictions necessarily conflicted with Hobbes's ideas. In the presence of Newcastle, the two Englishmen debated the point and subsequently Bramhall wrote out a series of objections to *De Cive*. While both men agreed not to publish their writings on the matter, a copy of Hobbes's manuscript was surreptitiously appropriated and published without his knowledge in 1654, notwithstanding the fact that Hobbes had since published *Leviathan*, in which his position was considerably refined.[38] Bramhall, feeling misrepresented as well as betrayed, was indignant since he assumed the manuscript had been released with Hobbes's permission, or perhaps he only pretended to assume it the better to villify his opponent. Whatever the exact circumstances were, Bramhall pro-

ceeded to have the original debate published, including both his original defense of freedom of the will and an added attack on the
"atheism" of Leviathan.[39]

With these publications was launched one of the classic battles on
a classic theme. Hobbes's polemic is always shrewd and powerful in
the fray, while Bramhall's logic moves with vigor and often with
elegance as well. Having begun in 1646, the quarrel continued until
1668 when Hobbes wrote a final volume against Bramhall's charges of
atheism (although the Bishop was already five years in his grave), a
rejoinder that was only published in 1681 after Hobbes himself had
died.[40] Longevity was clearly an important consideration for anyone
who hoped to get the last word in an argument with Hobbes.[41]

Hobbes's position was that when someone deliberates about
whether or not to perform a certain action, he imagines the consequences of the act with hope or fear as he considers them good or evil.
The whole sum of these alternating passions is what is called "deliberation," and the last appetite or aversion before the act is called
"will."[42] In the absence of external impediments, one is said to have
the liberty to exercise his will, but it is the individual who is free, not
his will. He cannot will to will, which is only another absurd use of
language; his will is not voluntary, but the actions he takes from will
are voluntary. Appetites, fears, and hopes, as Hobbes says, are not
willed because they do not proceed from, but *are* the will.[43]

Since an appetite or will is a response to external stimuli ("nothing taketh beginning from *itself,* but from the *action* of some other
immediate *agent* without itself"), the cause of his will is not the will
itself, and the will is not the necessary cause of voluntary actions.
Which is to say, since "the *will* is also *caused* by other things whereof
it disposeth not, it followeth, that *voluntary* actions have all of them
necessary causes, and therefore are *necessitated.*"*

This doctrine, said Bishop Bramhall ominously, "is of desperate
consequence, and destructive to piety, policy and morality."[44] On the
moral side, it seemed that if every human action was determined,

---

*E.W., IV, 274. In Hobbes's scheme, a sufficient cause is the same thing as a
necessary cause, a position he already adopted in the early *Short Tract.* To be a sufficient cause, nothing is wanting to produce a given effect. Should it not produce the
effect, it is not sufficient; but it is impossible to be sufficient and not produce the effect,
"then is a *sufficient* cause a *necessary* cause, for that is said to produce an effect *necessarily*
that cannot but produce it." Every effect is therefore produced necessarily, including
voluntary actions. Ibid., 275.

little meaning remained in such ideas as "virtue" and "vice." Moreover, there was the Hobbesian persistence in chaining all of men's behavior to his appetites. Was it not demeaning, asked another critic, Henry More?

For while all other Creatures have their Sences ty'd down to the service of the Body . . . [men] can mount aloft, and are enabled by a *Liberty* of their *Wills*, to shake off, or gradually destroy those ill desires, with which they are beset; and, by the help of Heaven, to assert that Liberty, which is most suitable to a Creature made by God's Image, and a partaker of Divine Sense.

And, as this is a most true Perswasion, and hath wonderful Power among Men, to draw them to Virtue. . . . Let those Men be asham'd who have so tamper'd with Mankind to perswade the contrary. This (in truth) has been vigorously and studiously attempted by Mr. Hobbs, in his Book, Of Liberty and Necessity.[45]

On the religious side, Hobbes himself was aware of the fact that his doctrine, imprudently considered, could have an undermining effect, "but only to such men as cannot reason in those points which are of difficult comprehension."[46] Most troublesome was the idea that the external stimuli to which appetites or will are responses were, in turn, produced by other causes in a continuous chain back to God, the first cause. "To him that could see the connexion of these causes," Hobbes concluded, "the necessity of all men's voluntary actions, would appear manifest."[47] While Hobbes's determinism here was not identical with an old-style Calvinistic doctrine of predestination, both the Bishop and Henry More found it no less pernicious, ungodly, and unfit to preach. It opened up a whole hornet's nest of theological problems as, for instance, that it seemed to imply that God was the cause of sin, it seemed to destroy the possibility of a Christian making a free vow to God, and it discouraged efforts toward a pious life. In Bramhall's words, "for repentance, how shall a man condemn and accuse himself for his sins, who thinks himself to be like a watch which is wound up by God, and that he can go neither longer nor shorter, faster nor slower, truer nor falser, than he is ordered by God? If God sets him right, he goes right; if God sets him wrong, he goes wrong."[48]

To all this Hobbes replied sharply that "truth is truth, and . . . the question is not, what is fit to be preached, but what is true."[49] He matched citations of chapter for chapter and verse for verse and pushed on. A rational man, he said, knows that God leads those he will save along a righteous way, while he hardens the hearts of those he will destroy. The rational man therefore examines his life to see if his path has been godly, and the examination itself is the necessary cause for one of the elect to work out his salvation with fear and trembling. But other, less prudent readers of his doctrine "are such as reason erroneously, saying with themselves, *if I shall be saved, I shall be saved whether I walk uprightly or no*: and consequently thereunto, shall behave themselves negligently, and pursue the pleasant way of the sins they are in love with."[50] To prevent that harm, Hobbes says he had hoped his debates with the Bishop would remain unpublished, and would not have picked up his pen had he not been "provoked by the uncivil triumphing of the Bishop in his own errors to my disadvantage."[51] Bramhall nonetheless continued to refuse to grasp how a Christian could be said "to return into the right way, who never was in any other way but that which God himself had chalked out for him,"[52] which he construed to be Hobbes's meaning. "So God bless us," the Bishop tells the reader, for those who follow Hobbes's principles "are fitter to live in hollow trees among wild beasts, than in any Christian or political society."[53]

The lengthy dispute between Hobbes and the Bishop goes to some depth, and it may still be profitably studied by those who are concerned about the issue, or who have never seen a scholastic confrontation that is also scurrilous, witty, and learned all at once. In general, however, Hobbes's controversies with his critics are too often stopped once the exposition of initial and fundamental positions has been completed. Their assumptions were so radically opposed, their first principles so disparate, that it was difficult even to make contact; Hobbes and his opponents often seem simply to glower at each other across an unbridgeable distance. Some basics have to be agreed upon, after all, even to begin a fruitful debate.

"I have been publicly injured by many of whom I took no notice," said Hobbes, "supposing that that humour would spend itself; but seeing it last, and grow higher . . . I thought it necessary at last to make of some of them . . . an example."[54] Indeed, Hobbes became an active polemicist, for which occupation his temperament supplied him with a certain natural pugnacity and a sometimes mordant style. However useful these were in single combat with his critics, they were less adequate when he faced official disapproval. With due promptness, for instance, *Leviathan* appeared in the Papal Index of

1654, and after the plague and great fire in London, Hobbes had to defend himself against a bill then in committee, which was enjoined to collect information on blasphemous and atheistic books (*Leviathan* included, as was the work of Thomas White, the Catholic priest and friend of Hobbes), and to report back to the House. Hobbes protected himself first by burning some papers, and then, characteristically, by writing an historical narration of heresy, showing why he himself should not be burned.

Hobbes was fortunate at the Restoration to find his way again into the good graces of King Charles, without whose favor one can only wonder what his fate would have been. The exiled Earl of Clarendon, writing in "the Leisure to which God hath condemn'd me," said that after the return of the king, Hobbes "came frequently to the Court, where he had too many Disciples," and that he continued to have them in 1670, the year in which Clarendon wrote.[55] Had Hobbes's theories remained in obscurity or cloistered in the universities, the consequent storm of controversy might have remained more subdued and philosophical, but because of the publicity he received through the press, much of the criticism was popular or semi-popular, and Hobbes's ideas drifted into a more general circulation. Through the court, moreover, they were made not only popular, but fashionable as well, catching on among the younger elements of the better classes.

Writing to a more academic audience a generation later, Richard Cumberland was still concerned about "Hobbists": "I did not think it worth while to spend the whole Book . . . confuting Hobbes' Errors, tho' I judged it necessary to be at some Pains in refuting his Mistakes, which had so grossly perverted so many."[56] "Hobbism," a witty version of the ideas of its venerable progenitor, was to linger on in society and the schools. In courtly circles, it was apparently employed partly for sophistic purposes, and also for justifying the comfortable manners of the Restoration court in good King Charles's golden days. It was this fact, as much as any other, which cast Hobbes in the role of a corrupter of the young and of those men of quality who were, one day, to take over the offices of England's public servants.

Hobbes faced institutional protests not only from the Roman Catholic Church (through its Index) and Parliament, but also from the schools. In 1669, one Daniel Scargill, a dismissed fellow of Corpus Christi College, Cambridge, was forced to recant his Hobbism publicly as the condition for his reinstatement in the university.[57] Still later, the philosopher's reputation was to reach even greater heights of a sort in the period of royalist reaction following the dissolution of Parliament in 1681, when Tory vengeance was turned against the dissenters and posthumously against Hobbes. The dominant political creed was then complete concurrence with the will of the sovereign, and the church complied by espousing a doctrine of nonresistance to the monarch. It is therefore somewhat curious, at first sight, to find the University Convocation of Oxford in 1683 delivering a proclamation against Hobbes, who professed to be a true son of the Anglican Church, a monarchist, and an enemy of Dissent. Yet *Leviathan* was adjudged fit for burning, and the tenets of its author were condemned as worthy of "detestation and abhorrence." Thus the irony which often plagued Hobbes in his life—that supporters of the king could find this monarchist an enemy as dangerous as the Presbyterians—continued after his death. The philosopher was condemned by the Convocation under three articles, and as if underscoring the ironies produced by the caprices of history, he shared his odium in one article with John Owen, the preacher, and the saintly Richard Baxter. The three men were named as sponsors of the doctrine (article ten) that "Possession and strength give a right to govern, and success in a cause or enterprise proclaims it to be lawful and just; to pursue it is to comply with the will of God, because it is to follow the conduct of his providence."[58]

That same year, Hobbes again found himself with strange bedfellows, for so far from being seen as the philosopher of absolutism which modern students think him to be, he was depicted as the very opposite by a royalist divine. This was Edward Pelling, who preached a sermon before the Lord Mayor which expressed the feelings of his audience. He exhorted them to hinder by every possible means

the spreading of those Leud and Antimonarchical Doctrines, which for these Five years past have made the whole Nation to Shake: as, That the King hath not his Authority immediately from God . . . but that the People are the Fountain of all Authority; that He is Their Trustee, and that they have Reserved to themselves so much of their Power, that they can call a Prince to an Account, and dispose of his Crown. These are Principles, which . . . were first Begotton by the Jesuit (the Father of Ravillacs), then Nursed up by Buchanan (the Father of Rebels) and at last Adopted by the Leviathan (the Father of Atheists).[59]

On the political (Ravillac) side, one wonders to what extent, if any, Hobbes had "corrupted" William Cavendish, the Third Earl's son and

William Cavendish, Fourth Earl, First Duke of Devonshire (1640–1707) by Willem Wissing. Devonshire Collection, Chatsworth. Reproduced by permission of the Trustees of the Chatsworth Settlement.

the last of the line to be connected with the philosopher. Having risen to the rank of privy councillor to Charles in 1679, he subsequently supported the impeachment of Lord Chief Justice Scroggs, appeared in defense of Lord Russell at his trial, and joined in the invitation to William, Prince of Orange, to secure by arms the infringed liberties of England.

On the religious side, the myth of Hobbes the atheist has persisted to present times, despite the fact that if one had to choose a single social value which Hobbes worked toward, it would perhaps be the idea of a Christian peace. The *terms* under which such a peace could be achieved have been disputed since his scheme holds in equilibrium both the possibilities of a thorough absolutism and a liberal individualism, his interpreters having stressed one or the other element according to their own historical and political circumstances. That he rested his doctrine on an egoistic psychology offended many to the extent they could not benefit from whatever truth is in it, while the "Hobbists," in particular, never realized that his ethical values quite transcended their psychological roots. "This set of [the philosopher's] notions came to spread much," wrote Bishop Burnet, thinking mainly of the "Hobbists"; "the novelty and boldness of them set many reading them. The impiety of them was acceptable to men of corrupt minds, which were but too much prepared to receive them, by the extravagancies of the late times."[60] How startled Hobbes must have been, having spent his personal life in a scholarly and temperate fashion, to find himself named the father of a large brood of profligate offspring.

VI

Hobbes Among the Muses

> ... both *fancy* and *judgment* are commonly comprehended under the name of *wit,* which seemeth to be a tenuity and agility of spirits....
>
> Hobbes, *Human Nature*
> (written c. 1640)
>
> For what authority is there in wit? A jester may have it; a man in drink may have it; be fluent over night and wise and dry in the morning. What is it? Or who can tell whether it be better to have it or be without it, especially if it be pointed wit?
>
> Letter from Hobbes to Edward Howard
> (1668)

URING his prolific Paris years, when Hobbes reached full maturity as a political and moral thinker, he turned his attention in still another direction—poetics. Early in 1651, the year of *Leviathan*, William Davenant published his poem *Gondibert*, together with a preface addressed to Hobbes. The philosopher responded with a short piece complimenting *Gondibert*—a sign, one hopes, more reflective of his courtesy than of his literary taste—and exploring the nature of poetry.[1] His *Answer to the Preface of Gondibert*, his literary observations in the Thucydides essay, and his *Virtues of an Heroic Poem*—the 1675 preface to his translation of Homer—plus remarks scattered through his other texts is all Hobbes left in writing concerning literature. It is small in volume and strung out over nearly half a century, yet it is of substantial importance in at least two ways: from the point of view of literary history, scholars have credited it with having exerted considerable influence on the course of English

133

critical thought, and from the biographical point of view, it allows us to see how this scientific philosopher regarded art throughout his adult years.

It is customary to observe that in the period covered by Hobbes's life, English literary thought underwent a profound change. In the earlier part, English literary criticism was still largely an eclectic composite of ideas and formulae from the rhetorical tradition, including a noticeable strain of classical idealism, and it was in no way as systematic as the French, which had earlier begun to absorb the teachings of the Italian critics and to codify the principles of Aristotle and Horace into the "Rules"—those literary regulations about nature to which every poem was obliged to conform. The French influence is frequently cited for having effected, in part, the transformation of the earlier kind of criticism in England and for having ushered in the highly ordered literary theory of the Augustan age during the latter part of the seventeenth century.

Hobbes has often been regarded as a significant stepping-stone in this transition, most importantly by virtue of having promulgated a mechanical view of nature which, in turn, became the nature which poets were to imitate. As J. E. Spingarn, who has done so much to shape our view of the period, has said: "The mechanical universe of the philosophy of Hobbes and Locke is thus the basis of seventeenth century criticism; and the sense of mechanical order in nature was implicit in all thought. This was the highest justification of the Rules: they represent the order found in nature."[2] As the idea of nature changed in the course of the century, in short, so did the idea of poetry. As nature was increasingly regarded as mechanistically regular and devoid of the rich variety of correspondences and relationships of the earlier humanist universe, so the logical component in literature was accorded a new respect at the expense of its less "orderly," more individually fanciful elements. Human nature itself is conceived of in literature as conforming to a more restricted, "reasonable" norm, and the metrics of Waller and the prose rhythms of Dryden attain a heightened regularity to approximate the symmetry of nature. The "Rules," in fact, were but "nature methodized."

My concern is to find out in just what way Hobbes fits into this rather oversimplified account of the development of the Augustan literary world. In general, as Spingarn's remarks suggest, where Hobbes's philosophy is construed as merely mechanistic and this interpretation is carried over into readings of his literary thought, scholars find that he has small regard for the creative spirit and that he propounds a literary theory in which "the imaginative process is no longer sufficient or even vital."[3] Another critic similarly holds that "Hobbes ignores the transforming power of the imagination," and that "the supremacy of judgment is already patent" in his theory—a theory which triumphs in Dryden's prose, where "denotation is immense but... suggestiveness is almost nothing."[4] This picture of Hobbes as the purely rationalistic philosopher is extended further when Restoration theories of prose style are discussed, especially when the anti-ciceronian movement for a plainer literary style is linked to the Royal Society's program to reform language by making it a more suitable vehicle for scientific purposes. Hobbes is then included as representative of the group and we are led to see him as a kind of early protagonist in that conflict, so familiar to us today, between science and the humanities.

Before turning to Hobbes's place in this transition, certain problems must be pointed out in this standard reconstruction of its nature. The first is more a matter of emphasis than of substance: that there was a decided shift in literary sensibilities between the Jacobean and Augustan periods is beyond question, but it makes a great difference if Donne and Dryden are taken to mark the two extremes of that shift, or if Jonson and Dryden are. In the first instance, there seems to be a radical discontinuity between the intensely personal, tough, and paradoxical expression of the metaphysical mind and the smooth, sophisticated expression of the Augustan one. In the second instance, if we begin with Jonson, the shift is more muted. There appears, instead, a steady growth of force in the already present neoclassical impulse, an impulse then common to much of Western European culture but earlier already discernable in poets like Sidney. Granted that factors external to literary theory may have encouraged that impulse, such as the advance of science, their effect is diminished in proportion as the shift toward the classical itself seems less extreme.

This brings us to the second problem, the influence of science on poetry and poetics. While science certainly affects our way of looking at the world and thus affects our poetry, it is to be doubted whether the relationship is tantamount to a direct correspondence. If the regularity of the mechanistic universe as espoused by Hobbes and seventeenth-century science can cause a new regularity in an Augustan poet's line, then it follows analytically that Hobbes and the mechanistic philosophers of science could be responsible for Augustan poetics. But mechanical science caused in Donne not regularity, but a poetry of doubt, and it caused the nineteenth-century poets, who lived in an equally mechanistic world, to "drink confusion to mathematics" as they created new myths. To accept scientific theories as facts that cause new feelings (as Donne did), or to accept them by assimilating them into poetic method (as some Augustans did), or to try to forget about them (as we have done), is a choice society at large and poets make, not science.

It is true that the seventeenth-century spokesmen of science advocated a clearer, non-metaphorical use of language for their purposes and consequently seem to us to deny what we call the imagination its former freedom. But poets of the period did not see it that way, and writers like Cowley continue to have the friendliest feelings toward science, responding to the Royal Society's exhortations about language not by dropping metaphors, but by using them to write odes in praise of the Society. Either the poets were too naive and unaware that they were working their own destruction, or we have misread the relations between science and poetry. It may be argued that the *kind* of metaphor the later Cowley uses and his emphasis on clarity of prose style is itself indicative of the influence of scientific rationalism, but clergymen and teachers were calling for a like clarity, and the classicism which enters English poetry was probably at least as much a cause as an effect of the rise of modern rationalism. These preliminary caveats take us into deep water and cannot be pursued here, but they have been necessary since literary historians who exaggerate the direct influence of scientific thought on poetry and who see it as destructive of metaphorical language and the imagination are apt to read the scientific Hobbes in a fashion that confirms these assumptions.

Whatever the general influence of mechanistic science on poetics, Hobbes's position in the shift toward neoclassicism hinges most directly on what he had to say about poetry, and what he had to say is by no means easy to determine, being beset by certain restrictions and by special semantic problems. Among the restrictions is the fact that both of his works devoted exclusively to criticism are almost wholly focused on discussions of the epic, the favored form of the period, and thereby give us a very partial view of his opinions which it is dangerous to generalize. Secondly, the examples he cites are almost exclusively from the classical literature of antiquity, so that whatever clarification might have been derived by comparing his theory to his taste in contemporary authors is practically excluded. We know, for instance, that he thought Milton's Latin prose as excellent as his reasoning was poor, but there is no extrapolating from this judgment to what Hobbes's opinion of *Samson Agonistes* might have been.

The semantic problems are more intricate, but bear directly on the changing concepts of poetry in the period. The literary vocabulary of critics remained fairly stable during the course of the seventeenth century, but the meanings of their crucial terms—"wit," "fancy," and "judgment"—underwent tacit reformation which reflected shifting aesthetic attitudes and which were, indeed, a measure of them. Throughout the first part of the century, for instance, "wit" in its broadest designation referred to the whole intellectual vitality of the mind, combining both the abilities of judgment and fancy in its designation, as in the first quotation from Hobbes which heads this chapter. Its secondary meaning was more narrow, and instead of designating a general agility of the mind it referred to a mere agility with words, a gift for pointed speech or clever repartee. As such, it tended to usurp its primary meaning and set wit (as fanciful speech) *opposed* to reason or judgment. The paradoxes and extravagant conceits of the metaphysical poets could thus, in the earlier part of the century, be truly praised for their wit, but as the word moved toward its more trivial meaning and the fashion of metaphysical poetry passed, so they were later damned by the same word, a shift indicating a changing perception of the metaphysical style as well. By mid-century, the word loses its bearings altogether, sometimes solidly associated with fancy and poetry, occasionally with reason, and one picks one's way from text to text with an open mind, but its former comprehensive sense is largely lost, and with it an appropriate word for what is now called poetic talent. The association of wit with fancy became most prominent, the word by then rather degraded, so that one finds Hobbes complaining in 1675, that the pleasantness of fancy makes men "give to it alone the name of Wit." By the end of the century, however, the word had been refurbished again and restored to its comprehensive designation in literature, but the yoked abilities of fancy and judgment in wit now described the propriety of word and thing in neoclassical poetry, not the paradoxes of Donne or even the masculine poise of Jonson.

These changes occurred over the whole span of Hobbes's writing so that his usage in earlier texts sometimes seems to disagree with his later one. Moreover, in any given time period when a word like "wit" may be assumed to have a stable meaning for him, he used it differently as he wrote on different levels of diction or in different contexts, picking up varying nuances of the term. Finally, even within the same text he did not altogether escape inconsistency when he shifted from one topic to the next. This adds up to a situation in which definitions must be regarded with some flexibility (Hobbes's constant injunctions to the contrary notwithstanding) and meanings must be culled carefully from the context. As Spingarn points out, Hobbes was a pioneer in literary theory by virtue of investigating with some care the psychological aspects of poetry, but it was precisely those psychological terms, "fancy" and "judgment," which were caught up in linguistic fluctuations in his texts. Spingarn therefore grants Hobbes too much, perhaps, when he says that "Hobbes's aesthetic is consistent and logical throughout, the first of its kind in English literature,"[5] for what one must seek in the semantic confusion is not absolute consistency, but a firm and general coherence.

The general contours of Hobbes's *Answer* fit broadly within the still somewhat eclectic framework of critical theory as it emerged in the Jacobean period, but the *basis* for his literary ideas in his psychological theories is wholly his own and the place where his philosophy most nearly meets the concerns of literature. But another place where the relationship between philosophy and literature can be tested is in Hobbes's own prose style, the characteristics of which will also be explored here.

The Critical Theory
and Its Psychological Basis

It is fundamental to Hobbes's literary thought that poetry is not distinguished from many other activities as "art" or "imitation." Since Hobbes considers nature itself an art (that of God), and since man imitates nature in his social and political organization, most of civilized life is "artificial," a construct imposed on the raw materials of the state of nature. Political society is as much a "made object" or *fictum* as a poem. Poetry, as only one among the many arts of man, cannot be distinguished from the others by the fact of imitation, but rather by the different ends and means of poetic imitation, and by the way the faculties function in the production of a poem.

Hobbes speaks of poetry as an imitation of "human life" or of "nature" or of "the manners of men," and its effect is to avert men from vice and incline them to "virtuous and honourable actions."[6] In the epic, the values conveyed are covered by the term "heroic virtue"—the same term he used in the Thucydides—which includes "settled valour, clean honour, calm counsel, learned diversion, and pure love."[7] Epic poetry, like history, therefore instructs and the virtues communicated are essentially the same (though "pure love" appears only on poetry's list), but unlike history, it must do so by delighting. It is further distinguished from other literature by its use of verse, but here he follows Aristotle in holding that not everything in verse is poetry. Lucan and Lucretius are excluded from the ranks of the poets in the *Answer* as being rather an historian and a philosopher, for "the subject of a poem is the manners of men, not natural causes; manners presented, not dictated; and manners feigned, as the name poesy imports, not found in men."[8] Prose fiction is therefore closer to poetry than philosophy in verse because its object of imitation is the same as poetry's, but prose is less effective than poetry since it lacks the ornament of verse. It might have been more consistent for Hobbes, for whom all pleasure is ultimately the enhanced vital motions around the heart, to have found it a matter of indifference what the subject of a poem was as long as it was instructively pleasurable, but that was not his position in the *Answer*.

The system of poetic genres is derived by Hobbes from the different spheres in which men act: as philosophers divide the world into celestial, aerial, and terrestrial regions, he says, so poets divide it into court, city, and country. When the poet's characters are drawn from the court, the poem will be heroic in accordance with their noble natures and it will take the form of either an epic or a tragedy, depending on whether it is narrative or dramatic. In the same way, city dwellers yield satire or comedy, and country folk give us bucolics or pastoral comedy, this whole division of the genres with reference to social rank being very common during the Renaissance and long after.[9] Like Bacon (with whom he has not much else in common), Hobbes leaves little room in this scheme for the shorter verse forms such as the sonnet and epigram, considering them "essays" or the parts of one of the larger genres.

As for the fable of a poem, there is no exaggerated formalism in Hobbes, who praises an organic unity of action, but nowhere mentions unity of place or time as requirements. Since poetry is an imitation of nature, Hobbes makes "the resemblance of truth . . . the utmost limit of poetical liberty": "Beyond the actual works of nature a poet may now go; but beyond the conceived possibility of nature, never."[10] In the examples he gives, these limits preclude such things as "iron men" and "flying horses" in a fiction; they allow a geographer to draw a fish in his map of the sea which would be two hundred miles long by scale, though not an elephant, the fish being "done within the precincts of [the geographer's] undertaking," but the elephant not. A fish is certainly the kind of thing that nature put in the sea, no matter how large, but flying horses are not the kind of thing that nature put in the air and they will not convince. This criterion is sometimes taken as indicative of an extreme reliance on empirical reality as the "nature" which poetry is to imitate, but as Hobbes well knew, what falls within the "conceived possibility of nature" is not a matter of empirical reality, but a matter of belief. He does not therefore object to the "strange fictions and metamorphoses" in classical literature since such things were "not so remote from the articles of faith" in ancient times.[11] It may be supposed that he would similarly not oppose "iron men" in fairy tales for children since their idea of nature is more extravagant.

Most of the other aspects of poetry treated by Hobbes touch on his psychological explanations of the creative process and on the previously mentioned semantic problems connected with them. To sort them out, a detour is required through Hobbes's psychological theory, some elements of which were noticed briefly in an earlier chapter, but which must now be reviewed in greater detail, and a good starting point is his idea of the imagination. As reason is usually associated by Hobbes with the use of words, the employment of method and the acquired abilities needed for science, so imagination is usually associated with sense perception, the growth of experience, and the natural aptitudes that develop prudence. Reason is a relatively late acquisition (children before the age of speech being called reasonable creatures only by anticipation), but imagination is man's basic equipment. It is born with his senses, and by providing images of his passions, it is the source of his voluntary motions. In fact, as will be shown and as it was already implicit in Hobbes's epistemology, Hobbes conceives of humanity as inherently and irretrievably imaginative to the core. It will therefore not do to dismiss Hobbes as a rigid rationalist simply by quoting his definition of imagination as "decaying sense," as often happens. A nicer discrimination of his contexts is required. The word "imagination" does not itself appear in

the *Answer*, though "fancy" does, and the frequently quoted definition of imagination as "decaying sense" in *Leviathan* belongs to a
discussion of the retention of sense images in perception, not to a
discussion of the creation of significant images in poetry.

In *Leviathan*, imagination or fancy—the terms are used there
synonymously—is described as the phantasms caused in the mind by
motion from external bodies, that is, sense: "sense, in all cases, is
nothing but original fancy."* A little later, fancy (as opposed to "original fancy") is those same phantasms as retained in the mind, Hobbes
noting that after an object of perception is removed or the eyes shut,

> We still retain an image of the thing seen, though more obscure than
> when we see it. And this is it, the Latins call imagination, from the image
> made in seeing: and apply the same though improperly, to all the other
> senses. But the Greeks call it fancy: which signifies appearance, and is as
> proper to one sense, as to another. IMAGINATION therefore is nothing
> but decaying sense. . . .[12]

The decay of sense is due to the influx of subsequent sense impressions which obscure preceding ones; an earlier impression is made
weak by being crowded, or as Hobbes says in his own apt image, it is
"as the voice of a man is in the noise of the day.[13] In Hobbes's
philosophic vocabulary, therefore, fancy or imagination is the apprehension and continued existence of sense impressions in the mind,
and while imagination conceived in this way may be "insufficent" for
making a poem, one can almost say that it is the entire foundation for
the life of man, for its phantasms are our only connection with the
external world.

Less familiar is Hobbes's significant refinement of this notion of
imagination when he distinguishes between "simple" and "compound" imagination, the former being described as "imagining the
whole object as it was presented to the sense," and he gives the
example of imagining a man or horse one has seen before. Compound
imagination, on the other hand, combines elements of former perceptions into new wholes, "as when, from the sight of a man at one time,

---

*E.W., III, 3. The motion that is the phantasm is not sharply distinguished by
Hobbes from the act of sense that apprehends it; as explained in *De Corpore:* "For a
phantasm is the act of sense, and differs no otherwise from sense than *fieri*, that is,
being a doing, differs from *factum esse*, that is, being done; which difference, in things
that are done in an instant, is none at all; and a phantasm is made in an instant." Ibid.,
I, 392.

and of a horse at another, we conceived in our mind a Centaur." In a more complex instance, Hobbes gives the example of "when a man compoundeth the image of his own person with the image of the actions of another man, as when a man imagines himself a Hercules or an Alexander," which we would call identification. It is, properly speaking, he says, "a fiction of the mind,"[14] and it gives imagination a scope and synthetic component closer to what was and is called imagination in more popular parlance.

The active element in compound imagination is already evident in the act of sense, which should not be thought of as a simple reaction to external stimuli. To perceive something entails comparisons and distinctions—an act of judgment—the basis for which is the presence of previously perceived impressions, so that sense must have in it "a perpetual variety of phantasms." If sense impressions were not distinguished but passed before a man's eyes "without the least appearance of variety, he would seem to me, whatsoever others may say, to see, no more than I seem to myself to feel the bones of my limbs by my organs of feeling." A man might *look* at an appearance and even be astonished by it, "but I should not say he saw it, it being almost all one for a man to be always sensible to one and the same thing, and not to be sensible at all of any thing."[15]

Insofar as comparisons and contrasts are required, sense perception therefore "hath necessarily some memory adhering to it," but "memory" is simply another name for imagination, the name we give it when we want to express the fact that the images are of absent objects and faded or "decayed," "so that imagination and memory are but one thing, for which diverse considerations hath diverse names."[16] Hobbes frequently remarks that two or more names pertain to the same thing when considered differently, as we have had occasion to see before. It is a procedure inherent in his methodology, allowing him to build from a few basic terms and to clear away that proliferation of entities he found so misleading in philosophy. Here he sweeps away the clutter of species, forms, and faculties accumulated by medieval psychology and builds simply from the senses, which are all that men are born with, and imagination. In this way, having extended the notion of imagination by observing that memory is only another name for it, he notes that memory of many things has yet another name, which is "experience." Imagination evoked by words has a special name of its own, "evidence" or "understanding"—that central concept in Hobbes's epistemology. But all these are still imagination, not new or different entities.[17]

Fancy or imagination acquires several more important names in the course of Hobbes's potent elaboration of its meaning, names requisite for describing all the activity in that phantasm-thronged place called the mind. Fresh phantasms continuously flow in with sense perception, and old phantasms perpetually arise prompted either by a variety of appetites (when our minds wander or dream) or by one strong desire which guides them in a more ordered sequence (when we "think"), and all this busyness Hobbes calls "discourse of mind." There is nothing to observe in these phantasms except, as noted before, their likenesses and differences ("what they serve for, or how they serve to such a purpose"). If the likenesses observed are between remote things, Hobbes says it is called "good fancy," the important word being "good" since it apparently differentiates this fancy from its ordinary perceptual function in that the things compared are "remote."[18] The discernment of differences is "judgment," or, when times, places, and persons are to be discerned, "discretion."[19] Judgment is thus an analytic component proper to intelligent perception; in its broader application, it is the source of propriety, and Hobbes associates it frequently with scientific knowledge as he associates fancy with poetry. The mechanics of judgment are described in *De Corpore:* judgment is "not perception made by a common organ of sense, distinct from sense of perception properly so called, but is memory of the differences of particular phantasms remaining for some time; as the distinction between hot and lucid, is nothing else but the memory both of a heating, and of an enlightening object."[20] As judgment is based on memories, and memory consists of imagination, it follows that judgment is a function of imagination, and is given a different name for its specific operation. And what else could it be since imagination is all the natural intellectual equipment we have? The only ability that Hobbes accepts as learned is reasoning (adding and subtracting the consequences of general terms), and that is a development of understanding, raised to a new power by the trained use of language.[21]

The general coherence of this position has been challenged in literary history because of certain passages in *Leviathan* where Hobbes describes wit in terms of fancy and judgment and seems to get tangled in his own definitions. The centrality of "wit" in seventeenth-century criticism has already been touched upon, but since its importance was largely in discussions of lyric poetry, the term does not become fundamental for Hobbes's poetics nor does it even appear in the *Answer*. Nonetheless, since Hobbes's remarks on it in *Leviathan* are said to have been influential for the last part of the century's criticism, they require some attention for their interpretation.

Wit, said Hobbes, "consisteth chiefly in two things: *celerity of imagining*, that is, swift succession of one thought to another; and *steady direction* to some approved end."[22] Both the steadiness and the swiftness result from some strong guiding passion, "for the thoughts are to the desires as scouts, and spies, to range abroad, and find the way to the things desired . . . for as to have no desire, is to be dead; so to have weak passions is dullness; and to have passions indifferently for everying, GIDDINESS. . . ."[23] In discussing the imaginings themselves, Hobbes then makes the aforementioned distinction between fancy and judgment, with fancy described in these words: "those that observe similitudes, in case they be such as are rarely observed by others, are said to have a *good wit*; by which, in this occasion is meant a *good fancy*."[24]

Now Spingarn and others have understood Hobbes to mean that fancy and wit are identical (as opposed to judgment), an identification tending toward that narrowing of wit's meaning which, as a name for poetic ability, would in turn limit the scope of poetry.[25] But Hobbes seems rather to be specifically distinguishing common parlance from his own: the observation of similitudes is *said* to be good wit, but what is *meant* is good fancy. Indeed, the whole import of the passage is to distinguish fancy from judgment, not wit from judgment, and he apparently does so with a literary example in mind. As he explains at the end of the passage, a person with a good fancy harnessed to judgment and a steady purpose "will be easily fitted with similitudes, that will please, not only by illustrations of his discourse, and adorning it with new and apt metaphors, but also, by the rarity of their invention."[26] Given this literary application, one could say that a poet is a man of wit; that is, a man of strong passions and a copious stock of images, who has the good judgment to know how to use them to further his design.*

---

*I believe Hobbes was consistent here in joining fancy and judgment in "wit," not only in *Human Nature*, as quoted at the head of the chapter, and in *Leviathan*, but also in the *Virtues* of 1675. But if Hobbes was generally consistent, he did have a lapse in

Unlike *Leviathan* or *De Corpore*, Hobbes's *Answer* provides only a highly condensed version of these relationships between "imagination" or "fancy" and its allied psychological terms. *Leviathan*, after all, was a sustained and systematic philosophical effort; the *Answer*, an occasional piece allowing Hobbes to make a brief foray into poetics. Hobbes nonetheless wanted to present certain salient features of his psychology to establish a minimum framework within which to work, and this he did in one packed and famous passage in the *Answer:*

> Time and education beget experience; experience begets memory; memory begets judgment and fancy; judgment begets the strength and structure, and fancy begets the ornaments of a poem. The ancients therefore fabled not absurdly, in making Memory the mother of the Muses. For memory is the world, though not really, yet so as in a looking-glass, in which judgment, the severer sister, busieth herself in a grave and rigid examination

---

another passage in *Leviathan*, where he can (and has been) read to identify wit not with fancy, but with judgment: "Judgment therefore without fancy is wit, but fancy without judgment not." How he arrived at this startlingly contradictory conclusion can only be seen in the context of the whole remarkable passage where it occurs. It is worth quoting at length, not only to settle Hobbes's terminology, but also because of the vividness of the prose, which catches his voice clearly:

> The secret thoughts of man run over all things, holy, profane, clean, obscene, grave, and light, without shame, or blame; which verbal discourse cannot do, farther than the judgment shall approve of the time, place and persons. An anatomist, or a physician may speak, or write his judgment of unclean things; because it is not to please, but profit: but for another man to write his extravagant, and pleasant fancies of the same, is as if a man, from being tumbled into the dirt, should come and present himself before good company. And it is want of discretion that makes the difference. Again, in professed remissness of mind, and familiar company, a man may play with the sounds and equivocal signification of words; and that many times with encounters of extraordinary fancy: but in a sermon, or in public, or before persons unknown, or whom we ought to reverence; there is no gingling of words that will not be accounted folly: and the difference is only in the want of discretion. So that where wit is wanting, it is not fancy that is wanting, but discretion. [E.W., IV, 59.]

Hobbes then concludes, with a grand non sequitur, "Judgment therefore without fancy is wit, but fancy without judgment, not." Given that elsewhere Hobbes has wit comprehend both judgment and fancy, the logic of this paragraph does not allow his conclusion. Properly speaking, he could conclude from his examples, as he does, that fancy without judgment is not wit, but not that judgment without fancy is. The lapse does not recur, and he may have been led into it by changing his examples from poetry and rhetoric to examples of social manners, where "wit" covers a different territory and thus caused Hobbes to shift his ground inadvertently. Whatever the reason, the passage may be admired for some of its prose and forgiven its concluding logic.

of all the parts of nature, and in registering by letters their order, causes, uses, differences, and resemblances; whereas the fancy, when any work of art is to be performed, finds her materials at hand and prepared for use, and needs no more than a swift motion over them, that what she wants, and is there to be had, may not lie too long unespied. So that when she seemeth to fly from one Indies to the other, and from heaven to earth, and to penetrate into the hardest matter and obscurest places, into the future, and into herself, and all this in a point of time, the voyage is not very great, herself being all she seeks. And her wonderful celerity, consisteth not so much in motion, as in copious imagery discreetly ordered, and perfectly registered in the memory; which most men under the name of philosophy have a glimpse of.[27]

It is clear that Hobbes is not writing in technical terms here; he does not assume that the audience is familiar with *Leviathan* and the special way he construes memory, experience, or fancy there, but simply writes in the popular literary idiom—a warning for us not to look for total consistency on every point between his texts when they are written at different levels of diction. "Fancy" is employed here only for the constructive side of imagination, the combining of elements of memory (discreetly ordered by judgment) into the new creations of the poet. It assimilates the meaning of "compound imagination" into its range, or at least a highly constructive aspect, a meaning which approximates general literary usage of the term. It does *not* conform to the meaning of imagination for those who belonged to the inspirational school, but indicates rather an affinity to thinking of artists as people with heightened talents and, as we shall see, a sense of craftsmanship: it tends not toward Milton's outlook, but toward the later Jonson's. Since poetry, fancy, and everything else in the mind of man come first from his contact with nature through his senses, Hobbes wonders why "a man, enabled to speak wisely from the principles of nature, and his own meditation, loves rather to be thought to speak by inspiration, like a bagpipe."[28]

Judgment and fancy work together in poetry, as they do in most human activities in various proportions, but fancy is the more important in poetry. As he says in *Leviathan*, "In a good poem... both judgment and fancy are required, but the fancy must be more eminent; because they please for the extravagancy; but ought not to displease by indiscretion."[29] Despite this statement and the primacy of pleasing in poetry, scholars have often felt that Hobbes elevated judgment at the expense of fancy, and the first sentence of his structure-and-ornament paragraph is often cited—"judgment begets the strength and structure, and fancy begets the ornaments of a poem"—as proof that he was moving toward an Augustan rationalism in poetry. Such a reading is possible only if Hobbes supposed that poetry has a "structure" somehow separable from the "ornaments" that bespangle it. But there is no evidence that he or any other serious reader or writer of his generation did make such a supposition, though such artificial distinctions, then and now, are made for teaching or analytic purposes. Moreover, seventeenth-century diction did not invariably relegate the meaning of "ornament" to things inessential or merely decorative, as is usual today.[30] Dozens of citations from Hobbes's contemporaries could be presented in evidence, but looking only in the *Answer* itself, the term can be found again in a sentence on heroic poems:

As the description of great men and great acts is the constant design of a poet; so the descriptions of worthy circumstances are necessary accessions to a poem, and being well performed, are the jewels and most precious ornaments of poesy. Such in Virgil are the funeral games of Anchises, the duel of Æneas and Turnus, &c.[31]

These "necessary accessions" of the poem are "ornaments" but not *mere* ornaments. They are "most precious" and "jewels." They include, for Hobbes, not only the fable and its variety of incident (rhetoric gave these to "inventio"), but also the style (rhetoric's "elocutio"), with the poet making his choices in both these areas under the guidance of his judgment, which also organizes his work (the part of rhetoric called "dispositio").[32] While fancy is "eminent," judgment must discern the aptness and propriety of fancy's invention and elocution to ensure that they serve the poet's design. This is Hobbes's meaning in the *Virtues*, though somewhat unguardedly phrased, when he says that "the virtues required in an heroic poem, and indeed in all writings published, are comprehended all in this one word—discretion."[33] The sentence suffers from that wish for nutshell formulations which is so characteristic of Hobbes's writings and which is often responsible for both the vice of minor inconsistency and the virtue of powerful expression. In this case, his meaning is more precisely stated a few pages later when he speaks of "elevation of fancy, which is generally taken for the greatest praise of heroic poetry; and is so, when governed by discretion."[34] All of this is well within the guidelines set down by Tudor literary critics and passed on to the Jacobean writers, Hobbes developing it only by his referral of the various parts of poetry and rhetoric to their psychological sources, a referral already suggested, though hardly elaborated, by Bacon before him.[35]

Hobbes's Puck-like imagery in his description of fancy quoted in the structure-and-ornament passage a few pages back is itself a fine "ornament" of his prose, amplifying his notion of fancy by showing its characteristic speed and scope and by relating them to a richly stocked memory, the materials of which fancy shares with philosophy. The functions of poetry and philosophy are correlative as Hobbes conceives of them in the rest of the passage, quoted below. There fancy is the active agent of the mind, the architect that realizes concretely in the outer world all the theory of philosophy; as it figures forth in poetry the actions and passions of men, so it builds in the world what philosophy makes conceivable:

So far forth as the fancy of man has traced the ways of true philosophy, so far it hath produced very marvellous effects to the benefit of mankind. All that is beautiful or defensible in building; or marvellous in engines and instruments of motion; whatsoever commodity men receive from the observations of the heavens, from the descriptions of the earth, from the account of time, from walking on the seas; and whosoever distinguisheth the civility of Europe, from the barbarity of the American savages; is the workmanship of fancy, but guided by the precepts of true philosophy. But where these precepts fail, as they have hitherto failed in the doctrine of moral virtue, there the architect Fancy must take the philosopher's part upon herself. He, therefore, who undertakes an heroic poem, which is to exhibit a venerable and amiable image of heroic virtue, must not only be the poet, to place and connect, but also the philosopher, to furnish and square his matter, that is, to make both body and soul, colour and shadow of his poem out of his own store. . . .[36]

It is hard to see, after this extraordinary praise of human imagination, how Hobbes can be said to have conceived of it in a way that was not "vital." Without fancy, philosophy would lose all efficacy or concrete representation in the world, the scope given to the constructive imagination by Hobbes apparently embracing all kinds of reasoned work on nature's materials and having affinities in its grand sweep to Aristotle's notion of art.

There are many places, it is true, where Hobbes voices his distrust of fancy, but this is never in the context of poetry. It is almost always true where fancy intrudes into scientific demonstrations or

counsel, although even there he allows that "sometimes the understanding have need to be opened by some apt similitude."[37] Fancy, in
the form of metaphors, slips unannounced into definitions and
thereby diverts the true course of reasoning, and it presents in language images which rouse the passions and make necessary objective
judgments impossible. In stirring the emotions, he says, "it is no
matter whether the opinion be true or false, or the narration historical
or fabulous, for *not* the *truth*, but the *image*, maketh passion: and a
tragedy, well acted, affecteth no less than a murder."[38] Hobbes warns
chiefly, and repeatedly, against these images of fancy when they are
in the service of rhetoric, most especially political rhetoric, since they
are the sparks that ignite revolutions. His most violent charges
against rhetoric are perhaps those in a chapter of his *Philosophical
Rudiments Concerning Government and Society* entitled "Of the Internal
Causes Tending to the Dissolution of any Government":

Sallust's character of Cataline, than whom there never was a greater artist
in raising seditions, is this: *that he had great eloquence, and little wisdom.* He
separates *wisdom* from *eloquence;* attributing this as necessary to a man born
for commotions; adjudging that as an instructress of peace and quietness.
Now eloquence is twofold. The one is an elegant and clear expression of
the conceptions of the mind; and riseth partly from the contemplation of
the things themselves, partly from an understanding of words taken in
their own proper and definite signification. The other is a commotion of
the passions of the mind, such as are *hope, fear, anger, pity;* and derives
from a metaphorical use of words fitted to the passions. That forms a
speech from true principles; this from opinions already received, what
nature soever they are of. The art of that is logic, of this rhetoric; the end
of that is truth, of this victory. Each hath its use; that in deliberations,
this in exhortations; for that is never disjoined from wisdom, but this
almost ever.[39]

Hobbes had earlier found in Thucydides, and later in Sidney Godol-
phin, examples of people who had merged the various uses of speech
successfully—the ability of logic to deliberate with the ability of
rhetoric to move—and in no other passage is he quite so pessimistic
and stern on the question as here. But how deeply felt and understood this theme of the separation of wisdom from eloquence was can
be seen in Milton (no enemy of fancy), who was led to make it a major
attribute of Satan in *Paradise Lost* and to conceive of him as the great
demagogic figure he is. While the poet made it central to the story of
the Fall itself, the philosopher made it fundamental to man's con-

tinual re-enactment of that Fall in all his civil wars. Both address the theme as a problem in politics, not in poetry, and the asperity in Hobbes's tone seems to reflect his exasperation that the radical weaknesses of man's nature should be so perfectly mirrored in his most essential instrument of progress, his language.

At this point, we have clearly linked up with Hobbes's Thucydidean themes. That we should do so is not surprising since the poet as well as the orator and philosopher of the time turned to the rhetoric books for his elocution and the relationship between passions and truth was a question common to them all. Poetry is exempt from Hobbes's strictures against rhetoric since all kinds of art are to be judged according to how well they realize their ends. Thus, following Quintilian, Hobbes censures Lucan for the flaw of writing as a rhetorician rather than as a poet when he overtly favors the Pompeian faction against Caesar, putting victory above the poetic end of a true imitation of the manners of men.[40] By the same token, when Hobbes takes unscrupulous orators to task, he is judging their truthfulness and virtue, not their art in rhetoric. In short, in all disciplines and in every case, Hobbes's evaluation of the utility of fancy and its relationship to judgment hinged on the particular end sought: fancy has no place in demonstrations since their purpose is to find truth, which is arrived at by a correct use of words in their proper signification and the accurate observation of things; there is eminent place for fancy in poetry because *its* end is to imitate nature in language that delightfully instructs. Fancy is not problematic in poetry as it is in rhetoric by virtue of its fictions or its ability to stir the emotions—those are poetry's avowed means to its end. It only becomes problematic in poetry when fancy is unchecked and fails to shape its flight toward serving the poet's design, his imitation.

Needless to say, perhaps, Hobbes's strictures concerning an unbridled fancy were hardly unique with him, having a venerable and continuous tradition behind them among materialists and idealists alike. Unfettered fancy was traditionally associated by writers of every stripe and to different degrees with insignificant or indecorous speech, and by philosophers with confusion and various forms of madness. That touch of madness, the *furor poeticus*, which is so frequently spoken of by Renaissance writers as the sign of inspiration, is of a different type, involving divine influence. Hobbes identifies it as "elevation of fancy" in his more psychological language, and he grants that in it "consisteth the sublimity of the poet."[41] But not belonging to the vatic school, Hobbes considered it of natural, not divine origin, that neoplatonic notion of a poetic frenzy having already become muted by the time of Jonson's *Timber* and in other quarters where the element of craftsmanship in poetry was given new attention. Both schools would have agreed, however, that inspiration or elevated fancy must be joined with an astute judgment of the fitness of word and expression to the matter—a quality usually called "decorum" or "decency" or, in the case of Peacham, "prudence." These terms suffered the same vicissitudes as "wit" did, however, and their precise connotations are often as hard to pin down, as we shall see.

If Hobbes was inclined to view poetry as a craft, he did not follow the neoclassical critics in finding that the best way to learn it was always by imitating the great writers of the past. Expression in a poem, "the countenance and colour of a beautiful Muse," if it were to be true and natural, was best drawn from the poet's own experience, and for this the poet had to *"know well"* and *"know much."*[42] Knowing much provides the poet's words with variety and novelty, but Hobbes warns that he is not referring to "the affectations of words newly brought home from travel, but in new, and withal significant translation to our purposes, of those that be already received; and in far-fetched, but withal, apt, instructive, and comely similitudes."[43] That significant translation is, of course, what all poets want, while variety of expression (and, in the *Virtues*, of incident) is as necessary for meaningful language as it is for meaningful perception, Hobbes understanding the two as exactly correlative: "for the phrases of poesy, as the airs of music, for often hearing become insipid; the reader having no more sense of their force, than our flesh is sensible of the bones that sustain it."[44] As for novelty or freshness of perception, the high value Hobbes puts on it stems from the fact that it stimulates the reader's "admiration," an emotion to which he attributes poetry's ability to instruct. As an element in epic poetry, admiration was apparently introduced into Continental criticism by the Italian writer Minturno, and subsequently gained wide currency, but it was used in such a different sense from Hobbes's that the variation is more interesting than the similarity.[45] For Sidney and others, admiration is the emotion which leads readers to emulate the idealized image of the hero in epic poetry and thus accounts for its efficacy as a teaching vehicle. But for Hobbes, admiration comes not from the image of the hero necessarily, but from newness of any kind, from novelty itself, and it leads to instruction in a wholly different way. Admiration, he says, causes curiosity, "which is a delightful appetite of knowledge,"[46] and which is the basic impulse toward learning. It is the intellectual passion which makes us educable, which is ultimately responsible for our development of language and therefore of science, and it is the fulfillment of this "lust of the mind" that poetry promises and that holds our attention. So in *Leviathan*, Hobbes defines admiration as "*Joy*, from apprehension of novelty," and he finds it "proper to man, because it excites the appetite of knowing the cause."[47]

As novelty of expression is a sign that the poet knows much and a cause of our admiration and curiosity, so perspicuity, propriety and decency in a poem are a sign that he "knows well," and delights "all sorts of men, either by instructing the ignorant, or soothing the learned in their knowledge."[48] Knowing well involves having clear and distinct images lodged in the memory. If a poet has a firm image in his mind of a character who is introduced speaking in the poem, that character will be maintained to the end, and this is what Hobbes means by "propriety." Odysseus will always sound like the shrewd hero he is and not, say, like the petulant hero that Achilles is. Were Odysseus to suddenly sound like Achilles, it would be "a change of pace, that argues the poet tired."[49]

"Perspicuity," as in the Thucydides essay, is still associated with clear images, but Hobbes was concerned in the earlier work with the vivid images effected in the reader's mind by perspicuous prose, while in the *Answer* he is concerned with the clarity of images in the author's mind which are a *source* of perspicuous language. There is also no broad methodological application of the term as there was in Thucydides, Hobbes using it here in a purely stylistic sense, much as Jonson does, to refer to the poet's choice of words and effectiveness of style. Jonson, in the name of perspicuity, disallowed terms of art in poetry or words either too new or too archaic,[50] and Hobbes on the same grounds is averse to foreign words or terms not known in accepted literary English, as well as "empty" words.[51] There is no exclusion of words as being intrinsically "unpoetic," however, and no application of a criterion of "easiness" or, of what often went with it in later writers like Dryden, a polished fluidity in meter.

Here a word might be said about metrics, although Hobbes does not take it up under "perspicuity." His ideal style for an epic— "known words and style unforced" in the *Virtues*—also depended on meter; and comparing Virgil and Homer, Hobbes notes that Latin is more apt to fall into hexameters with less difficulty. This makes Latin appear "more grave and equal," he observes, but the evenness is not valued for its easiness, but because it gives the impression of "majesty" appropriate for an epic. Even this is disposed of as not of the first significance, since "in truth there be no majesty in words, but then when they seem to proceed from a high and weighty employment of the mind."[52] In the same way, while he approves of rhyme, he does not see much benefit in difficult rhyme schemes as being too much of a constraint on the matter of an epic. It is "but a difficult toy, and forces a man sometimes, for the stopping of a chink, to say somewhat he did never think," and he therefore approves of the looser stanza form of Gondibert, which was made up of pentameters with alternating rhymes.[53] By extension, he would not have been enamored of the closed couplet. The gravity and dignity of the pentameter recommends it for the epic, a longer line being too unwieldy ("not far from ill prose") and a shorter one too light ("a kind of whisking, you know, like the unlacing, rather than the singing of a muse").[54] But even this recommendation relates only to the special problems of the epic, and poets writing in shorter verse forms may vary their measures or "seek glory from a needless difficulty, as he that contrived verses into the forms of an organ, a hatchet, an egg, an altar, and a pair of wings."[55] This suggests that Hobbes's tastes and poetics were sufficiently broad to accommodate at least Herbert from among the metaphysical poets.

Whether or not a writer shares the Augustan dislike of metaphysical poetry, associated with "strong lines," elaborate conceits, and unequal rhythms, is frequently used as a measure of taste for the period. Hobbes alludes to them in a brief passage on perspicuity, which he finds wanting in

the ambitious obscurity of expressing more than is perfectly conceived; or of perfect conception in fewer words than it requires. Which expressions, though they have the honour to be called strong lines, are indeed no better than riddles, and not only to the reader, but also after a little time to the writer himself, dark and troublesome.[56]

This is not very helpful since the criterion of perspicuity was used in prose and verse as a restraint against excessive compression even among writers of strong lines,[57] and it is unclear whether Hobbes was thinking of accomplished poets like Herbert, or only the worst ones. The latter possibility arises since Hobbes himself favored a "close," sinuous style as we know from his Thucydides essay, where he also uses the ratio of thoughts to words as a test for compactness—indeed, it was widely used by critics—and he praises the historian for it in the words of Cicero:

> Thucydides . . . is so full of matter, that the number of his sentences [thoughts] doth almost reach to the number of his words; and in his words he is so apt and so close, that it is hard to say whether his words do more illustrate his sentences, or his sentences his words.[58]

Moreover, Hobbes had excused Thucydides for passages where he had been charged with obscurity and over-compression on the grounds that the difficulty lay in the matter, not the expression, and would remain hard to grasp regardless of what words Thucydides had employed. Whether, as Williamson suggests, Hobbes subsequently regarded obscurity with an intolerance which would agree with neoclassical criteria,[59] or whether in the *Answer* Hobbes's dislike is addressed only to a modishly enigmatic manner of writing is impossible to determine from the passage. His liking of "far-fetched" figures and his emphasis generally on sense or matter suggests that he would not find either the unusualness of metaphysical conceits or their intellectuality necessarily offensive.

Lastly, "knowing well" gives rise to "decency," which regulates the fitness of the characters depicted to their actions, and the relation of the poet to his poem—relationships that establish the character and tone of the genre. "Indecencies" of the first kind include the representation of cruelty, lust, or drunkenness in great persons—an injunction which only pertains to the epic, not the tragedy—not because they are flaws, but because inhumanity and sordidness are inconsistent with the greatness of the actions that are the subject of an epic. Hobbes's heroes need not be perfect, for he allows the failing of ambition in heroic characters,[60] but flaws should be of a kind that contribute to the imitation of actions of heroes, not mar it. This has not so much to do with a theory of universal types as it does with sense of genre. Heroic character cannot be realized in drunken action, and if you have no hero, you have no epic. Actions or language causing much laughter are similarly improper, offenses against the genre since laughter is proper to comedy and satire, but ill-suited to the dignity of heroic characterization or the gravity of epic action. Of indecencies of the second type, Hobbes mentions the use of humble rather than courtly language in an epic, or metaphors and similies based on comparisons taken from "mean conversation, and experience of humble or evil arts."[61] All of these principles of decency are meant to provide the high tone and grandeur of the epic, and to serve as guidelines to the proprieties required in a long, dignified, and complex verse form.

A clearer picture of Hobbes's outlook might have emerged had he dealt with more forms, but it can be said of his approach to heroic verse that his theory is prudent and sensible. The classical strand in earlier poets was greatly emphasized and systematically developed in the Restoration, but it had not yet happened in Hobbes's work: there is no exaggerated rigidity about form, no calcification of the concept of decorum into a kind of social etiquette as found in Thomas Rymer, no doctrine of poetry as a sugar-coating of a pre-established moral pill, no catering to a broad audience, no particular reverence for the French critics. If his views on the epic are indicative of his general views, they probably conformed more closely to the moderate classicism of the kind found in such transitional Jacobean poets as Jonson.

His rationalism is most apparent in his view of the poet since he found the writing of poems an entirely reasonable pursuit, comparable to other kinds of productive art. It is, for him, dependent on heightened talents and knowledge, not divine assistance, and it consequently yields insights into human nature and the manners of men, not divine truths. Having already deprived the monarchs of the world of their divine sanctions, he could not reasonably be expected to endow poets with them.

Partisans of the metaphysical school, in particular, have found this order of truth disappointing, laying the destruction of the scope of Donne's poetic world at Hobbes's philosophic doorstep, although a poet like Cowley managed to be both metaphysical in his poems and anti-metaphysical in his philosophy, as Williamson notes. Hobbes's rationalism, it is said, is reflected in his elevation of judgment over fancy, but this is to find an elevation where there is none and it probably misconstrues the basically Aristotelian intention of the *Answer*. That is, Hobbes was writing about epic poems—not dreams, madness, verbal repartee, or the numerous other situations where fancy is prominent. A poem is a consciously made object and differs from fancy's other manifestations in that it has a design and a purpose; and the poet critically evaluates how well his fancies are being made to serve that purpose. Judgment, therefore, is not supreme, but essential.

Hobbes and the scientists, it is sometimes also said, by conceiving of everything as matter in motion rather than as a value-infused universe left no room for the subjects of poetry. To this Hobbes would probably be the first to say that, nonetheless, we experience our thoughts and passions as intensely and variously as if we didn't live in a mechanical universe, and poems deal with the way men feel and act, not natural causes. Among those who do not think Hobbes denied fancy's role, there remains the objection, best stated by Douglas Bush, that "while Hobbes desiderates the fruitful union of imagination and judgement, his whole manner of thinking proves the division between them."[62] To this I think Hobbes would enter an eager guilty plea. He was writing philosophy, not poetry, and as he might say: in this, there is no place for fancy, except sometimes to open the understanding by an apt similitude; in that, it is eminent.

If one were looking for the most evident connection between Hobbes's mechanistic materialism and his poetics, it can be found in the very late *Virtues*, which is tacitly dependent on his materialism, rather than the *Answer*, which he relates to his psychology. In the *Virtues*, the psychological aspects are largely relinquished, the organization into form and expression is dropped, and his major divisions of the epic become words, sentence construction, contrivance of the fiction, elevation of fancy, the impartiality of the poet, clearness of descriptions (imagery), and the amplitude of the subject, in that order. Dryden, expressing the prime importance form had for the Augustan age, berated the *Virtues* for starting where it should have ended— with the choice of words. But for Hobbes to have begun with the choice of words was really more in harmony with his method of analyzing things down to their individual material units, more reflective of his mechanistic outlook. In such a scheme, the work of the poet and the historian, building from the same materials, becomes comparable, and Homer is treated in the *Virtues* as a poetic historian or an historical poet, differing from prose history mainly in narrative style. It is a more deeply Epicurean stance, with less consideration of the moral consequences of poetry, "for all men love to behold, though not to practice virtue," and poetry and history are finally meant simply "to furnish an ingenuous reader, when his leisure abounds, with the diversion of an honest and delightful story, whether true or feigned."[63] It is somewhat paradoxical, then, considering the influence physical science is sometimes said to have on shaping the neoclassical age, that where Hobbes's poetic is most consistent with his mechanistic outlook, he is *least* consistent with neoclassical theory. The approach in the *Virtues*, so far from looking forward toward the eighteenth century, regresses to the methods of the older rhetorical texts, which began with individual words and tropes, not the theories of forms favored by the Augustan authors. What may be said of the *Answer* is all the more true of the *Virtues*, therefore—that if Hobbes's influence was rationalistic, it is everywhere mitigated by his basic individualism, for his continual emphasis on the diversity of the objects of men's passions would by itself have prevented him from trying to measure beauty too much by a rule.

Hobbes as Stylist

If Hobbes could reply to a modern literary historian who charged him with a clangorous style, he would doubtlessly snort that philosophy "professedly rejects not only the paint and false colours of language, but even the very ornaments and graces of the same." He cultivated a style that suited his subject matter, a *philosophic* rhetoric, "plain and evident," fit for reasoning from definitions and for setting forth the first grounds of his science: "and the first grounds of all science are not only not beautiful, but poor, arid, and, in appearance, deformed."[64] That Hobbes chiefly aimed for perspicuity and not for the opulence of, say, Santayana's prose, partly reflects a different concept of the philosophic enterprise and a different range of things to express, but to call it a "plain and evident" style as he did, or clangorous as others have, does not do it full justice.

In the context of his century, it is a style that belongs to the broad spectrum of prose manners called anti-ciceronian, and his contemporaries would probably have regarded it as generally "senecan," where that was taken to mean a style favoring brevity, fullness of matter, spare ornamentation, and an unaffected vocabulary. The dispute between rhetoric and philosophy was reflected in the contemporary discussion of styles, and Hobbes opted for a prose considered to be more compatible with philosophic sobriety than swelling periods, carefully calculated rhythms, and highly figurative language was.

Bishop Sprat, a man mindful of the meaning of style, did not find Hobbes's prose unpleasant when he compared it with Bacon's:

> I scarce know Two Men in the World that have more different Colours of Speech than these Two Great Wits: The Lord Bacon short, allusive, and abounding with Metaphors, Mr. Hobbs round, close, sparing of Similitudes, but ever extraordinary decent in them. The one's Way of Reasoning proceeds on Particulars, and pleasant Images, only suggesting new Ways of experimenting, without any Pretence to the Mathematicks. The other's bold, resolv'd, settled upon general Conclusions, and in them, if we will believe his Friend, *Dogmatical*. [65]

The comparison is particularly apt, grasping the way their differences as philosophers are reflected in their different styles.

As Hobbes's philosophic objectives and his strong impulse toward clarity made him an anti-ciceronian, so the same factors made him moderate the possible extremes of an anti-ciceronian style. The two extremes of crabbedness and looseness are equally unknown to him, the one exiled from his prose because it obscures meaning and the other because it weakens the solid joints of reasoning. The cadence and balance of his prose usually flow from the progress of philosophy's logical movement—from the balanced opposition of differing views and frequent distinctions, from the disjunctive constructions of alternative considerations, and from the rhythmical sequence of principle and example, definition and deduction. His expository prose is usually cast in periods of middling length, well-knit without being forced, and everywhere shaped to his meaning with great vigor. Unaffected and resolute, it aims to bring light by which the reader can master the course of an argument:

> For the order of words, when placed as they ought to be, carries a light before it, whereby a man may foresee the length of his period, as a torch in the night shows a man the stops and uneveness in his way. But when placed unnaturally, the reader will often find unexpected checks, and be forced to go back and hunt for the sense, and suffer such unease, as on a coach a man unexpectedly finds in passing over a furrow. [66]

Naturalness of construction here is not the imitation of the polite conversation of gentlemen, or the loose, familiar manner of Restoration senecanism. It is rather syntax disposing of sense in such a way that its relations are shown most lucidly, and it is what Hobbes calls "good style." It is not a "polite" style—it has too much business to attend to—but when occasion requires that Hobbes bend his prose to make a knee, even then he is more concerned with the matter of his compliments than with giving his expression an airy turn.

Hobbes's prose is thus usually neither curt nor rambling, neither harsh nor pointed—all possibilities of senecan style—but Hobbes avails himself of most of these qualities from time to time, varying his manner freely with his topic and purpose. One of his frequent variants, his terse, emphatic manner, is most evident in his definitions and most often associated with his name:

> Eloquence is power, because it is seeming prudence.[67]

> *Honourable* is whatsoever possession, action, or quality, is an argument and sign of power.
>
> . . . .
>
> Dominion, and victory is honourable; because acquired by power; and servitude, for need, or fear, is dishonourable.
> Good fortune, if lasting, honourable; as a sign of the favour of God. Ill fortune, and losses, dishonourable. Riches are honourable; for they are power. Poverty, dishonourable.[68]

The manner is logical and direct to bluntness; clear-eyed, but with an edge of irony since it is aware of its own outrageous frankness. Applied to an analysis of the passions and the bitter truths of emotional life, this conciseness can move toward the epigrammatic:

> To have done more hurt to a man, than he can or is willing to expiate, inclineth the doer to hate the sufferer. For he must expect revenge, or forgiveness; both which are hateful.[69]

Where Hobbes deals with emotions less familiar or darker, he can lengthen his period and make it more complex, suggesting more than it denotes, but without sacrifice of compactness, force or light:

> For to some men, as well sleeping as waking, but especially to guilty men, and in the night, and in hallowed places, fear alone, helped a little with the stories of such apparitions, hath raised in their minds terrible phantasms, which have been and are still deceitfully received for things really true, under the names of *ghosts* and *incorporeal substances*.[70]

The sentence is made to follow the contour of Hobbes's thought as it moves from the event to its name, from the observation to the judgment. "Fear alone," nestled in the middle, both climaxes the first part of the sentence with its short phrases and suggestion of solitary terror, and it is syntactically the subject of the second part, which lengthens into an analysis of the mere superstition of such terror, abetted (as usual) by the careless naming of things. It is the true sound of Hobbes's voice, authoritative, purposeful, debunking, exceptionally skillful in the presentation of instances.

Among the felicities of Hobbes's style, Bishop Sprat noted the decency or aptness of his similitudes, though sparsely employed. This is the wholly fitting result of Hobbes's attitude toward figurative language: metaphors are useful because they help to "open the understanding," but they are apt to deceive. The exactness of his comparisons would enhance the former possibility without unduly encouraging the latter. The neatness of his similes can be seen in his explanation of remembering or reminiscence:

Sometimes a man knows a place determinate, within the compass whereof he is to seek; and then his thoughts run over all the parts thereof, in the same manner as one would sweep a room, to find a jewel; or as a spaniel ranges the field, till he find a scent; or as a man should run over the alphabet, to start a rhyme.[71]

Similies are preferred to metaphors for the obvious reason that there is no improper signification of words involved, and notwithstanding the sparseness of both in Hobbes's prose, the passage quoted above proves that he was not averse to using them rather lavishly where he felt them to be useful. When Hobbes is in a defensive stance, his comparisons maintain their aptness, but lose some of the dignity of philosophic exposition. More homely, more pungent, his manner approaches what has been called a "pert" style, as when he explains why in Leviathan he has not followed the custom of quoting profusely from the ancient authors. In his list of reasons for his practice, we find:

Fourthly, such opinions as are taken only upon credit or antiquity, are not intrinsically the judgment of those that cite them, but words that pass, like gaping, from mouth to mouth. Fifthly, it is many times with a fraudulent design that men stick their corrupt doctrine with the cloves of other men's wit. . . . Seventhly, it is an argument of indigestion, when Greek and Latin sentences unchewed come up again, as they use to do, unchanged.[72]

How sharp Hobbes could become in polemic is seen in his reply to an opponent who objected to his doctrine of state determination of the forms of religious worship. Pertness gives way, and a roughness, by no means uncommon in seventeenth-century polemics, enters: "Down, I say: you bark now at the supreme legislative power."[73] Hobbes sometimes protested, probably correctly, that his language was more civil than that of his opponents. But for covering his enemies with scorn, he gave at least as well as he took.

This disputatious side of Hobbes can be found even in his earliest work, but it grew bolder and erupted more frequently as he gained confidence in his mastery of philosophy. What need is there for caution, after all, if a man is armed with the *certainty* of his truth? The entire development of Hobbes's style, in fact, was toward a greater trenchancy that reflected not only increasing confidence, but also increase of depth and control, so that despite his railing against orators, his rhetoric was welded to his thought and both gained new strength in every area as Hobbes matured. Inessentials were stripped away from his doctrine, bringing more succinctness to his prose and centering everything more firmly and cleanly on his basic tenets. Points passed over in his earlier works as minor were given more ample treatment as they were seen to have richer relationships to his themes, and his prose gained proportionately in force. To illustrate this mutual reinforcement, it is worth quoting at some length Hobbes's parallel treatments of felicity in *Human Nature* (1640) and *Leviathan* (1651):

But for an *utmost* end [of human appetites], in which the ancient *philosophers* have placed *felicity*, and disputed much concerning the way thereto, there is no such thing in this world, nor way to it, more than to Utopia: for while we live, we have desires, and desire presupposeth a further end. Those things which please us, as the way or *means* to a further end, we call *profitable;* and the *fruition* of them, use; and those things that profit not, *vain*.

Seeing all *delight* is *appetite,* and presupposeth a *further* end, there can be *no contentment* but in *proceeding:* and therefore we are not to marvel, when we see, that as men attain to more riches, honour, or other power; so their appetite continually groweth more and more; and when they are come to the utmost degree of some kind of power, they pursue some other, as long as in any kind they think themselves behind any other: of those therefore that have attained to the highest degree of honour and riches, some have affected mastery in some art; as Nero in music and poetry, Commodus in the art of a gladiator; and such as affect not some such thing, must find diversion and recreation of their thoughts in the contention either of play or business: and men justly complain of a great grief, that they know not what to do. *Felicity*, therefore, by which we mean continual delight, consisteth *not* in *having* prospered, but in *prospering*.

[*Human Nature*, E. W., IV, 33]

To which end we are to consider, that the felicity of this life, consisteth not in the repose of a mind satisfied. For there is no such *finis ultimus*, utmost aim, nor *summum bonum*, greatest good, as is spoken of in the books of the old moral philosophers. Nor can a man any more live, whose desires are at an end, than he, whose senses and imaginations are at a stand. Felicity is a continual progress of the desire, from one object to another; the attaining of the former, being still but the way to the latter. The cause whereof is, that the object of man's desire, is not to enjoy once only, and for one instant of time; but to assure for ever, the way of his future desire. And therefore the voluntary actions and inclinations of all men, tend, not only to the procur- ing, but also the assuring of a contented life; and differ only in the way: which ariseth partly from the diversity of passions, in divers men; and partly from the difference of the knowledge, or opinion each one has of the causes, which produce the effect desired.

So that in the first place, I put for a general inclination of all mankind, a perpetual and restless desire of power after power, that ceaseth only in death. And the cause of this, is not always that a man hopes for a more in- tensive delight, than he has already attained to; or that he cannot be content with a moderate power: but because he cannot assure the power and means to live well, which he hath present, without the acquisition of more. And from hence it is, that kings, whose power is greatest, turn their endeavours to the assuring it at home by laws, or abroad by wars: and when that is done, there succedeth a new desire; in some, of fame from new conquest; in others, of ease and sensual pleasure; in others, of admiration, or being flattered for excellence in some art, or other ability of the mind.

[*Leviathan*, E. W., III, 85–86]

In point of theory, one of the major changes Hobbes makes in the later version of the first paragraph is to bring out more clearly the notion of futurity in desire, its inability to rest in any present because it must, in the nature of man, strive to assure its future fulfilment. In the earlier version, Hobbes is caught up distinguishing means and ends, dispatched in a couple of words in *Leviathan*, rather than de- scribing the compulsive motion in desires. In the *Leviathan* version also, desires are more closely linked to life itself, for there is a great difference in force between observing that we have desires as long as we live (a commonplace), and saying that to be without desire is as much as being senseless. Felicity consequently undergoes different redefinitions in the two passages: in neither is it the respite from passions in the classical sense, but in *Human Nature* it is "prospering"—a quality we associate with general well-being—whereas in *Leviathan* it is ceaseless motion, "a continual progress of the desire, from one object to another," and any connotation of pause or anything more than partial fulfilment is wholly eradicated.

In point of style, these changes are perfectly expressed in *Leviathan* in Hobbes's great opening sentence of the second paragraph. There is nothing comparable in the earlier version either in its power of generality or the propulsion of the prose. Desire, motion, and life are merged, and we have been prepared for the necessary eminence of power in the life of man, expressed by the driving repetition of the word in the sentence. In *Human Nature*, Hobbes had not yet completely thought out the idea of power or seen the full dynamic relation it would have to his psychology; in *Leviathan*, it dominates his second paragraph in preparation for a wide-ranging discussion of the appetites, and it is brought into a nearer relation with politics. The line Hobbes draws there from the basic ingredients of instinctual life to the life of kings is carried through with unbroken vigor in thought and expression, the clarification of the idea of power giving it new logical prominence in the second paragraph and the prose investing it with new energy and authority.

"There is nothing I distrust more than my elocution," said Hobbes, worried about being obscure,[74] but if doubts remain about Hobbes's ability to create a philosophic style, a rhetoric shaped to present his logic with extreme illumination while moving the reader to ponder its meanings, it might suffice to let one last example speak for itself. After the famous passage in which Hobbes infers that the life of man in the state of nature is "solitary, poor, nasty, brutish, and short," he brings additional proof to the heart of his doubting readers in an equally fine passage:

It may seem strange to some man, that has not well weighed these things; that nature should thus dissociate, and render men apt to invade, and destroy one another: and he may therefore, not trusting to this inference, made from the passions, desire perhaps to have the same confirmed by experience. Let him therefore consider with himself, when taking a journey, he arms himself, and seeks to go well accompanied; when going to sleep, he locks his doors; when even in his house he locks his chests; and this when he knows there be laws, and public officers, armed, to revenge all injuries shall be done him; what opinion he has of his fellow-subjects, when he rides armed; of his fellow citizens, when he locks his doors; and of his children, and servants, when he locks his chests. Does he not there as much accuse mankind by his actions, as I do by my words?[75]

The basic ingredients of Hobbes's style are all present in his earliest published work, the Thucydides translation, where the preface is written in a clear, direct fashion, and the style changes only in the sense that Hobbes became more adept at it. Its preference for "plainness" can in no way be attributed to the influence of mid-century English science since, in its earliest appearance, it antedates the Royal Society's program for language reform by some thirty-five years. It may be more truly explained by saying that the Attic current in English prose suited his purposes best, and that he shaped it into a flexible instrument for conveying what he considered the only true way of philosophizing, which is from clear definitions. He did not say that it was the only proper use of speech, but the only proper one for philosophy. In *Leviathan*, he gives four special uses of speech: to register the causes of things, or their past or possible future effects; to counsel and to teach; to express our wills and purposes, so that we may help each other; and "to please and delight ourselves and others, by playing with our words, for pleasure or ornament, innocently."[76] The techniques appropriate to the last two categories, he used sparingly in his published works (except in his poems), and then only as aids to to his work in the first two categories. Of those, he was a master.

VII

Hobbes in the Scientific World of the Restoration

> All men by nature reason alike, and
> well, when they have good principles.
> For who is so stupid, as both to mistake
> in geometry, and also to persist in it,
> when another detects his error to him?
>
> E. W., III, 35

H O B B E S ' s prose style was one area, at least, in which his contemporaries had little to criticize, though his opponents complained of his frequently assertive tone and of "peevishness" and "morosity" in his polemic. His scientific method was another area in which he encountered relatively little opposition, perhaps partly because he shielded it with the honored name of Euclid. If the method itself offended no one, many abhorred his application of it to social phenomena, an application which was the basis for his claim to having founded a new science. Since his deterministic materialism rendered the socio-political world as mechanistic as the natural one and seemed to erase the ethical significance of human activity, most of his critics attacked him on ethical or metaphysical rather than methodological grounds. It is therefore not very surprising that relatively little attention has been given to Hobbes's relationship with other scientists of the period, notwithstanding Hobbes's own emphasis on science. This is further explained by the fact that Hobbes's purely technical conjectures on scientific problems such as squaring the circle have proven erroneous, and although his reasoning is sometimes interesting, it is of little significance compared to the work produced by the giants of his time. Yet Hobbes spent much of the last quarter-century of his life in this area, and to evaluate his relationship to the swiftly changing world of science in the Restoration is to enter into a complex subject that offers us many insights into the intellectual character of the era.

Broadly speaking, Hobbes's mechanical conception of the universe was generally associated with the doctrine of the atomists. Although the atomic structure of matter was merely hypothetical in Hobbes's view and his position on the material nature of the universe is essentially simply that of a plenist,[1] his outlook was roughly in accord with the current revival of the atomic and materialistic theories that could be seen in the new popularity of Democritus, Epicurus, and Lucretius. His espousal of a theory of the subjectivity of secondary qualities was in the very mainstream of scientific thinking, while his theory of the ideal nature of space and time was astonishingly modern. His presentation of an idea of proper scientific method is both lucid and cogent, his criticism of purely empirical and inductive methods was persuasive and preceded the work of Berkeley and Hume. He expressed distrust of a merely experimental basis for science in scornful tones, but this should not be exaggerated into a contempt for its usefulness, for Hobbes did attempt to work experimentally in optics, mechanics, anatomy, and physiology.[2] He thought the contemplation of nature a noble pastime, if it were but understood that the "doctrine of natural causes hath not infallible and evident principles,"[3] and if the experimenters would leave reasoning about their results to the philosophers.[4] For the best that could be done to establish natural science was to find hypothetical motions which would cause the observed effects, and Hobbes himself spent a great deal of time doing that in his discussions of the tides, the effects of gravity, the existence of the vacuum, hardness and softness, and many other physical phenomena.

The exact nature of Hobbes's ideas on specific physical questions is not so pertinent as the more general one of his relationship to the scientific world, his relationship, that is, to a small but increasingly important segment of the intellectual community. Science was beginning to organize itself in England, notably in the formation of the Royal Society, and with organization came a new power and prestige among the educated classes. The professional scientist with his new definition of knowledge had to effect a transformation in the meaning of the idea of an intelligentsia, and he brought with him as tools for the job his professional journals, his professional organization, and his new textbooks that allowed him to add his field to the curricula of the universities. Hobbes, with some claim to being a philosopher of science and with his heavy emphasis on the scientific nature of his system, also had a certain reputation at large as a practitioner of science, and to this extent he managed to identify himself and his method in the public mind with the whole idea of science. The reaction of the scientific world to Hobbes thus reveals a good deal about the way scientists regarded themselves in their growing self-awareness during the seventeenth century, and about Hobbes's status in the early modern period of scientific development.

When Hobbes returned to England from his exile in France, his reputation as a man of science was at its peak. In Paris he had been chosen tutor to the Prince of Wales in mathematics, and he had instructed George second Duke of Buckingham as well; he had the respect of both English and French mathematicians of the first rank. Yet Hobbes never became a member of the Royal Society when men far less distinguished and far less scientifically inclined were quickly welcomed. Aubrey tells us that Hobbes "had a high esteeme for the Royall Societie, . . . and the Royall Societie (generally) had the like for him: he would long since have been ascribed a member there, but for the sake of one or two persons, whom he took to be his enemies."[5] Aubrey specifically mentions as antagonistic John Wallis and Robert Boyle, adding Sir Paul Neile, whom, Aubrey said, "disobliges everybody."[6] That Wallis and Boyle, two leading figures of the organization, should have opposed Hobbes is significant since the Society represented science at its most professional, advanced, and disinterested level in England. One would therefore expect that if its members disagreed with any of Hobbes's scientific work, they would have opposed him on a dignified and objective basis as colleagues trying to correct the work of a fellow savant. The Society, after all, had been formed without regard to social distinctions or political convictions; it professed to have aims which would benefit the whole of mankind by the advance of knowledge. Had their criticism of Hobbes been wholly motivated by purely scientific interests, it would not fall within the scope of this study, but this was not the case. Moreover, regarding Aubrey's remark that Hobbes would "long since" have been elected to the Society, there does not seem to be any evidence that he was even ever a candidate for election, although a number of the members were personal friends of his (including the third Earl) and he stood in favor with the Society's Royal Patron,[7] who adorned his closet with a portrait of the philosopher and settled a pension of £100 on him.

The story of Hobbes's war with the Royal Society properly dates from the publication of *Leviathan*, which occurred a decade before the Society's establishment. In *Leviathan*, Hobbes roundly and frequently attacked the Aristotelianism of the teachings of the universities and their foisting of metaphysical ideas upon students of the sciences. Their teaching of the existence of invisible and independently existent essences, species, and forms was an absurdity resulting from the careless use of language (inexcusable in geometers and logicians), and it was entirely repugnant to Hobbes's own orientation which was, as we would say, distinctly anti-metaphysical. In the natural sciences, such incautious ways of speaking had led to attributing appetites to things which do not possess them (stones fall because they endeavor to reach their place of rest), or to the uncritical acceptance of such meaningless terms as rarefaction and condensation, which purportedly explain why the same body is greater at one time than another, without adding anything to it. "As if there could be matter that had not some determined quantity; when quantity is nothing else but the determination of matter," Hobbes said scornfully, "or as if a body were made without any quantity at all, and that afterwards more or less were put into it, according as it is intended the body should be more or less dense."[8] As for geometry, which is the very root of all science, "till of very late times it had no place at all [in the University]; as being subservient to nothing but rigid truth."[9] To these charges, Hobbes had added remarks implying that the teaching of the efficacy of spirits and similar phenomena produced papist tendencies in the schools, and that these together with "Aristotelity" in turn led to pernicious political doctrines regarding the balance of power between church and state.[10] Now while the religious doctrines embraced by the universities did indeed have political ramifications since the universities produced the bulk of the clergy, Hobbes's criticism of the schools compounded religion, politics, and scientific doctrine from the very onset.

In effect, Hobbes had declared war along two fronts, and a dual counteroffensive was opened by the two Savilian Professors, Seth Ward and John Wallis, both of whom were clergymen. In 1654, Ward, who had thought well enough of Hobbes to write a preface to his *Human Nature* just four years before, now invited the philosopher to submit the geometrical discoveries of which he had been boasting to the examination of the schools, which he was assured he would find much advanced in geometry since his student days. At the same time, in his *Vindiciae Academiarum*, Ward claimed precedence for Descartes,

Gassendi, and Sir Kenelm Digby in propounding a theory of the subjectivity of secondary qualities, and accused Hobbes outright of plagiarism. Undoubtedly stung, Hobbes took the opportunity offered by his forthcoming publication of *De Corpore* to insert a chapter that allegedly solved the problem of squaring the circle. This problem and a number of closely related ones, such as the determination of the value of π, had obsessed mathematical cranks and geniuses since at least the time of Archimedes, and would continue to do so until it was proven that they were unsolvable by Euclidean methods.[11] The second half of the seventeenth century was a period of great attempts at their solution by a number of outstanding mathematicians who made substantive contributions in the course of their essays.[12] Hobbes unfortunately failed to distinguish himself as even an illustrious failure; his solution was very wrong. What was worse, John Wallis, one of the most astute and respected mathematical minds of the period, knew as much and promptly released a refutation, his *Elenchus geometriae Hobbianae*.

Hobbes saw that he had blundered, and a somewhat revised and less assertive version, though scarcely a better one, appeared in the English edition of *De Corpore* in 1656. To this volume he appended his *Six Lessons to the Professors of Mathematics of the Institution of Sir Henry Savile*, in which Hobbes reaffirmed the principles of his geometrical procedures and systematically castigated Ward and Wallis for the charges of self-conceit, injury to the universities, and enmity to religion which they had incidentally brought against him while correcting his mathematics and physics. In the case of the latter, Hobbes again took up the matter of rarefaction and condensation: "I understand very well," he said, "that bodies may be sometimes thin and sometimes thick, as they chance to stand closer together or further from one another."

So in the mathematic schools, when you read your learned lectures, you have a thick or thronging audience . . . which in a great church would be but a very thin company. I understand how thick and thin may be attributed to bodies in the plural, as to a company; but I understand not how any one of them is thicker in the school than in the church. . . . For I conceive the dimensions of the body, and of the place, . . . to be coincident and the same.[13]

Rarefaction and condensation, said Hobbes, were meaningless terms in the sense assigned to them by the two professors, and they would be as well understood if they said that the same body took up sometimes a greater, sometimes a lesser place, by "wallifaction and warden-sation, as by rarefaction and condensation."[14] As for their continued insinuations of atheism, Hobbes suspected (or at least accused) them of writing to stir up "the multitude . . . to attempt upon my life; and if it succeed, then to sneak out of it by leaving the fault on them that are but actors."[15]

In the same year, Ward issued a rejoinder, *In Thomae Hobbii Philosophiam Exercitatio Epistolica*, and Wallis replied with his *Due Correction for Mr. Hobbes, or School Discipline for not Saying his Lessons Aright*, while Hobbes, although in the midst of fending off Bishop Bramhall's attacks, still found time to make his response of 1657, *Stigmai, or the Marks of the Absurd Geometry, Rural Language etc. of Doctor Wallis*.[16] By that time, this supposedly scientific dispute had, on the one hand, degenerated into irrelevant quibbles (e.g., the use of the ablative in Latin), while on the other hand it had grown to include a large variety of political, philosophical, mathematical, and physical points. Wallis had assailed Hobbes anew with charges of plagiarism, finding his mathematical propositions in Cavalieri, Mersenne, Fermat, Descartes and Robervall,[17] and now in 1657 he kept close to Hobbes's heels by publishing a reply to Hobbes's last assault under the chiming title, *Hobbiani puncti dispunctio*. Even taking into consideration the raciness of polemical writing in the period, the language in which this dispute proceeded sometimes got out of hand, particularly on Wallis's part. Hobbes, at his worst, calls all of Wallis's charges "error and railing, that is, stinking wind; such as a jade lets fly, when he is too hard girt upon a full belly,"[18] but his opponent could go him one better in this style. Henry Stubbe, who wrote in Hobbes's defense, rightly remarks with indignation that "the Doctor (Sir Reverence) might have used a cleanlier expression than that of a 'shitten piece,' when he censures Mr. Hobbes's book."[19] Sorbière went so far as to suggest, somewhat improbably, that the king gave Hobbes his pension to console the philosopher for the injuries he suffered from Wallis.[20]

The dispute subsided for awhile after the exchange of 1657, but the perverseness of Hobbes's stubborn refusal to be corrected by one more knowledgeable than he in mathematical matters was soon to acquire the virtue of error that is at least carried out on a grand scale. Wallis had published a work on the elements of calculus in that year, his *Mathesis Universalia*, quite independently of his controversy with Hobbes, and it was with a criticism of the volume that Hobbes renewed the war in 1660 with his *Examinatio et emendatio mathematicae hodiernae*. The volume evoked no reply, so Hobbes apparently resorted to dissimulation. He now imagined that he had solved yet another great and ancient problem, that of the duplication of the cube, and this solution he published anonymously in France. Unaware of its author's identity, Wallis took the bait and wrote a refutation, whereupon Hobbes immediately announced his authorship and sallied forth once more to defend his errors. What Wallis was to say in mockery of Hobbes, one might say in sympathy for him: it had "so unhappily fallen out, that Geometry, which he thought his greatest Sanctuary, hath most failed him."[21]

Not yet satisfied with the extravagant scale on which he had conducted this campaign, Hobbes chose to republish his solution coincidentally with a criticism of Robert Boyle's experiments with the air pump, recently made public in his *New Experiments touching the Spring of the Air*. In Hobbes's new work, the *Dialogus physicus, sive De Nature aëris*, Boyle's labors "seemed to him only to confirm the conclusions he had reasoned out years before from speculative principles," as Robertson says. Under the misguided idea that Boyle's volume somehow represented an official statement of policy by the group that was even then forming the Royal Society, he deplored the experimental techniques it propounded, which seemed to be consciously and directly in contradiction to the methods he had put forth, and he evidently thought (perhaps less incorrectly) that it was the express wish of Boyle and Wallis to exclude him personally from the scientific life of the nation.

For his part, Boyle wrote a firm reply, while Wallis, taking the opportunity of supporting his friend, produced his *Hobbius Heuton Timorumenos, or a Consideration of Mr. Hobbes, His Dialogues*, a bitingly satirical work which incidentally, but maliciously, accused the philosopher of writing *Leviathan* in defense of Cromwell's title. The long round of criticism and insult finally drew to a temporary close when Hobbes, certainly well-battered mathematically and perhaps frightened by the aspersions Wallis had cast upon his politics, made two moves. He dedicated to the king a series of seven short dialogues on physics, the *Problemata Physica* of 1662, including an apology for his *Leviathan*, mostly for any of its religious doctrines which may have been troublesome to the king. He begged the king not "to think the worse of me, if snatching up all the weapons to fight against your enemies, I lighted upon one that had a double edge,"[22] and this may be taken as a response to the growing hostility towards Hobbes's work which has already been discussed in an earlier chapter. Secondly, he protected himself further by writing a *Consideration upon the Reputation, Loyalty, Manners and Religion of Mr. Thomas Hobbes* in the same year and in rebuttal of Wallis, where he pointed out that the mathematician had conveniently forgotten his own services to the parliamentary army, for whom he had deciphered some of the king's coded messages. To the charge that he defended Cromwell's title in *Leviathan*, he rightly responded by asking, "What was Oliver, when that book came forth?"[23] In fact, Cromwell had no title in 1651, so Hobbes could not have written in defense of it. Both contestants now held their peace.

The controversy, while it had continued to refer to matters mathematical and physical, had clearly lost much of whatever scientific character and motivation it originally possessed. But Hobbes's silence was not a sign of loss of interest nor a confession of weakness, for he reopened the dispute in 1666, at the age of seventy-eight, and for a dozen years thereafter, he published anti-Wallis literature with a kind of pugnacious regularity matched only by the persistence of Wallis's replies. Hobbes sent six more anti-Wallis works to press and addressed at least four papers to the Royal Society of the same nature between 1666 and 1678.[24] The last of these appeared only a year before his death, thus prolonging the controversy to the very end and continuing to suffer the rebuttals of Wallis, a man truly and deeply talented in the art of verbal demolition.

As a practicing mathematician, if not in his mathematical principles, Hobbes was an easy target for Wallis; indeed, as Wallis himself cruelly remarked, Hobbes lay so open to the lash at every turn that " 'Difficile est, Satyram non scribere.' "[25] Future mathematicians have found Hobbes's solution to the quadrature of the circle (and other problems) no less specious than Wallis did, and the eminent historian of mathematics, Montucla, even ventured that "on peut même dire qu'il surpassa en ridicule tous ses prédécesseurs en ce genre."[26] Hobbes no doubt failed to see his errors, but the simple foregoing catalogue of his disputes is of such magnitude that one must wonder at the energy he was willing to expend in his defense. The stakes involved must have been higher than reputation and pride, notwithstanding the importance Hobbes attributed to them.

The mystery of why Hobbes continued this controversy is almost inscrutable unless he believed his entire system hung in the balance, or unless it can be ascribed to the dogmatic streak in his character, or unless one accepts the not quite sufficient explanation he once gave, that he did so because the two professors represented the universities and clergy. While we have seen that Hobbes's criticism of the schools and clergy was not unrelated to his criticism of Wallis, mathematics was certainly a curiously circuitous way to go about rebuking them. Equally intriguing is the question of why Wallis did not simply allow Hobbes to work out his own destruction, especially since Hobbes's emendations of his solution to the quadrature of the circle in the English edition of De Corpore in 1656 indicated that he was not certain of his ground. Wallis was aware of this, as he was also aware that Hobbes would not take his refutations kindly.

Aside from Hobbes's errors in working with specific mathematical problems, it was clear that he failed to see the value of the new mathematical analysis, his own self-education having largely limited his thinking to the methods of the older standard geometry. He was convinced, moreover, that numbers were meaningless unless they signified ("exposed" is his word) magnitudes, that is, unless they had reference to bodies.[27] Arithmetic was therefore necessarily spatial in character, and one could encounter difficulties applying algebraic methods to geometry. So confident of this was he that in one of his dialogues, he has the character who is converted to his principles remark: "I see you have wrested out of the hands of our antagonists this weapon of algebra, so as they can never make use of it again. Which I consider as a thing of much more consequence to the science of geometry, than either of the duplication of the cube... or the quadrature of the circle, or all these problems put together."[28] In Wallis's advanced notation he could find nothing, he said, "but only of certain characters, as if a hen had been scraping there."[29] Yet it was precisely in this area that mathematics was taking giant strides forward: while Descartes, Fermat, Pascal, and Leibniz used algebraic symbols in moderation, the neatness, compactness and increased utility of replacing rhetorical expressions by symbols was becoming increasingly clear, and a marked use of them is evident in the work of Herigone, Oughtred, and his disciple, Wallis.[30] Hobbes somewhat grudgingly recognized the advantageous brevity of this notation, but nonetheless insisted that such a procedure destroyed clarity since one had to translate one's thoughts twice.[31]

In truth, Hobbes's failure to grasp such fundamental technical advances might have led the younger generation of scientists like

Ward, Wallis, and Boyle to be content to ignore his scientific works and thus to consign them to oblivion, together with whatever philosophic points he had made in the course of his disputes. As it was, Hobbes's reputation as a scientist was exposed in his long and hopeless controversy, and it did him no good with some eminent figures. In 1656, when Huygens wrote to Wallis about Hobbes, it was already in a somewhat disparaging fashion, and the philosopher seemed to have lost a degree of the esteem among at least some mathematicians of Huygen's caliber.[32] Bredvold believes that Hobbes had been "discredited in discerning circles even before 1660" as both a scientist and mathematician,[33] and while this seems to be somewhat overstated, it is true that Huygens's attitude toward Hobbes continued to harden. In 1661, Huygens wrote Moray that Hobbes had lost all credit with him in geometric matters, and in 1663 he wrote to A. Bruce of Hobbes's geometry with mock pity, speaking of it as a disease of which the philosopher should be cured. "Je suis bien aise de ce que ma replique contre M. Hobbes n'a pas depleu a l'Illustre Assemblée, et le seray encore plus si elle peut guerir ce pauvre homme de sa maladie."[34]

In Boyle's reply to Hobbes's criticism too, there is at least a claim that Hobbes's prestige was losing ground. Boyle writes that "informed men (some of whom keep great correspondence with the Virtuosi abroad)" did not even think Hobbes worth the trouble of a refutation. They were of the opinion, Boyle reports, that "my publishing anything against his Objections would not be necessary nor was much expected."[35] Again, in 1662, Huygens wrote to Sir Robert Moray asking him to thank Boyle for a copy of his book, and he expressed surprise that Boyle should have "taken the pain to write so big a book against objections so frivolous."[36] Thus, in Huygens's words, Hobbes had become pleasant "by his abundance of absurdities,"[37] and was no longer taken seriously in at least some of the most advanced sectors of science.

This judgment must be sharply modified however, when speaking of other circles, for while Hobbes's reputation as a practicing scientist was severely impaired in the highest mathematical sectors in England, it did not have the same disastrous decline in France or other European countries, Huygens's words notwithstanding. There is firm evidence of the existence of a growing group of Hobbes admirers in France who formed something like a Hobbes group based on personal acquaintance and correspondence. Sorbière remained a stout admirer, and among Hobbes's correspondence preserved at Chatsworth there is a series of letters from a variety of other devotees written in the most adulatory language, and extending from the 1650s through the 1660s. These admirers were not mathematicians, to be sure, but they express a lively interest in Hobbes's views on the philosophical bases of scientific knowledge and on his physiological theories, and they point to a certain enduring strength in Hobbes's scientific reputation abroad. In this context, one recalls too, the long and admiring letter Hobbes received in 1670 from Leibniz.

More telling is the report of Col. Samuel Tuke to the Royal Society of the proceedings of the Montmor Academy during his visit to France, where he notes that Bacon, Gilbert, Harvey, Hobbes, and Digby among others were named by the French as especially representative of the English scientific genius.[38] Wallis, who was particularly sensitive about England's ability to establish itself as a learned nation in Europe, must have winced to hear the report. At one point in their controversy, Wallis asked why Hobbes had replied in English to a book Wallis had written in Latin, and he concluded that Hobbes's work was intended for people "who may understand *rayling in English*, that yet doe not understand *Mathematicks in Latin*."[39] He was implicitly accusing Hobbes of refusing to risk his European reputation, a reputation of which Hobbes boasted and of which both men were very conscious.[40] Hobbes seemed to have regarded science as an international pursuit, while Wallis, though not alone in seeking national prestige for scientific achievement,[41] was extreme and somewhat inclined toward chauvinism. He had "an unmistakable tendency to exalt the accomplishments of his fellow-countrymen" even when scientists of other nations sometimes had a better claim to priority.[42] It is entirely likely that Hobbes's acclaim abroad was thus another factor which prompted Wallis's attempt to discredit the philosopher's work. Although Hobbes was an Englishman, he was hardly the man Wallis would want to represent English science abroad, not only because his mathematics were in error, but for other reasons which will become clear.

Moreover, if Hobbes had lost the respect of mathematicians of Wallis's own rank, he nonetheless seems to have kept the esteem of many members of the Royal Society who were accomplished enough in their own fields and who considered him a kind of savant, but who could not judge the mathematical merits of the dispute between Wallis and him. These members would include some physicians (like

George Ent and Scarborough), virtuousi like Petty, and the dilettanti (like Aubrey and Cowley), who would be more and more relegated to the sidelines in the Society as its work grew both more intensive and technically difficult. Looking back on his dispute with Hobbes, Wallis himself suggested that the philosopher was one of those, like the dilettante, who "had in his younger years some little insights in Mathematics; & which at that time (when few had any) passed for a great deal." Upon the credit of these few insights, however, Wallis said "he did bear himself as a great Man, & ... somewhat singular."[43]

Despite supporters in England and in France, it remains true, nonetheless, that Hobbes was becoming ever more isolated from the center of scientific activity in the nation, and this was largely due to the strong governing hand which Wallis held over the organization and publications of the Royal Society after it was established. The correspondence between Wallis and Henry Oldenburg during the 1660s and 1670s indicates that while Oldenburg was the editor of the *Philosophical Transactions*, Hobbes's publications regularly passed through Wallis's hands and were, with equal regularity, given poor reviews by him in the journal.[44] On a number of occasions, Hobbes had tried to participate in the Society's activities or other people tried to introduce him to its work, but without success. In 1661, for instance, he presented a paper to the king, a proposition for finding the mean proportionals between two given straight lines, and the king sent it over to the Society where Lord Brouncker corrected it, but the hint by the king, if it was one, was studiously ignored.[45] In 1668, Hobbes sent a letter to Joseph Brooke concerning a woman who had reportedly lived without food for a year, and this quaint history was subsequently read to the Society in one of its meetings by Daniel Colwall, although Hobbes's name never appeared in the *Journal Book* of the Society as its author.[46] In 1671, Hobbes sent a copy of his *Rosetum Geometrium* and three printed papers to the Society through either Robert Hooke or Southwell, in an evident attempt to bring his dispute with Wallis within its walls or to gain the recognition of the organization. The *Journal Book* duly notes that it was ordered "that thanks be given to the Author, and the books themselves referred to the Consideration of the Mathematical Professors of Gresham College and Mr. Collins."[47] Nothing more is heard about them, but they seem to have been given to Wallis to review. In 1672, Hobbes again showed his esteem for the Society by sending them a copy of his *Lux Mathematica*, and once again he failed to evoke more than their formal thanks. "It was ordered," reads the *Journal Book,* "that Mr. Hevelius, Signor Malphighi [two correspondents who had presented volumes] and Mr. Hobbes should be thanked by the secretary for their respect to the Society, with an intimation that their books were committed to the perusal of some of the members."[48] While the cool neutrality of the Society seems to reflect an understandable wish not to become officially involved in the dispute, it was nonetheless a somewhat spurious neutrality since Wallis was a central figure in the organization.

It is some measure of Hobbes's inability to carry any weight whatever on the governing levels of the Society that when, in a final attempt to gain recognition there, Hobbes wrote to Oldenburg an official letter of criticism of Wallis and a request for publication privileges at the Society, he was flatly refused.[49] He found it improper, wrote Oldenburg in reply, to read publicly an invective against so eminent a member as Dr. Wallis. He continues, in a letter full of painful revisions, by saying that he would publish anything that would advance science if it were not too long "nor interwoven with personal reflexing."[50] It is a sign of Hobbes's helplessness in this situation that Oldenburg, an old friend of his and less a scientist than a devotee of science, should write to him in this manner in 1672, when in 1655 he had corresponded with the philosopher in the most deferential tones, asking his advice on mathematics.[51] Frithiof Brandt so far sees in the Royal Society a hotbed of Hobbes's opponents that he suggests that Isaac Barrow, though he was substantially indebted to Hobbes for his optical theories, would not acknowledge his source because "he was a close friend of Ward, . . . a professor in Gresham College. . . . In short, he belonged to the anti-Hobbes circle."[52]

Hobbes eventually gave up in the face of these continual rebuffs. In 1674, Robert Hooke, through Aubrey, sent out an inquiry to Hobbes apparently concerning any unpublished scientific work he might have that he would like presented to the Society by Hooke and published by them. At the age of eighty-six, Hobbes wrote back to Aubrey, from the bitterness of his heart, a letter quoted here almost in full:

As for that part of your letter, which concerns Mr. Hooke's desire I pray you present my humble service to him; for I have a great esteeme both of his good nature and of his Judgement in all manner of Phillosophie. And tell him first that I have no Treatises of Phillosophie or Mathematiques, but what are printed, which William Crooke only can lawfully Print. The coppies being his property. and though they were in my hands, does Mr.

Hooke think it fit that any thing of mine should passe through the hand of Dr. Wallis, (that is not only no Phillosopher at all nor Geometrician but also my enemy) or of any of his admirers? If I had any thing now in my hands towards the advancement of that Learning which the society pretendeth to, I could be content it should be published by the society much rather than any other, provided that they that continually attend the businesse, and are of the Society upon no other account then of their Learning, either had forborn to do me injury or made me reparation afterward. Do they thinke, that no body takes his Learning to be an honour to him, but they? But what reparation could they make? As for the members, I have amongst them for the most part a sufficient reputation, and I hope I have so of Mr. Hooke; and amongst the Learned beyond the Seas a greater Estimation, then the Society can suppresse; but that is nothing to the body of the Society, by whose authority the evil words and disgraces put upon me by Dr. Wallis are still countenanced, without any publique Act of the Society to do me Right. so that I am not to be blamed if I vindicate my self by my own pen till it be done by theirs. If Mr. Hooke consider this, I hope he will not take it ill that his Motion is not entertayned by me. This is all that I have now to write.[53]

Instead of letting Hobbes's technical failures silently disqualify him from serious scientific consideration, the deluge of books, pamphlets, and incidental criticism of his ideas inevitably brought the philosopher still more to the attention of the scientifically literate public, for criticism, no matter how scathing, is always better publicity than absolute disinterest. Bredvold has noted at least part of the reason why those members of the Royal Society felt obliged to persist in their campaign against Hobbes, observing that if Hobbes had lost the respect of many scientisits, "it was his reputation and influence with the larger public that made a continued polemic against him necessary."[54] This was certainly the case, but the campaign against Hobbes had its beginnings *before* the establishment of the Society in 1662, and it was largely due to Wallis's efforts, helped by Ward. In his correspondence with Huygens, Wallis spelled out his reasons, suggested earlier, for his animosity. In 1659, he wrote:

Our Leviathan is furiously attacking and destroying our Universities (and not only ours but all) and especially ministers and the Clergy and all religion, as though the Christian world had not sound knowledge... and as though men could not understand religion if they did not understand Mathematics. Hence it seemed necessary that some mathematician should show him... how little he understands the Mathematics from which he takes his courage; nor should we be deterred from doing this by his arrogance which we know will cast up poisonous filth against us.[55]

Wallis determined to be that mathematician. In the much later preface to his *Opera*, Wallis extended the charge, finding that Hobbes was corrupting the young in the guise of a geometer.[56]

Hobbes's attacks on the clergy and the universities were derived from and sustained by the groundwork of his philosophy. His philosophy, in turn, carried authority partly because it claimed to have the same invincible certainty as science itself. Wallis, appreciating this basic appeal of Hobbes's ideas, concluded that it was the place of a mathematician to defend both school and church by showing that the very core—the science—of Hobbes's system was flawed. Had there been no other attacks on the university and no Hobbes supporters, Wallis might have found little reason to take up his cudgels, but of course there were. There were people like John Webster and, more to the point, Henry Stubbe, and finally there was Hobbes's good standing with the king and various nobility to consider. Henry Stubbe, who had begun a translation of *Leviathan* into Latin and who had his own political interests at the university which were inimical to Wallis, entered the fray on Hobbes's side. Writing in Hobbes's defense, he brought to bear the full weight of his learning which, because it was so immense, so wildly utilized and occasionally so empty, could only be called grotesque at times. He then consolidated the forces of Hobbes's friends there and brought the philosopher's presence onto the very grounds of Oxford by arranging to have him send a copy of his works to Thomas Barlow, the Oxford librarian. Barlow was politically a most conservative man, and one who held traditional but judicious ideas about the role of the university, yet he is able to write Hobbes that "he never did, nor doe thinke, that you could condemne Universityes. . . . It is my hope, and prayer, that our University may be such, as they should, Seminaries of all good Letters; in which the young of this Nation may . . . be taught religion and Piety towards God, and obedience and duty to their Governor."[57] Barlow could not agree with all of Hobbes's tenets, but he gracefully concedes that he has learned "(both in yours and other learned mens writings) that to be true at last, which at first reading I much suspected as hereticall."[58] Aside from serving as a go-between with university people for Hobbes—a service much needed by a private scholar such as the philosopher was—Stubbe also kept Hobbes posted on university politics, and assured him of Wallis's darkening prospects and his own bright ones during a correspondence that lasted at least through the period 1656–1657.[59] In 1657, Stubbe himself was expelled from his college, Christ Church, Oxford, for writing against the university and clergy.

After the foundation of the Royal Society, this situation increased in complexity and urgency as more issues and more interests began to overlap. Justifying his reply to Hobbes's criticism, Boyle begins his defense in a vein similar to Wallis's:

It was also suggested to me that the dangerous Opinions about some important, if not fundamental, Articles of religion I had met with in his *Leviathan*, and some other of his writings, having made too great Impressions upon divers persons (who, though said to be for the most part either of greater *Quality*, or of greater Wit than *Learning*, do yet divers of them deserve better Principles) these Errors being chiefly recommended by the Opinion they had of Mr. Hobbes's demonstrative way of Philosophy; it might possibly prove some service to lighter Truths than those in Controversie between him and me, to show that in Physicks themselves his opinions and even his Ratiocinations have no such great advantage over those of some Orthodox Christian Naturalists.[60]

Wallis, the clergyman, defended the universities and his profession with his mathematics; Boyle, a profoundly religious man, protected his religion and his profession with his physical science. Like Wallis, he reasoned that Hobbes's theological position ultimately claimed its merit from his scientific method, and therefore an attack from a naturalist would cut to the heart of the matter, severing Hobbes's ideas from the source of their strength.

Boyle, too, explicitly ties the influence of Hobbes's ideas to his method, his "demonstrative way of Philosophy," and here Boyle was really confronted with two things to deal with: the materialistic basis of Hobbes's philosophy, and his deductive procedures—that steady march of conclusions necessarily derived from a small group of well-defined concepts. Now Boyle certainly did not believe that the strict observation of matter in its number and motions—that is, the mechanical conception of the universe which characterized the outlook of early modern science—was incompatible with the Christian religion; yet it is well known that the emphasis on material existence in science was itself associated with atheism in nonscientific circles. Boyle's remarks grew from his acquaintance with English public opinion in the period which had already begun to see science as equivalent to materialism, while materialism, in turn, continued to be associated with atheism. The equation of materialism with atheism was a facet of public thought which, as we have seen, Cudworth also had to struggle with as he attempted to distinguish between the "atheistic" materialism of Hobbes and his own materialistic foundation for his moral philosophy. In the case of Boyle and the Royal Society, the equation was simply carried one step further to include science under the name of materialism. Bredvold puts the matter concisely when he says that although Hobbes was dangerous to the Royal Society as an enemy, he "would have been far more insidiously dangerous as a friend. . . . Their most subtle and persistent difficulty was to explain to the public the difference between the Hobbists and the members of the Royal Society; to explain how it was possible for Christian scientists to accept the new philosophy of motion and yet escape an atheistic materialism."[61]

It was because of this public association of matter, science and godlessness, that Bishop Sprat, when he came to write his defense of the Society, did his best to turn a belief in the atomistic theory into a Christian virtue. " 'Tis true," he wrote of the Society scientist, "his *employment* is about *material things.*" Granting so much, however, he grants no more:

But this is so far from drawing him to oppose invisible *Beings,* that it rather puts his thoughts into an excellent good capacity to believe them. In every *work* of *Nature* . . . he knows that there is not only gross substance, which presents itself to all mens eies; but an infinit subtilty of *parts,* which come not into the sharpest sense. So that what the *Scripture* relates of the Purity of *God,* of the Spirituality of his *Nature,* . . . and the *Souls* of men, cannot seem incredible to him, when he perceives the numberless particles that move in every mans *Blood.* . . . Having found that his own *senses* have been so far assisted by the *Instruments* of *Art,* he may sooner admit, that his mind ought to be rays'd higher, by a Hevenly light, in those things wherein his *senses* do fall short.[62]

The difference between the defenses of Sprat and Boyle and the earlier one of Wallis is not so much in substance as of scale, for it was essentially the same dispute they had—the relationship between religion and various aspects of the new science—but it had a new meaning in the changed institutional setting. It was no longer a matter of a few schoolmen representing a certain part of a faculty at the university, it was now a separate and sizeable group of intellectuals, clergy, noblemen, and others, organized to speak as a new force in society which, they claimed, would bring the greatest benefit to all mankind. The Royal Society was more public, more visible, than its preceding group of gentlemen and scholars who met privately at Oxford and London, and it was to become increasingly engaged in a public dispute concerning what its influence on the community was to be.

The fact that Hobbes's controversy with various members of the Royal Society was deeply embroiled with social issues does not mean that it lacked a purely scientific component. It merely means that the scientific element could not survive unsullied in the midst of these other factors. To turn to the question of method, for instance, which was one of the main issues in contention between Hobbes and Boyle: the Baconian Boyle was incensed when Hobbes made his experimental methods a target through which the Society's program could be attacked. Hobbes was not satisfied, he wrote,

to fall upon the Explication of my Experiments, [but] has... endeavored to disparage unobvious Experiments themselves, and so discourage others from making them. Which if he could by his Dialogue effect, I dare be bold to say he would more prejudice Philosophy by this one Tract, than He... could promote it by all his other writing. Wherefore, though his disparaging of Experiments would probably have much more Authority... if he had been the Author of considerable ones, or did appear to be... skilled in them: yet left for all this his Fame and Confident way of writing might prejudice Experimental Philosophy in the minds of those who are yet strangers to it....[63]

Boyle found much to fault in Hobbes's conjectures about various specific natural phenomena such as the vacuum, but here he is largely concerned with methods rather than conclusions. While the Baconian, experimental side of the Society can easily be exaggerated, Boyle seems to feel that Hobbes had done a real disservice to science by denigrating the experimental approach in favor of his own "demonstrative way" and its heavy reliance on deductive procedures. This was undeniably a legitimate point about which two men concerned with the methodological basis of scientific knowledge might profitably argue, but even here the issue of suspected impiety and immorality clouded the question. The very importance of "things" for the experimentalist's method was related to that same dreaded materialism in the public mind. In his defense, Sprat therefore also had to

take issue with those who thought it was "in vain to strive after the
Purity, and *Holiness* of our minds, while we suffer them to spend so
much time, on the labors of our Senses,"[64] and he concludes his
argument by asserting that "the diligent *Observer* of *Nature*, is neerer
to make a modest, a severe, a meek, an humble *Christian*, than the
man of Speculative Science, who has better thoughts of himself and
his own *Knowledge*."[65] Hobbes's materialism and that of the pious
Boyle were, of course, of an entirely different order, but that was not
very easy to make clear to the popular mind. The fact that in Hobbes
materialism is a metaphysical principle and the basis for the genetic
definitions from which his deductive system flowed, while in Boyle
the observation of material phenomena was linked to an inductive
process meant ultimately to reveal the working hand of God in nature, was not a distinction easily conveyed to the general public. The
philosophic points in question were thus largely confused by the
simple identity in the public mind that materialism is, after all, materialism.

The Royal Society had been experiencing considerable difficulties
in countering this kind of public thinking almost from the time of its
foundation. Moreover, as the Society grew in strength and prestige in
some circles, it still had to concern itself not only with its general
reputation in the community, but also with opposition within the
universities where conservative elements had doubts regarding its
influence on education.[66] The pulpit too, could be damaging, despite
the fact that two of the society's founders were clergy who later
became bishops, and despite the fact that for scientists like Boyle, part
of the utility and benefit of their work for the world was the en-
hancement of religion. In 1667, for instance, one finds Robert South
preaching at Westminster Abbey about a "diabolical society" devoted
to "new experiments in vice," a society in which only the judgments
of the senses were accepted as evidence of the truth. Not as damning,
but no more helpful, was the ridicule of the seemingly esoteric nature
of the Society's work by writers; even King Charles, though he was
their patron, never could take them very seriously.

From an acute awareness of the Society's leaders of the necessity
for public support sprang its request that Bishop Sprat write his *History of the Royal Society* in 1667, "the weightiest, and most solemn
part" of which was "to make a defence of the Royal Society and this
new Experimental Learning, in respect of the Christian Faith."[67] Not
wholly satisfied with it, Glanville was recruited for the same pur-

pose, and in the following year he produced his apology for the Society, *Plus Ultra*. While Glanville was more concerned with explaining the actual substance of the Society's achievements and its procedures—"Their aims are to free Philosophy from the vain Images and Compositions of Phansie, by making it palpable, and bringing it down to the plain objects of the senses"[68]—he still felt obliged to preface his work by reminding the audience that "We of the Clergie have no reason to apprehend danger from that Constitution."[69] Attacks against the Society nonetheless seemed to increase rather than diminish. As University Orator, Dr. South took the opportunity of the dedication of the new Sheldonian Theatre at Oxford in 1669 to deliver a long speech condemning both the Royal Society and its new learning, and religious fanatics. So outspoken was he that the correspondence of the Society's members buzzed with the scandal, the whole incident being all the more dramatic since a Society member, Christopher Wren, had designed the Theatre.[70] Because so many scholars like Ward and Wallis were also clergymen in the period, such a confrontation between the old and new learning within the university bespoke a certain tension within the ranks of the clergy as well; but the Society, meanwhile, needed the clergy to lend it social and intellectual respectability, and it needed the universities to establish itself as a full-fledged learned profession.

At this point, the acrimonious Stubbe once more picked up his pen, this time in the employment of one of the fellows of the Royal College of Physicians, who feared that the new Society was encroaching on its professional jurisdiction in surgery and anatomy.[71] With startling speed, Stubbe issued no less than seven books and pamphlets in the period 1670–71, deploring the Society's ignorance and methods, and salting the whole heavily with scurrilous insinuations concerning the organization's papist designs. In these embattled circumstances, the leaders of the Society were anxious, indeed zealous, to disavow anything that smacked of an affiliation with Hobbes, and they used any means at their disposal—books, pamphlets, correspondence. The pages of the highly successful *Philosophical Transactions* were also called into service, not only to criticize Hobbes's scientific volumes, but also to review favorably some of the anti-Hobbes literature, notwithstanding the fact that, having nothing whatever to do with science, such titles as *The Creed of M. Hobbes* looked strangely out of place in the journal.[72] In such circumstances too, where Hobbes was no less embattled than the Society, the philosopher was frankly delighted when, through Aubrey, he received a request from Josias

Pullen (or Pulleyn), Vice-Principal for Magdalen College, Oxford, for a copy of his works for the library. Oxford, after all, was Wallis's home ground as well as his own alma mater, and Hobbes wrote to Pullen in 1672 that he would long ago have offered the library a copy of his works except that "you know how much they have been decryed by Dr Wallis & others of the greatest sway in the University; and therefore to offer them to my colledge or Hall had been a greater signe of humility than I have yet attained to."[73]

Considering Wallis's connections to school, church, Royal Society, and politics (he was a parliamentarian who managed to shift gently with the times), the prudence of continuing his battle against Hobbes had some grounds, to which personal venom might well be added. On Hobbes's part, while his mathematical solutions and proofs were effectively crushed at every turn, he never seems to have lost his faith in the principles upon which they were founded, and Wallis was astute enough to know that it was a question worth debating. As De Morgan has pointed out, Hobbes "was not the ignoramus in geometry that he is sometimes supposed. His writings, erroneous as they are in many things, contain acute remarks on points of principle,"[74] and he goes on to suggest that Hobbes was a remote precursor of the thought of George Boole.[75] It was in the course of these disputes with Wallis, for instance, that such issues as that of the definition of a point and line were thrashed out, and that Hobbes brought his charge against the ideas of condensation and rarefaction, with its demand for the clarification of fundamental terms in the physical sciences. These and other points were worthy of consideration, if they could only have been debated apart from the extra-scientific issues with which they were hopelessly compounded. And these points characteristically have to do with the purity of one's language and the rigor of one's logic, for as Hobbes said from the very beginning, it was using words with understanding that made science to be knowledge, as opposed to mere opinion.

What is one to conclude about this world of science in the Restoration from which Hobbes was excluded, but in which he had so actively participated in earlier years? It was surely very different from the one he had known. His own milieu in Paris and England in the 1630s and 1640s had been one in which science went on partly by correspondence, partly by conversation; the generally educated gentleman could participate as student and patron in the activities of the savants, and the distance separating them would not be unbridgable. A man of broad philosophic interests might comfortably include science in his reading or perform experiments at home, for while science was delimited by its methods and its subject matter, thinkers like Hobbes were always aware of its relationship to other kinds of language and endeavor and could therefore perceive them as unified interests. In these decades, it was people like Hobbes, his patron Cavendish, and talented amateurs like Digby, as well as men who were more exclusively interested in science, who introduced England to the work being done on the Continent, the problems being considered, the standards and the procedures which were the presupposition for the rapid professional development of English science. In R. A. Hall's words:

The men who brought English thought up to date in one way or another, like the Cavendishes, Sir William Boswell, Theodore Haak, Henry More of Christ's, William Oughtred and John Pell, Sir Kenelm Digby, Thomas Hobbes, Walter Charleton . . . performed a function without which enthusiasm for science in England would merely have beaten the air.[76]

This transmission of information which opened up science in England and brought it up to the more advanced European levels could be performed in the setting of private homes and meetings. The new Restoration world of science, however, while it still had its vast correspondence, also had its professional journals for disseminating knowledge; while it still had its generally cultivated men as students and patrons, this kind of popular participation diminished with time and was altogether lost after the first fifteen years or so. It had a nominal patron in the king and it had private contributors, but it raised its money by regular fees levied on its members. Its work became increasingly technical and lost the interest of novelty for its peripheral followers, who could contribute less and less of substance. It was interested in its reputation abroad as representative of the national endeavor and was competitive; it was concerned about its reputation at home as a professional and learned entity. Its leading members, sharply aware of the rapid growth of scientific knowledge, spent increasing amounts of time on it alone, and a payroll had to be established for members who devoted their whole time to the Society's labors, such as Hooke, who were their first "curator." In short, science had collected itself and taken on many of the characteristics of modern professional organization. How different from Mersenne's cell it all was, how public!

The transformation did not occur so quickly that Hobbes could not have survived in this atmosphere for the remainder of his active life, and he would have been no more out of place than a good many of the early members. But it was precisely the awareness of men like Wallis, Boyle, and Ward of the new public image of scientific knowledge—its reputation and prestige—which stood in his way, for Hobbes was tainted in the eyes of the clergy and was the progenitor of everything entailed by "Hobbism" in the eyes of the public.

The role played by personal animosity and Hobbes's personality in his controversies is difficult to evaluate since it can hardly be kept distinct from the other issues, but it may be noted that Hobbes was considerably older than his opponents, who represented a younger generation of scientist for the most part, and the disparity between Hobbes's world and that of the new scientific organization was underscored by his age. The disputes began when he was sixty-six and ended when he was ninety, and age itself became a symbol of their differences. He struck a venerable figure, but there was something about his still strangely active, strangely stubborn, somewhat rough yet magisterial manner which, together with his dangerous reputation, provoked an often mixed response. A number of stories about him circulated that indicate a conflicting fear, awe, dislike, and perhaps contempt, and which would finally issue in ridicule. Hooke, for instance, who found Hobbes disagreeable before he arrived at a more cordial relationship, wrote the following to Boyle:

I should have sooner given you an account of an interview I had of Mr. Hobbes, which was at Mr. Reeve's [an instrument maker], he coming along with my Lord De: [Devonshire] to be assistant in the chusing a glasse. I was, I confess, a little surpriz'd at first to see an old man soe vewe me, & survey me every way, without saying anything to me; but I quickly shuk off that surprizall, when I heard my Lord call him Mr. H: supposing he had been inform'd to whom I belong'd. I soon found, by staying that little while he was there, that the character I had formerly receiv'd of him was very significant. I found him to lard and seale every asseveration with a round othe, to undervalue all other men's opinions and judgments, to defend to the utmost what he asserted though never soe absurd, to have an high conceipt of his own abilitys & performances. . . . He would not be perswaided but that a common spectacle glass was as good an eye-glass for a 36 foot glass as the best in the world, and pretended to see better than all the rest by holding his spectacle in his hand, which shuk as fast one way as his head did the other, which I confess made me bite my tongue, but indeed Mr. Pells description of his deportment . . . surpasses all the rest.[77]

This was in 1663, when Hobbes was seventy-five and, from the description, struggling with a well-advanced tremor. Two years earlier, Wallis had written of his *"relenting thoughts . . .* to see an old man thus *fret and torment* himself, as now he doth in his Old Age, to no purpose" with his mathematics, although Wallis himself never relented for a moment.[78] Even Pell, Hobbes's friend of at least twenty years standing, seems to have taken part in this kind of sport,[79] which had its more popular, less nasty manifestation in the broadside ballads written about Hobbes in this period.

In this context, it is refreshing to read in Cowley a praise of Hobbes's youth-in-age, where the philosopher's continued intellectual vigor, which remained with him to the end, is seen as a kind of sustained flowering of the mind rather than as a species of unnatural folly:

> Nor can the Snow which now cold Age does shed
>   Upon thy reverend Head,
> Quench or allay the noble Fires within,
>   But all which thou hast bin,
>   And all that Youth can be thou'rt yet,
>   So fully still dost Thou
> Enjoy the Manhood, and the Bloom of Wit,
> And all the Natural Heat, but not the Feaver too.[80]

The poem was written before the establishment of the Royal Society, but Cowley does not seem to have changed his mind about Hobbes subsequently, and by writing an ode to the Society as well, this poetic Fellow effected a harmony between them in his mind that did not exist in fact.

Hobbes lived on for more than fifteen years after Hooke met him at Mr. Reeve's house. His final years were spent at the country homes of the Cavendishes, his association with that family having by then spanned four generations. When the end came on December 4, 1679, the news of his death flew about in letters; broadside elegies were written. "Mr. Hobbes is lately dead," wrote one correspondent, "in all the forms of a very good Christian."[81]

Concluding Remarks

> Lastly, though for nothing else, yet be-
> cause the mind of man is no less impa-
> tient of empty time than nature is of
> empty place, to the end you be not
> forced for want of what to do, to be
> troublesome to men that have business,
> or take hurt by falling into idle com-
> pany, but have somewhat of your own
> wherewith to fill up your time, I recom-
> mend unto you to study philosophy.
> Farewell.
>
> "Author's Epistle to the Reader,"
> *E.W.*, I

T H E twenty-odd years between the publication of *Leviathan* and *De Corpore* and Hobbes's death was largely taken up for him in the defense of his mathematics and physics, one vol-ume following after the next, and in the completion of several minor, but interesting other works. Some of these latter works were sup-pressed, notably his history of the Civil War, written about 1670 and entitled *Behemoth*, the publication of which was specifically forbidden by the king. His collected Latin works were issued in Amsterdam in 1668 since he failed to get a censor's license in England, and Robertson makes the very reasonable inference that after Hobbes's brush with the House of Commons in 1666, all works by him dealing with human nature fell under a ban by the king as the price for royal protection. What Hobbes would have written had he been allowed, and how he must have chafed at the bit during those years when he was under constant public attack but unable to reply, we can only speculate, for Hobbes was not one to suffer contradiction silently. He nonetheless practiced his doctrine of obedience with at least external patience, for when a pirated edition of *Behemoth* came out, he prohib-ited action on the part of his publisher, who apparently wished to release an accurate edition. Writing from Chatsworth to William

189

Crooke, his publisher, just six months before his own death, Hobbes bowed to the power of the throne:

The king knows better, and is more concerned in publishing of books than I am: therefore I dare not venture to appear in the business, lest it should offend him. Therefore I pray you not to meddle in the business. Rather than to be thought any way to further or countenance the printing, I would be content to lose twenty times the value of what you can expect to get &c. I pray do not take it ill; it may be I may live to send you somewhat else as vendible. . . .

The philosopher did not live to complete another work, though two months later he again wrote Crooke to say that he had something in English underway.

In these circumstances, we may add to the reasons already given for Hobbes's continued mathematical debates in his later life the fact that other outlets, which he might have preferred had his natural inclinations been free to express themselves, were closed to him. The directions in which his inclinations moved is suggested by the philosopher's *Dialogue between a Philosopher and a Student of the Common Laws of England,* an unfinished work from the same period, many points of which were treated in an earlier chapter. The volume evolved out of Hobbes's study of *Coke upon Littleton,* and since it energetically attacks the common-law justification of English constitutionalism, he may have left it incomplete in anticipation of the king's refusal to allow its publication as being too provocative. Hobbes's *Historia Ecclesiastica* apparently fell under the same ban. Among his other endeavors was a return to his humanistic studies, and in 1673 there appeared his translation of Books IX-XII of the *Odyssey,* entitled *The Travels of Ulysses,* which presents in isolation the tales of the Greek hero's adventures from the time he left Troy to his arrival at Phaeacia, as he told them to King Alcinous. Two years later, Hobbes issued his complete translation of both the *Iliad* and the *Odyssey* which, he said, he wrote "because I had nothing else to do," and which he published because "I thought it might take off my adversaries from showing their folly upon my more serious writings, and set them upon my verses to show their wisdom."[1]

But it is not quite correct to say that Hobbes had returned to his humanistic studies in these late works, for he had never really left them or really severed his links with his past. The continuity of his interest in poetic styles and forms is evident not only in his *Answer to the Preface of Godibert* and the very late translation of Homer, but also in his *Historia Ecclesiastica* and his *Vita*, both of which he chose to write in Latin hexameters and pentameters. The *Historia*, if we are to believe Aubrey,[2] was begun in his middle period in 1659, but not finished until 1671.[3] Furthermore, "humanism" must be construed in its broader sense to see the continuity it obtained in the philosopher's life. As Hobbes's earlier years have been reconstructed here, his initial thoughts on political theory grew out of a pedagogical and humanistic concern over the question of the education of the nobleman through the example of historical literature. His ideas on method and causality represented a solution to the problem of the opposition between reason and passion, logic and rhetoric—the traditional humanist's terms for discussing the moral education of gentlemen. Moral philosophy and rhetoric met in the problem of historical method, and Hobbes's *Behemoth* testifies to the fact that even after Hobbes had found his "demonstrative way," he did not wholly relinquish history as an alternative means of teaching. He never much changed his earliest idea of history, that its reasoning must come from logic, though its means must come from rhetoric, and yet the demands on rhetoric were somewhat more stern in the Thucydides than they were later. Hobbes's later historical narration of heresy is brief, straightforward, and had the practical purpose of protecting him from prosecution; his late *Behemoth*, on the other hand, is a history, but it is written in the popularly accessible form of a dialogue. Perhaps this is simply an allowance made for the fact that Hobbes's audience had now widened to include the literate public, not only the "better sort of reader," and he thus thought to make his instruction more entertaining.

One can point to apparent contradictions in Hobbes's attitude toward history, as in *Leviathan*, for instance, where he blames the ancient histories for inspiring rebellion:

And as to rebellion against monarchy; one of the most frequent causes of it, is the reading of the books of policy, and histories of the ancient Greeks, and Romans; for which, young men, and all others that are un-provided of the antidote of solid reason, receiving a strong, and delightful impression, of the great exploits of war . . . receive withal a pleasing idea, of all they have done besides; and imagine their great prosperity, not to have proceeded from the emulation of particular men, but from the virtue of their popular form of government.[4]

Hobbes reiterates this belief in *Behemoth*, but his reservations about history are essentially no different from his original ones in the Thucydides. It was never that Hobbes thought history lacked efficacy, but that histories were read for the wrong reasons or wrongly read, and these errors were to be combatted always in the same way—by the strong antidote of solid reason. Hobbes could, and did, bring the same charges against contemporary historical examples, and he deplored the political influence of the example set by the Low Countries.[5] But history usually meant ancient history for him, and it should be remembered that Hobbes's attitude toward the classical authors, whether historians or philosophers, was always complex and ambiguous. Like so many humanists of his period, he took more from them than he ever acknowledged or, perhaps, ever knew. Occasionally, he asserts that he honors those ancients who contributed to knowledge, but more often he follows the path of writers like Sir Walter Raleigh, who said he could not be persuaded that God had shut up all the light of learning in the lantern of Aristotle's brains.

Something more could be said about his choice of the dialogue form, a form he came to prefer in his older years, not only for histories like *Behemoth*, but also for some of his work in physics. It is a form which looks backwards rather than forwards, following the tradition that went back to Plato through Galileo and Bruno, and in which science and philosophy are something to be developed and taught at least in part by dialectic. It may seem strange that Hobbes, with his Euclidean model for methodology, should select this mode for developing his ideas, but he uses the dialogue form in a variety of ways for different purposes. In *Behemoth*, for instance, the Hobbesian figure delivers what is essentially a narrative of the Civil War, while the second character is an auditor who punctuates the tale with a series of "whys" or judgments. He is the perfect auditor inasmuch as he learns from history by keeping his attention riveted to the question of causality rather than being caught up in the passions of the tale, and he draws correct inferences. His queries are met with explanations of the possible intentions of the historical personages involved, by judgments on their consistency and by animadversions on their sense of honor and justice. Dialectic as a means for finding the truth has no place here, but only instruction by drawing a moral from the tale. In his *Seven Philosophical Problems*, Hobbes's procedure is somewhat different. Usually, the main function of the interlocutor there is to present a range of phenomena which the Hobbesian speaker must explain on the basis of his theories, thus assuring the reader that those theories are, if not necessarily true, at least sufficient hypotheses. Occasionally, Hobbes's approach is more Socratic, and he will follow out an argument of his interlocutor to arrive at an inconsistency, but at other times his dialogue is so much a monologue that little would be lost by changing the form, particularly where he deals with mathematics. When Hobbes does not use the interlocutor simply as an opportunity to affirm deductions from his principles, however, the dialogue is mainly employed to test verbally his hypotheses against a variety of presented instances or to match them against theories suggested by other people.

Hobbes does not discuss his late preference for the dialogue form, but it can be reasonably conjectured from his employment of it that natural history could be treated in this fashion because of its indemonstrable nature, and he presumably treated mathematics only rarely in this form because he thought the necessary character of its conclusions was better suited to straightforward logical exposition. Moreover, while the plain, daily language of the dialogues was admirably suited for a larger audience, such as he might have expected for *Behemoth,* it had the added advantage of reducing the possibility of confusion arising from treacherous technical jargon. The *Seven Philosophical Problems,* while a dialogue, was originally written in Latin and thus not intended for popular consumption until its later translation, but he asked the king, to whom it was dedicated, that his "writing should be tried by your Majesty's excellent reason, untainted with the language that has been invented or made use of by men when they were puzzled."[6] The dialogue was therefore a useful form for Hobbes, allowing him to propound both philosophical and scientific ideas in clear, well-formulated prose that was accessible to every man's reason.

It is difficult to reconcile this aim and the sweeping scope of Hobbes's philosophical endeavor with the increasingly technical and specialized aims of the scientific world as it was developing during the Restoration era. In this context, Hobbes's similarities with the kind of thought represented by the science of the Royal Society are limited, even apart from the question of their disparate methodology. Such traits as they shared—a distrust of scholastic learning or a wish for a reformation of English prose style—were either characteristic of the age and widespread, or in other ways not specifically related to scientific goals alone. In the case of language reform, Williamson has convincingly shown that the program for a "plain" style espoused by the Royal Society had a number of independent sources, among them the aim of distinguishing fact from conjecture in natural philosophy, but also the reaction against "metaphysical" writing in both poetry and pulpit prose.[7] Thus the poet or preacher might inveigh against metaphorical speech (as Hobbes did) or "excesses" and still remain innocent of any scientific thoughts whatsoever. In Hobbes's case, his criticism of incautious language preceded that of the Royal Society by two decades, and while the correct use of language was of the essence of his idea of scientific method, the question ultimately went back to his metaphysical propensities and his thoughts on the conflict between rhetoric and logic, reason and passion—that is, it went back to his Thucydides first, and only then to Euclid. On the issue of materialism, the resemblance between Hobbes's general outlook and that of scientists like Boyle was superficial, although of the greatest importance because of its ramifications in public opinion.

In short, there was no particularly close tie between the later Hobbes and the English scientific spirit if the opinions of figures like Wallis and Boyle are indicative, for even if they did not necessarily represent the numerical majority of the Society's membership, they were among the most influential of the group and they represented the direction that professional mathematics and physics would take in England. Humanists may still tend to think of Hobbes as the embodiment of early modern scientific attitudes,[8] but this opinion must be set against the judgments of historians of science who tend to regard him as one of those useful "diletantti, philosophers and literary men" whose major contribution was to make known in England the scientific literature of the Continent.[9] The truth lies somewhere in between, for while his whole approach certainly differed from that of Wallis and Boyle, yet he performed well enough when science could still go on in the atmosphere of the great Jacobean noble's country house or the philosophically lively Parisian gathering of savants. That was the era, and those the places, in which he flourished, but it was a stage soon superseded. Nonetheless, as earlier noticed, he respected the aims of the Royal Society, and despite his differences with it, it could no doubt have accommodated him as a member and profited from his outlook had he not been a figure of such notoriety.

If Hobbes did not long participate in English science in a substantive way, yet his political theory has an unmistakable spirit of modernity about it, and it derives this modern flavor and makes its distinctive contribution precisely because of its scientific orientation. By conceiving of the state and society as emerging simultaneously out of the state of nature by a covenant agreed to by individuals who do not reserve any of their prior rights to self-governance other than every man's right to try to preserve himself; by refusing to refer the creation of Leviathan to any final causes, and by holding his analysis aloof from any commitment to special sanctions of a particular religious or social group, he isolated the purely political factors in human behavior. The Leviathan was not necessarily a monarchy or a democracy, it could be Christian or Moslem, its moral code demanded only what human prudence is supplied by nature. Hobbes certainly hoped for a state both Christian and monarchist, but to a great extent he freed his language from conforming to his personal preferences, and by extricating political existence from the passions of special interests and extra-political functions of society, he hoped to give it over to the rule of reason. To modern critics, therefore, who say that Hobbes did not sufficiently consider economic and social factors in society, the answer must be that his abstraction of the purely political does not constitute his error, but his triumph.

These same factors, together with Hobbes's materialistic view of the world, account for the distinctive experience some people have in reading him. Somewhere, Lord Chesterton observed in materialistic philosophy a combination between "logical completeness and spiritual contraction." He found in it "a sort of insane simplicity" in which "we have at once the sense of it covering everything and the sense of it leaving everything out." Some of that sense may be gotten from reading Hobbes: it is the response of common sense to the methods of science. It is the reconstruction of complex phenomena in terms of a highly selective set of concepts which makes Hobbes so "scientific," and which, in distinction to earlier writers of books on polity, allowed him to write a Science of Politics instead of an Art of Government. Hobbes's basic terms—matter, motion, sense, fear, power, and so on—touch on every part of our existence, and thus seem to "cover everything," but they constitute only a small part of our experiential world, and thus seem to "leave everything out." It is a common characteristic of theoretical science and much analytical thought; it can understand more by trying to explain less.

Hobbes's science is based on the correct use of words, and it is the central place accorded language, his awareness of speech as the means by which social order is both created and destroyed, and his hope that an understanding of it would eventuate in civic peace, that leads us back to the classical humanism from which his thought originated.

Appendix

A letter from Hobbes to Cavendish dated Aug. 22, 1638, exists in two copies among the Rawlinson Manuscripts at Oxford, numbers 232, fol. 80, and D. 1104, ff. 14–15v. Neither copy seems to be in Hobbes's hand, but it is within the range of his style and I do not believe it has been previously published. It is useful not only as an indication of his relationship with the Cavendish family, but its central section also throws some light on Hobbes's definition of laughter in *Leviathan, E.W.*, III, 46, as "sudden glory," "caused either by some sudden act of their own, that pleaseth them; or by the apprehension of some deformed thing in another, by comparison whereof they suddenly applaud themselves."

To Mr. Cavendish.
Most Noble Sir:

I am far from beleiving the reports that come hither concerning your Conversation at Paris. Nevertheless for the satisfaction of my particular affection to yourself, & of my long Obligation to your House, I have taken Occasion thereby to use the Priviledge of my Study to write unto you a word or two touching the Nature of those faults that are reported of you: And seeing I believe you no more guilty of them than all other Men of your Age, I hope how severely soever I shall censure the Crime you shall have no cause to think I censure you, but that what I say is rather Counsel for the future than Reprehension of any thing past: which I shall leave to your Choice to weigh as the humble advice of a servant or to laugh at it, or call me fool or Thucydides for my Presumption. If therefore I must humbly beseech you to avoid all offensive speech not only open reviling but also that Satyrical way of niggling [?] that some use. The effect of it is the cooling of the Affection of your Servants, & the provoking of the hatred of your Equals, so that He which useth harsh Language whether downright or obliquely shall be sure to have many haters, & He that hath so, it will be a wonder if he have not many swift Occasions of Duel: of which tho the immediate cause be in them that give such Occasion, yet he is originally to blame that deserved their hatred; & of the two quipping & reviling the former is the worse, because being the same Iniquity, it seems to hide it self under a double construction, as if a man had a good will to abuse an-

197

other but were afraid to stand to it. whereas the words of a Gentleman should be perspicuous & justifiable & such as show greatness of Courage not of Spleen. To encourage Inferiors, to be chearfull with ones equals & Superiors, to pardon the follies of them one converseth withall, as to help them off that are fallen into the danger of being laught at, these are the signes of nobleness as the Master Spirit, wereas to fall in Love with ones self on the sight of other mens infirmities as they doe that mock & laugh at them is the Propertie of one that stands in competition with such a Ridiculous man for Honor. They are much deceived that think mocking wit for there be few that cannot doe it, & what Wit is it to loose a friend tho the weakest in the World for the appluse of a jest. This fault I know is no more yours than every ones whom Adversity of Age hath not driven from it, & therefore I think I may without offence represent it to you in its own Nature that is as the most unnoble thing in the world. If a Man could value himself moderately, & at the rate that other Men hold him currant, examining what true & just Title he hath to pretend to more respect & Priviledge than others & that done would not, as Children that cry for every thing that is denyed them, expect more than is due, & when He cannot have it fall into Choller, I think it were not possible for that Man either out of Passion or in Passion to be offensive.

Secondly I beseech you to take no occasion of querrell but such as are Necessary, & from such men only as are of Reputation. For neither Words uttered in heet of Anger, nor the Words of Youths unknown in the world, or not known for Vertue are of Scandal sufficient to ground an Honourable Duel on. When two Boys goe out of the Academie to Pre aux cleres no man but thinks them Boys as before, nor is their Act valour for having engaged themselves rashly they are forced to the field with shame & cold hearts & prayers that He may be prevented. Does the World call this Valour?

Lastly I think it no ill counsell that you profess no Love to any Woman which you hope not to Marry or otherwise to enjoy. For an Action without Design is that which all the World calls Vanity. And now I have done my tedious discourse which I would not have written without a great Opinion that you can heer Reason patiently, & that your Nature is so good as to Pardon the Boldness & Indiscretions that proceed from true Affection, & duty as this does from me who am your most Obedient &

Most Humble Servant
Tho: Hobbes.

Chatsworth
Aug. 22, 1638.

Notes

Introductory Essay

1. *B.L.*, I, 387.
2. *L.W.*, I, lxxxvi:

> Atque metum tantum concepit tunc mea mater,
> Ut pareret geminos, meque metumque simul.

3. *E.W.*, I, "Epistle to the Reader."
4. Ibid., II, xix–xx.
5. *L.W.*, I, lxxxvii.
6. *B.L.*, I, 350.
7. "[Hobbes] was splendidly one-sided. . . . a most valuable quality . . . more likely to bring into relief whatever truth [an hypothesis] may really contain." Sir Leslie Stephen, *Hobbes* ("Great Men of Letters Series"; London: Macmillan, 1904), p. 71.
8. *L.W.*, I, xxxvi.
9. Stephen, *Hobbes*.
10. John Laird, *Hobbes* (London: Ernest Benn Limited, 1934).
11. Leo Strauss, *The Political Philosophy of Hobbes: Its Basis and Its Genesis*, trans. Elsa M. Sinclair (Chicago: University of Chicago Press, 1952). In his very stimulating book, Strauss fails to account for Hobbes's early scientific "Short Tract," which falls in his "humanistic period."
12. E.g., F. C. Hood, *The Divine Politics of Thomas Hobbes: An Interpretation of Leviathan* (Oxford: Clarendon Press, 1964), p. 14. "Hobbes's passion for philosophy, apparently dormant for twenty years, was reawakened by his discovery of Euclid."
13. Howard Warrender, *The Political Philosophy of Hobbes: His Theory of Obligation* (Oxford: The Clarendon Press, 1957).
14. A. E. Taylor, "An Apology for Mr. Hobbes," *Seventeenth Century Studies Presented to Sir Herbert Grierson* (London: Oxford University Press, 1938).
15. Laird, *Hobbes*, pp. 73–76.
16. T. S. Eliot, *Selected Essays: 1917–1932* (New York: Harcourt, Brace & Co., 1932), p. 305.
17. H. R. Trevor-Roper, *Men and Events* (New York: Harper & Bros., 1957), p. 236.
18. Particularly conducive to the formulation of injudicious generalizations about the transition in Hobbes's life is a marked preference for subjects and philosophies not "narrowed" by a scientific "positivism." E.g., "Hobbes deserted the cause of humanism for a philosophy mastered, from its inception in his mind, by mathematical abstractions. . . ." D. G. James, *The Life of Reason: Hobbes, Locke, Bolingbroke* (London: Longmans, Green, & Co., 1949), p. 1.

199

19. *E.W.*, I, 7.
20. Stephen, *Hobbes*, p. 56.
21. *E.W.*, VIII, xv.

Chapter I

1. Basil Willey, *The Seventeenth Century Background: The Thought of the Age in Relation to Religion and Poetry* (New York: Columbia University Press, 1934), p. 125.

2. These consist of Aubrey's *Brief Lives*, Hobbes's own *Vita carmine expressa*, his prose *Vita* (largely duplicating the material in the verse version), and Richard Blackbourne's *Vitae Hobbianae Auctarium*, a composite work based on Aubrey's account. Except for Aubrey's work, these are all reprinted in *L.W.*, I.

3. *B.L.*, I, 328.

4. Ibid., p. 325.

5. *The Academy of Eloquence*, ed. R. C. Alston ("English Linguistics, 1500–1800," no. 347; Menston, England: The Scolar Press, 1971), "Introduction," n.pag.

6. *B.L.*, I, 329.

7. *L.W.*, I, xxiii: "in literatura tam Latina quam Graeca progressus fecit, ut Euripidis Mediam simil metro Latinis versibus expressit."

8. Hobbes did later use the Medea myth in this context, but the comparison was always with the daughters of Pelius who, on Medea's counsel, cut up their father and boiled him in hopes of making him a new man, a procedure Hobbes found analogous to that of "reformers" in politics. These events, however, are prior to those related by Euripedes.

9. The provisions of the *Nova Statuta* of Elizabeth I for the undergraduate course at Oxford are summarized in M. H. Curtis, *Oxford and Cambridge in Transition: 1558–1642* (Oxford: The Clarendon Press, 1959), p. 86–94.

10. *L.W.*, I, lxxxvii.

11. Curtis, *Oxford and Cambridge*, pp. 96–101, is particularly helpful in analyzing the discrepancies between statutory demands and actual practice in the school curricula at both Oxford and Cambridge.

12. *L.W.*, I, lxxxvii; *B.L.*, I, 329.

13. *B.L.*, I, 329.

14. *L.W.*, I, lxxxvii.

15. The importance of the spoken word is emphasized in other areas by other studies. See W. F. Mitchell, *English Pulpit Oratory from Andrewes to Tillotson* (New York: Russell & Russell, 1932), pp. 41–46, a discussion of the influence of patristic oratory in the "rhetorical world" of the English Renaissance; and Walter Ong, S. J., in "Oral Residue in Tudor Prose Style," *PMLA*, LXXX, 3 (1965), 145–54, has written of the influences of language patterns from spoken rhetoric on prose style.

16. Foster Watson, *The English Grammar Schools to 1660* (Cambridge: Cambridge University Press, 1908), p. 440.

17. *B.L.*, I, 330–31.

18. Ibid., p. 347.

19. *L.W.*, I, xiii.

20. Ibid., xiv.

21. *L.W.*, I, lxxxviii.

22. *B.L.*, I, 361.

23. Ibid., pp. 331, 347.

24. Ibid., p. 331. Aubrey thinks that Hobbes's contact with Bacon dated from after his first Lord's death, as he says. This could refer to the second Earl, but the second Earl died *after* Bacon's death in April 1626. Either Aubrey is mistaken (which is easily possible), or he is referring to the first Earl, who died in March 1625/26, which would make the acquaintance a short one. William Harvey, who was a near enough friend to Hobbes's to leave him £10 at his death, was then Bacon's physician, and it is possible that Hobbes first met him at this time.

25. Bodley, *Rawlinson MSS. D. 1104*, fols. 18–20. Letter of Dec. 10, 1622, Cambridge. A slightly inaccurate version is in F. Tönnies, "Contributions à L'Histoire de la Pensée de Hobbes," *Archives de Philosophie*, XII, 2, 81–84.

26. Some thirty years after writing them, the verses came back to haunt Hobbes in his vitriolic and lengthy dispute with John Wallis. Everything that was attackable was attacked in the course of the dispute, including the poem. Hobbes's reply to Wallis makes no defense of their quality, saying that the verses were "as ill in my opinion as I believe they are in yours, and made long since...." *E.W.*, VII, 389.

27. Bodley, *Rawlinson MSS. 232*, fol. 79; cf. copy in *Rawl. MSS. D. 1140*, fol. 15v.

Chapter II

1. *E.W.*, VIII, xx.

2. Ibid., p. vii.

3. George Croom Robertson, s.v. "Hobbes," *Encyclopaedia Britannica*, 11th ed., XIII, 545.

4. Henry Burrowes Lathrop, *Translations from the Classics into English from Caxton to Chapman: 1477–1620* ("University of Wisconsin Studies in Language and Literature," No. 35; Madison: University of Wisconsin Press, 1933), p. 67.

5. *E.W.*, VIII, ix.

6. It ought to be added that this preference, which persisted throughout Hobbes's life, never assumed any major importance in his systematic philosophy. In *De Cive*, twenty years later, he reiterates it, but carefully points out that it is merely his *opinion*, and that he cannot *demonstrate* the superiority of the monarchical form of government. *E.W.*, II, xxii.

7. The great gap that separates the early Italian form of civic humanism from the later English kind can be gauged by comparing Hobbes's use of Pericles here (to support monarchy) with Leonardo Bruni's use of him in his *Oratio Funebris* of 1428 (to defend the republican ideals of Florence). In this, Hobbes was not particularly behind his time; republicanism was slow to grow in England.

8. *E.W.*, VIII, xxi–xxii, xxvi.

9. Ibid., p. xxvi.

10. Ibid., p. 24 (*History*, 1, 21.)

11. *Hypercritica*, in *Critical Essays of the Seventeenth Century*, ed. J. E. Spingarn (Bloomington: Indiana University Press, 1957), I, 91.

12. Similar strictures, with some variations, can be found in historical and educational writers throughout the period, ranging from Amyot and Bodin to Blundeville and Cleland. Many examples can be found in Leonard F. Dean's "Tudor Theories of History Writing," *Contributions in Modern Philology* (April 1947), no. 1, pp. 1–24, and

need not be repeated here. Dean's fine study also synthesizes many of the current conventions under discussion here to arrive at an outline of what might be called the traditional theory of writing history in Tudor England.

13. In his letter to Lord Henry De Brass of July 15, 1657, Milton lauds Sallust, "for I want a Historian, not an Orator. Nor yet would I have frequent maxims, or criticisms on the transactions, prolixly thrown in, lest, by interrupting the thread of events, the Historian should invade the office of the Political Writer; for, if the Historian, in explicating counsels and narrating facts, follows truth most of all, and not his own fancy or conjecture, he fulfils his proper duty." *The Works of John Milton,* ed. F. A. Patterson *et al.* (New York: Columbia University Press, 1936), XII, 93–94.

14. *Rhetoric,* i. e, 1356ᵃ. So in Cicero also, *De Leg.,* i. 1, 5, and *De Oratore,* ii. 15, 62.

15. James Cleland, *The Institutions of a Young Noble Man,* ed. Max Molyneux (New York: Scholars' Facsimiles & Reprints, 1948), p. 83.

16. *E.W.,* VIII, vi–vii.

17. Strauss, *Political Philosophy of Hobbes,* p. 82. In its full-blown form, this conflict usually included a third contestant, of course—poetry. The classic discussion in the period is perhaps Sidney's in the *Defense of Poesie.*

18. Thus Amyot: "Forasmuch as examples are of more force to move and instruct, than are the arguments and proofes of reason, or their precise precepts, bicause examples be the very forms of our deedes, and accompanied with all circumstances." Thomas North, trans., *Plutarch's The Lives of the Noble Grecians and Romans, from James Amyot's French* (Stratford-Upon-Avon: Shakespeare Head Press, 1928), p. xvi. See also the many examples in Strauss, *Political Philosophy of Hobbes,* pp. 79–86, drawn from a whole array of representative writers on the same theme, especially Bacon.

19. Strauss, *Political Philosophy of Hobbes,* p. 86.

20. *E.W.,* VIII, p. ix.

21. Ibid., p. xx.

22. Werner Jaeger's *Paideia: The Ideals of Greek Culture,* trans. Gilbert Highet (2d ed.; New York: Oxford University Press, 1945), especially I, 287–331 and III, 46–105, still provides a classical treatment of this debate. Also, H. I. Marrou, *A History of Education in Antiquity,* trans. George Lamb (New York: Sheed and Ward, 1956).

23. See Plato's polemic against the Sophists, most notable in the *Phaedrus* and *Gorgias,* and Aristotle's in, for instance, the *Ethics,* x. 9, 1181ᵃ, and *De Sophisticis Elenchis* i. 165ᵃ19–31, 183ᵇ–184ᵇ.

24. *Politics,* vii. 13, 1332ᵃ39–1332ᵇ11.

25. *Rhetoric,* i. 1. 1354ᵃ1; i. 1. 1355ᵃ5.

26. Ibid., 18–20.

27. *E.W.,* III, 701.

28. Ibid., p. xvi.

29. Ibid., pp. 348–49.

30. Ibid., III, 315.

31. This conclusion diverges from the viewpoint of J. W. N. Watkins in his *Hobbes's System of Ideas* (2d ed.; London: Hutchinson University Library, 1973), p. 15, where he says that "the political content of *Thucydides* [Hobbes's essay] is meagre." For the humanistic mind in Hobbes's period, the relations between rhetoric and history had considerable implicit political content, and in Hobbes's case these became explicit when dealing with the Thucydidean theme of the inflammatory effects of political rhetoric.

32. In acknowledging Thucydides' influence on him, Hobbes does in fact associate

his name with both politics and rhetoric. Having learned from Thucydides how much wiser one man is than a democracy, Hobbes says, he translated the book so that those who spoke English would flee the demagogues.

> Is Democratia ostendit mihi quam sit inepta
> et quantum coetu plus sapit unus homo.
> Hunc ego scriptorem verti, qui diceret Anglis,
> Consultaturi rhetoras ut fugerent.
>
> L.W., I, lxxxviii.

33. *E.W.*, VIII, xx–xxi.

34. The ubiquitous influence of rhetorico-logical training in Hobbes's period has received much scholarly attention recently and justifies, I think, the emphasis given it here in reconstructing his thought. Hardin Craig's *The Enchanted Glass* (New York: Oxford University Press, 1936), has for long presented a good general survey of the subject, and W. S. Howell's *Logic and Rhetoric in England: 1500–1700* (New York: Russell & Russell, 1961), a more technical and more recent synthesis. The far-reaching formative effect of these studies in other fields can be seen in Mitchell, *English Pulpit Oratory*, Ong, "Tudor Prose Style," and in its literary aspects, in Rosamund Tuve's *Elizabethan and Metaphysical Imagery* (Chicago: University of Chicago Press, 1947).

35. The first two chapters of the *Rhetoric*, Bk. I, are concerned with the scope, methods, and relations of rhetoric. As for the overlapping between rhetoric and dialectic, any well educated person in Hobbes's time was acquainted with it. It was first learned in Aristotle's *Rhetoric* or other school text, and would be encountered again in the comparison between argument by example and induction in the *Prior Analytics* (Bk. II, ch. 27, 69) and the comparison between syllogism and enthymeme (Bk. I, ch. 1 and 70ª). The whole matter would be brought to mind again in the *Topics* (Bk. I, ch. 1 and 12), and technical competence in such things comes with repetition. Thus Cowley could casually remark that "old fashioned writing, was like *disputing* in *Enthymemes*, where half is left out to be supplyed by the Hearer; ours is like *Syllogism*, where all that is meant is exprest."

36. *E.W.*, VIII, xv, xxiii, xxx xxxii.

37. See Richard Rainolde, *The Foundations of Rhetoric* (1563), ed. R. C. Alston ("English Linguistics 1500–1800," No. 347: Menston, England: The Scolar Press, 1972), fol. xiiv., on historical narrations. Also, Dean, "Tudor Theories of History Writing," p. 2.

38. *E.W.*, VIII, pp. xxvi–xxvii, xxx–xxxi.

39. *Ibid.*, p. xxii.

40. Commenting on the weightiness of Thucydides' prose, Hobbes says that "his eloquence [was] not at all fit for the bar; but proper for history, and rather to be read than heard. For words that pass away (as in public oration they must) without pause, ought to be understood with ease, and are lost else: though words that remain in writing for the reader to meditate on, ought rather to be pithy and full." *Ibid.*, p. xxxi. This is also an expansion of Cicero's remarks in *De Oratore*, Bk. ii.

41. In the somewhat chaotic rhetorical terminology of the time, the compounding of the three terms *perspicuitas, evidentia,* and *enargeia* is worsened by a confusion of the last, *enargeia,* with *enargia.* Nonetheless, the scope of the term is clear enough. In Richard Sherry's 1550 *Treatise of Schemes and Tropes*, he speaks of "enargia, evidence or perpicuitie called also description rhetoricall, that is when a thynge is so described

that it semeth to the reader or hearer yt he beholdeth it as it were in doying." In W. G. Crane, *Wit and Rhetoric in the Renaissance* ("Columbia University Studies in English and Comparative Literature," No. 129; New York: Columbia University Press, 1937). In Hobbes's digest of the *Rhetoric* of Aristotle, words are said to be perspicuous if they are "proper," which he associates with using "received" words and good metaphors. "For in a metaphor alone there is perspicuity, novelty, and sweetness." *E.W.*, VI, 488–89.

42. *E.W.*, VIII, xxii.

43. Ibid., p. viii.

44. Ibid., p. xxviii.

45. Ibid., p. xxvii.

46. The discussions of Thucydides' technique in Jaeger, *Paideia*, I, 382–411, and Richard McKeon's essay, "Freedom and Disputation," in his *Thought, Action and Passion* (Chicago: University of Chicago Press, 1954), pp. 89–101, have been helpful for me.

47. Ibid., p. xxviii.

48. Ibid., p. xxi.

49. A markedly different outlook on the seventeenth-century context yields a markedly different evaluation of Hobbes's importance to historiography. F. Smith Fussner, who is mainly concerned with the advance of historical technics toward modern ideas of massive documentation, quantification, criteria for periodization, etc., in *The Historical Revolution: English Historical Writing and Thought; 1580–1640* (New York: Columbia University Press, 1962), pp. 170–73, remarks on other aspects of Hobbes. His suggestion of a correlation between historiographical and scientific advances has since been elaborated by G. Wylie Sypher, "Similarities between the Scientific and the Historical Revolutions at the End of the Renaissance," *JHI*, XXVI (July-Sept. 1965), 353–68.

50. Dean, "Tudor Theories of History Writing," p. 4, points out the acceptability of the set-speech convention, but also the criticism this rhetorical style was receiving from contemporaries like Thomas Blundeville and William Camden.

51. Frithiof Brandt, *Thomas Hobbes' Mechanical Conception of Nature* (Copenhagen: Levin & Munksgaards, 1928), pp. 198–202.

52. Hist. MSS. Comm., 13th Report, Appendix, Part II, *The Manuscripts of His Grace the Duke of Portland Preserved at Welbeck Abbey* (London: Printed for H. M.'s Stationery Office, Eyre and Spottiswoode, 1893), II, 128. Hereafter cited as *Welbeck Abbey MSS*.

53. Peter Burke, "A Survey of the Popularity of Ancient Historians, 1450–1700," *History and Theory*, V (1966), 135–52.

54. Lathrop, *Translations from the Classics*, p. 183.

55. Strauss, *Political Philosophy of Hobbes*, pp. 30–45, elaborates on some aspects of Hobbes's substantive debt to Aristotle's psychology.

56. *E.W.*, VIII, vii.

57. *B.L.*, I, 357.

58. See above, pp. 19–22 for the "problematic" nature of this question. Since Hobbes's ideas in the Thucydides essay have a clear bearing on philosophical questions of method and the kinds of knowledge various subjects yield, it is unnecessary to continue the commonplace assertion repeated by generations of Hobbes scholars that he did not become a philosopher until he had learned geometry, i.e., a year after his translation. The assumption underlying this commonplace is that the humanities are philosophically negligible—a position not unusual among twentieth-century

philosophers, but one which would have astounded many a seventeenth-century thinker.

59. i. 3, 1359^b2 [W. R. Roberts trans.].

60. *E.W.*, VI, 250.

61. Ibid., IV, 165.

62. *E.W.*, III, 702. Cf. Aristotle's defense of eloquence in the *Rhetoric*, i. 1. 1355^a22–1355^b8, where he argues along much the same lines.

Chapter III

1. *E.W.*, VII, 451. With respect to dating the letter, see G. R. de Beer, "Some Letters of Hobbes," *Notes and Records of the Royal Society of London* (hereafter cited as *Notes and Records*), VII (April 1950), 199–200.

2. Letter to Robert Leeke, Aug. 4 (N.S.), 1630. Hist. MSS. Comm., *Report on Manuscripts in Various Collections*, VII, "Additional Manuscripts of Sir Hervey Junkes Lloyd Bruce" (London: His Majesty's Stationery Office, 1943), 396.

3. Tönnies, "Pensée de Hobbes," pp. 84–86. This Aglionby, whoever he was, is apparently the same man as the Aglionby whose name regularly appears in the account books of Chatsworth and a long-time friend of Hobbes's.

4. *L.W.*, I, xiv; De Beer, "Some Letters of Hobbes," p. 205.

5. *B.L.*, I, 332.

6. *L.W.*, I, xiv.

7. *E.W.*, IV, "Dedication."

8. Ibid., I, 13–16; III, pp. 19–22.

9. Ibid., IV, 16.

10. Ibid., p. 18.

11. Ibid., III, 15.

12. Ibid., p. 16.

13. Ibid., IV, 21.

14. Ibid., III, 21–23, 33.

15. Ibid., pp. 23, 25.

16. Ibid., p. 33.

17. Ibid., p. 27.

18. Ibid., IV, 28.

19. Ibid.

20. Ibid. The relation between perception and conception has been studied astutely by T. A. Heinrichs, "Language and Mind in Hobbes," *Yale French Studies*, No. 49 (1973), pp. 56–70.

21. Ibid., III, 29.

22. "The [*dogmatici*] are they that take up maxims from their education, and from the authority of men, or of custom, and take the habitual discourse of the tongue for ratiocination. . . ." Ibid., IV, 73.

23. Ibid., III, 55.

24. Ibid., VII, 212.

25. See J. W. Young, *Lectures on Fundamental Concepts of Algebra and Geometry* (New York: Macmillan, 1911), especially pp. 8–9.

26. *E.W.*, VII, 202.

27. This exchange between the two philosophers is taken up again on pp. 76–79, below.

28. *L.W.*, V, 271–72.

29. The Ockhamite cast of his thinking has been noted most emphatically by John Herman Randall, Jr., in *The Career of Philosophy* (New York: Columbia University Press, 1962), I, 536, but the works of the Franciscan philosopher do not appear to have been in Hobbes's library.

30. "und wir können ihm nie durch äussere Erfahrung das beibringen, was nicht zur äussern Erfahrung gehört; . . . nie einen Punkt ohne Ausdenhung und eine Linie ohne Breite vorzeigen. . . . weil er sich nun einmal jeder nicht empirischen Erkenntniss verschliesst." Schopenhauer, "Die Welt als Wille," *Sämmtliche Werke* (Grossherzog Wilhelm Ernst Ausgabe: Leipzig, n.d.), I, 451.

31. *E.W.*, VII, 222, 225.

32. Of course there are geometries based on many different sets of primitive terms and they are all equally true and necessary if the logical inferences are faultlessly derived, notwithstanding the fact that these geometries may be applicable to nothing whatever in the physical universe except themselves. Hobbes naturally could not have known about modern non-Euclidean geometries; had he known, he might have considered "lines without breadth" to belong to just such a geometry, such lines referring to some other linguistic universe.

33. "Unusquisque autem qui dubitatione caret, talem lucem praetendit, et habet propensionem voluntatis ad affirmandum id de quo dubitat, non minorem quam qui revera scit. Potest ergo lux haec causa quare quis obstinate opinionem aliquam defendat vel teneat, sed non quod sciat veram eam esse." *L.W.*, V, 270.

34. Sheldon Wolin, *Politics and Vision* (Boston: Little, Brown & Company, 1960), p. 258.

35. *E.W.*, VII, 199; I, 82.

36. Ibid., I, 43.

37. Ibid., VII, 183–84.

38. Harald Höffding, *A History of Modern Philosophy*, trans. B. E. Meyer (New York: Dover Publications, 1955), I, 265–66.

39. *E.W.*, VII, 184.

40. Ibid.; also I, 82–83.

41. When geometry *is* regarded as a constructive science, "motion" becomes a primary term, as it is in Hobbes and in some modern geometries. When geometry is *not* construed as a constructive science, "congruence" becomes the important primitive idea. In the former, geometry is a study of simple motion; in the latter, it is a science comparing given relationships in space. Euclid himself seemed undecided between the two outlooks and thus laid the basis for these two ways of understanding the initial concepts of the *Elements*.

42. Höffding, *Modern Philosophy*, I, 266.

43. *The Philosophy of the Enlightenment*, trans. F. C. A. Koelln and J. P. Pettegrove (Princeton: Princeton University Press, 1955), p. 254.

44. *E.W.*, III, 36.

45. Neal W. Gilbert divides Renaissance concepts of method into two groups: a humanist-rhetorical group which was primarily concerned with method for its usefulness in organizing and teaching material, and a scientific group, which was mostly concerned with method as an instrument that provided strict demonstrations and

proofs. *Renaissance Concepts of Method* (New York: Columbia University Press, 1960), pp. 21–23. The division stems from the rivalry between philosophy and rhetoric: in Hobbes, both objectives and tendencies merge.

46. Hobbes's relationship to the Paduan school has been noted by several authors, but it remains to be treated definitively. See J. H. Randall, Jr., "The Development of Scientific Method in the School of Padua," *JHI*, I (1940), 177–206; Watkins, *Hobbes's System*, pp. 32–34; Gilbert, *Renaissance Concepts*, p. 211, and Richard Peters, *Hobbes* (Baltimore: Penguin Books, 1956), pp. 63–64.

47. *E.W.*, III, 23–24.

48. Ibid., III, 36–37.

49. *B.L.*, I, 347–48.

50. Ibid., p. 332.

51. *L.W.*, I, xxv.

52. Hist. MSS. Comm., *Welbeck Abbey MSS*, II, 124.

53. In that year, Mersenne dedicated several volumes of his *Harmonicum Libri* to Cavendish, although he does not appear in the preserved correspondence until August 1639.

54. It is usually conjectured that Cavendish's interest in mathematics dated from the correspondence between F. Derand and Oughtred; that is, from not later than October 9, 1634, when a letter from Derand was sent in his care to Oughtred (Jean Jacquot, "Sir Charles Cavendish and his Learned Friends: A Contribution to the History of Scientific Relations between England and the Continent in the Earlier Part of the 17th Century," *Annals of Science*, VIII [March 28, 1952], 13; Cornélis de Waard, *Correspondance du P. Marin Mersenne: Religieux Minime* [Éditions du Centre National de la Recherche Scientifique: n.p., 1960], VI, 65). However, the earlier date of 1631 can be established from a letter of June 22 of that year from one Richard Andrews in London to the Earl of Newcastle. It reads, in part, "My service to Sir Charles Cavendish to whome I sent a Letter this Last weeke, which came from Monsieur Mydorge from Paris." *Vere-Cavendish Papers*, B. M. Loan 29/235, fol. 62. The question is of significance here only as it relates to Hobbes's possible contacts with other scientists at an early date.

55. Hist. MSS. Comm., *Welbeck Abbey MSS.*, II, 125. On August 25, 1635, Hobbes (then in Paris) wrote to the Earl of Newcastle to thank him for a gift, also speaking warmly of Payne: "though I honour you as my Lord, yet my love to you is just of the same nature it is to Mr. Payne, bred out of private talke, without respect to your purse."

56. Ibid., p. 126. Letter from Hobbes to the same. Paris, August 25, 1635.

57. One was *de Loco imaginis in visione a speculo spherico concavo reflexâ et a speculo cylindrico concavo reflexâ*, to which is attached the *Radii optici definitiones, pro triplici visionis differentia*, in B. M., *Harl.* 6756. The manuscripts are dated February 16, 1934, and are first mentioned in a letter from Charles Cavendish at Welbeck, to Walter Warner at Cranborne Lodge, May 2, 1936, in B. M., *Birch Mss. 4407*, fol. 186. The letter was printed by James O. Halliwell, *A Collection of Letters Illustrative of the Progress of Science in England from the Reign of Queen Elizabeth to that of Charles the Second* (Historical Society of Science; London, 1841), p. 66, and reprinted in de Waard's edition of Mersenne, *Correspondance*, VI, 66; however, both editors cite *Birch MSS. 4405*, fol. 161.

58. Hist. MSS. Comm., *Welbeck Abbey MSS.*, II, 128–29. Letter from Hobbes to the Earl of Newcastle, Paris, July 29/August 8, 1637.

59. Halliwell, *Collection of Letters*, p. 65. Walter Warner in a letter to Robert Payne, October 17, 1634, Westminster.

60. Hist. MSS. Comm., *Welbeck Abbey MSS.*, II, 131. In a letter from the Earl of Newcastle to the Earl of Devonshire, May 2, 1637.

61. For Charles Cavendish's importance to the history of science in his role as intermediary, see Jacquot, "Sir Charles Cavendish," pp. 13–27.

62. A. R. Hall, in *The Scientific Revolution, 1500–1800: The Formation of the Modern Scientific Attitude* (Boston: Beacon Press, 1956), p. 191, points to the importance of private correspondence in furthering scientific organization: "In the mid-seventeenth century a number of men occupied a prominent position, less on account of their own intellectual capacities, than because of their indefatigability as correspondents." Cavendish, in his own way, was one of these "philosophical merchants."

63. Stephen Potter Rigaud, *Correspondence of Scientific Men of the Seventeenth Century* (Oxford: Oxford University Press, 1841), I, 23.

64. *E.W.*, I, viii.

65. On this question, see Brandt, *Hobbes' Mechanical Conception*," p. 78, and Ferdinand Tönnies, "Hobbes-Analekten," *Archiv für Geschichte der Philosophie*, III, 232.

66. *L.W.*, I, xx–xxi.

67. *E.W.*, I, 103.

68. Ibid., I, 69.

69. While it is of little importance here, Hobbes vacillated somewhat on whether the heart or brain was the seat of sense perception, and one can find both opinions in his work. On this and the bearing it has on dating his work, see Brandt, *Hobbes' Mechanical Conception*, p. 91.

70. *E.W.*, III, 2.

71. Ibid., p. 352.

72. Ibid., IV, 8.

73. Ibid., I, 485.

74. Ibid., IV, 8.

75. Ibid., I, 93–94; 105–6. Hobbes shrewdly realized that if matter was the only reality and if he postulated the reduction of all physical phenomena to motion, it still would not follow of itself that the space through which matter moves is "real." He distinguishes this "imaginary" or psychological space from "real space"; that is, the space occupied by bodies, which he calls "place."

76. *L.W.*, V, 303.

77. The problem of dating the *Short Tract* is one of the thorniest in the Hobbes corpus, and its importance hinges on the fact that it involves dating his development of a doctrine of subjective secondary qualities. Brandt's discussion of this, *Hobbes' Mechanical Conceptions*, p. 40ff., is indispensable.

78. Jacquot, "Sir Charles Cavendish," p. 18.

79. *E.W.*, VII, 339–40.

80. *E.W.*, I, 121–22. Thus Brandt, *Hobbes' Mechanical Conception*, pp. 274–75, argues that Hobbes's concept of causality does not derive from an analysis of experience, but from an analysis of the idea of necessity.

81. "Ita quod eorum esse est eorum cognosci." *Sent.*, I, dist. 2, qu. 8F.

82. *E.W.*, I, 32–33.

83. T. A. Heinrichs, "Language and Mind," pp. 68–70, is helpful here, approaching the issue somewhat differently but coming to very similar conclusions.

84. See Brandt, *Hobbes' Mechanical Conception*," pp. 225–30, where he argues that Hobbes drops his concept of evidence altogether to avoid a contradiction in his

nominalist position, Brandt holding that the idea of evidence points to a really existent universal concept behind names.

85. *E.W.*, I, 92.

86. Ibid., III, 39, 42; Ibid., I, 206.

87. See the discussions of Brandt, *Hobbes' Mechanical Conception,"* pp. 294–316, Peters, *Hobbes*, pp. 83–87, and Watkins, *Hobbes's System,"* 87–96, on the various aspects of the concept of endeavor.

88. De Waard, *Correspondance du P. Mersenne*, I, xlvii–xlviii, speaking of the monk's talent for stimulating fruitful discussion, remarks on some of the topics under consideration by the group: "La plus connue de ces questions est celle de la cycloïde *[i.e., that of the plane locus of a point fixed on the circumference of a circle as the circle rolls on a straight line]*, mais c'est aussi dans la cellule du Minime que Hobbes discuta en 1634 avec Beaugrande le problème du retour de l'arc, et que Hobbes et Roberval trouverent, en 1642, les premiers moyens de résoudre celui de l'égalisation des arcs de la parabole et de la spirale d'Archimède; c'est enfin avec Mersenne que Roberval et Cavendish s'appliquent peu après á la recherche du centre de percussion des différent corps."

89. *L.W.*, I, xc.

90. Hist. MSS. Comm., *Welbeck Abbey MSS.*, p. 129. Letter of October 16, 1636.

91. Ibid., p. 130. Letter from Hobbes to the same, Byfleet, Oct. 26, 1636. The warmth and concern Hobbes felt for the Cavendish family by this time is evident in the letter, though its purpose is to be excused from service. Perhaps a still better indication of the relationship can be found in a letter to young Cavendish two years later, which I have quoted in its entirety in Appendix I, for that purpose.

92. Ibid., p. 128. Letter of June 13/23, Paris.

93. Bodley, *Rawlinson MSS. D. 1104*, fol. 18; also in Tönnies, "Contributions," pp. 86–87.

94. Ibid., fol. 13. Also in Tönnies, *Pensée de Hobbes,"* p. 86.

95. Tönnies, *"Pensée de Hobbes,"* pp. 88–89. Letter from Digby to Hobbes, London, September 11, 1637.

96. *E.W.*, IV, 414.

97. *B.L.*, I, 334.

98. *E.W.*, IV, 414.

99. *Hobbes*, p. 28.

100. Marjorie Nicolson, "The Early Stage of Cartesianism in England," *Studies in Philology*, XXVI (1929), 358.

101. E. S. Haldane and G. R. T. Ross (trans.), *The Philosophical Works of Descartes* (Cambridge: Cambridge University Press, 1931), II, 61–62.

102. Ibid., p. 65.

103. Ibid.

104. *B.M.*, *Birch MSS. 4280*, fol. 107. Letter from Amsterdam, Sept. 7/17, 1644.

105. Brandt, *Hobbes' Mechanical Conceptions*, pp. 138–42, 179.

106. *L.W.*, V, 278.

107. Ibid., p. 303.

108. Ibid., p. 298.

109. Brandt, *Hobbes' Mechanical Conceptions*, p. 74, discusses Hobbes's work in the light of seventeenth-century atomism.

110. *E.W.*, VII, 340.

111. *B.M.*, *Birch MSS. 4278*, fol. 273.

112. The first part of the "little treatise" had Hobbes's ideas on psychology outlined in *Human Nature*; the second part was political, *De Corpore Politico, or the Elements of Law*, and they were subsequently published separately under those titles.

113. Descartes found Hobbes's moral philosophy in *De Cive* more clever than either his physics or metaphysics, although he disapproved of Hobbes's moral principles as well. These he found wicked and dangerous, in particular Hobbes's view of human nature, and he thought that Hobbes's argument for monarchy could be made more solid if based on more virtuous maxims: "Je le trouve beaucoup plus habile en Morale qu'en Métaphysique ni en Physique; nonobstant que je ne puisse aucunement approuver ses principles ni ses maximes, qui sont très mauvaises et très dangereuses, en ce qu'il suppose tous les hommes méchants, ou qu'il leur donne sujet de l'être. Tout son but est d'écrire en faveur de la Monarchie; ce qu'on pourrait faire plus avantageusement et plus solidement qu'il n'a fait, en prenant des maximes plus vertueuses et plus solides." Descartes, *Correspondance*, ed. C. Adam and G. Milhaud (Paris: Presses Universitaires de France, 1956), VI, 88.

114. *B.L.*, I, 333.

115. Hobbes's influence on Petty in subjects other than anatomy was enduring. Many years later, in 1685, Petty wrote of him as belonging to that "species of Transcendentall Men" which included, among the ancients: "Archimedes, Aristotle, Hippocrates, Homer, Julius Caesar, Cicero, Varro, Tacitus," and among the moderns: "Moliere, Swarez, Galileo, Sir Thos Moore, Sir Fra Bacon, Dr Donne, Mr Hobbs, Des Cartes." *The Petty-Southwell Correspondence, 1676–1687*, ed. the Marquis of Lansdowne (London: Constable and Company Ltd., 1928), II, 158–59. The same editor also compiled *The Petty Papers: Some Unpublished Writings of Sir William Petty from the Bowood Papers* (London: Constable and Company Ltd., 1927), which is also thoroughly permeated by Petty's peculiarly practical version of the Hobbesian spirit.

116. B.M., *Birch MSS. 4278*, fol. 196. Letter of June 27 o.s., 1645. Part of the fascinating Pell-Cavendish correspondence contained in *Birch MSS. 4278–4280* has been printed in Robert Vaughan's *The Protectorate of Oliver Cromwell and the State of Europe during the early part of the reign of Louis XIV* (London: 1838); other parts appear in Helen Hervey's "Hobbes and Descartes in the Light of some Unpublished Letters of the Correspondence between Sir Charles Cavendish and Dr. John Pell," *Osiris*, X (1952), 69–90, and some additional letters are in Halliwell, *Collection of Letters*. The large collection of Pell Papers in other parts of the *Birch MSS.* offer in themselves the materials for a short history of mathematics during the 1640s.

117. B.M., *Birch MSS. 4278*, fol. 227. Letter of Nov. 8/18, 1645.

118. *E.W.*, I, "Author's Epistle."

Chapter IV

1. The Cavendish family, which was related to the royal family through Arabella Stuart and which had risen to their great prominence under Stuart patronage, distinguished itself in the royalist cause. Hobbes's former pupil, the third Earl of Devonshire, supported the king financially and politically; he was impeached by Parliament and fled in 1642, returning to England in 1645 to save his estate. His younger brother, Charles, displayed conspicuous courage at Edgehill, and rose to the rank of Colonel in a brief but dazzling career; a dashing cavalier, he also became a popular and gallant

officer. In the battle for Gainsborough, he refused quarter from Berry, Cromwell's captain-lieutenant, and throwing blood from his wounds into the faces of his captors, he died magnificently and young in 1643. The Earl of Newcastle was "governor" to the Prince of Wales for a time, and fled after his part in Marston Moor. Charles Cavendish, Hobbes's friend and correspondent, was consigned by a physical deformity to a scholarly life. Francis Bickley, *The Cavendish Family* (Boston: Houghton Mifflin, 1914), p. 49.

2. B.M., *Birch MSS. 4278*, fol. 265. Letter of Dec. 7, n.s., 1646. It is suggested by Stephen, *Hobbes*, p. 38, that Newcastle procured this position for Hobbes, but on the basis of this letter he seems to be mistaken. Cavendish is a reliable source, and as Newcastle's brother, a well-informed one on this matter. Neither would he gain by dissimulating in this case.

3. Ferdinand Tönnies, "Siebzehn Briefe des Thomas Hobbes an Samuel Sorbière, nebst Briefen Sorbière's, Mersenne's u. Aa.," *Archiv für Geschichte der Philosophie*, III (1889), 194. Letter from S. Germ. *[St. Germain]*: Octob. 4. 1646.

4. Ibid., pp. 199–200. Parisiis 22 Martii 1647.

5. *B.L.*, II, 277.

6. Ibid., I, 352.

7. *E.W.*, I, ix.

8. The differences between *De Cive* and *Leviathan* are quite considerable, showing Hobbes working for greater internal consistency in his system, but they cannot be discussed here. Hood, in his *Divine Politics of Thomas Hobbes*, examines them intelligently. In particular, he argues that Hobbes's dispute with Bishop Bramhall in 1646 (discussed below) forced him to rethink his stand on the question of freedom of the will between the time of the second edition of *De Cive* and *Leviathan,* thus explaining certain irreconcilable differences.

9. A letter from R. P. *[Robert Payne]* to Dr. *[Gilbert]* Sheldon suggests that Hobbes merely *allowed* the publication of the little treatise. He writes, March 26, 1650, "Do your eyes begin to clear up again? If they do you may read a little Tract of Human Nature, printed lately by Fr. Bowman, out of a MS copy of Mr. Lockey's, who persuaded Bowman to publish it, as the Second part of Mr Hobbes's intended work. But I conceive it is but his first Draught; & I have sent him Word, that if he will add to, or alter any thing in it the Stationer hath promised to do him right in a second Edition." B.M., *Birch MSS.* 4162, fol. 112.

10. In a letter from Paris, September 22, 1651, Hobbes's physician, Gui Patin, wrote to M. Andre Falconet in Lyon, that Hobbes was "un philosophe stoicien, melancolique, et outre cela Anglois." As for the illness, he does not seem to have been dangerously ill, although he felt very miserable indeed. *Lettres de Gui Patin*, ed. J. -H. Reveille-Parise ("Libraire de l'Academie Royale de Medecine;" Paris: J. -B. Balliere, 1846), II, 593–94.

11. Hobbes's work schedule, as well as information regarding the dangers of a pirated translation, is derived from another letter of R. P. *[Robert Payne]* to Gilbert Sheldon. He writes from Oxford, May 13, 1650: "I sent notice to Mr Hobbes, that his book *de Cive* is translated into English, & desired him to prevent that translation by one of his own. But he sends me word he hath another task in hand, which is politics in English, of which he hath finished 37 Chapters (intending about 50 in the whole) which are translated into French by a learned Frenchman of good quality as fast as he finishes

them. And that his book *de Cive* is translated into French & printed already; And now I am come hither, I meet with the two first parts of that *de Cive* printed in English; but the last, *viz. Religio,* left out; a copy whereof I propose to send him by the next Opportunity: And this I do to urge him to hasten the Edition of all his Works intire, & not suffer him self to be thus mangled by Strangers." B.M., *Birch MSS. 4162,* fol. 111.

12. It is not correct to imply that Hobbes's embroilment with the clergy began only with *Leviathan.* Payne writes to Sheldon, March 7, 1649/50, that as early as that date Hobbes's mail to the Earl of Devonshire was being intercepted, and that one such letter contained a passage to the effect that he had lost the reward of his labors with the Prince "by the sinister suggestions of some of the Clergy." B.M., *Birch MSS. 4162,* fol. 111.

13. Robertson, "Hobbes," p. 548.

14. B.M., *Birch MSS. 4162,* fol. 111. Payne writes of him, "I am sorry to hear any of our Coat have had the ill fortune to provoke so great a Wit against the Church. I am confident, had you been on the place, you would have thought fit to deal with him another way."

15. Letter of Aug. 19, 1650. B. M., *Birch MSS. 4162,* fol. 113. While Hobbes is not mentioned by name, and much of this correspondence is carried on in the most elliptical language, it is evident that Payne is referring to the philosopher.

16. *E.W.,* III, 697–98.

17. Sir Edward Nicholas in a letter to William Edgeman. *Clarendon State Papers,* ed. H. O. Coxe (Oxford: Clarendon Press, 1869), II, 122.

18. *E.W.,* II, iv.

19. Ibid., p. vi.

20. Ibid., p. xiv.

21. Hobbes unfortunately used the American Indians as an example of man approaching the state of nature (*E.W.,* III, 114), conceiving of them as lacking in a highly developed society. While his anthropology is wanting here, Hobbes's meaning is clear and he does not think of man in the state of nature as an actual historical event.

22. *E.W.,* IV, 70.

23. Ibid., II, xiv.

24. Ibid., III, 110–13.

25. Ibid., p. xi.

26. Ibid., I, 73–74.

27. Ibid., II, xv.

28. Ibid., I, 72–74.

29. One can see the direction Hobbes was moving in to effect this derivation of psychology from geometry and physics in his "endeavor" concept. Stephen, *Hobbes,* pp. 72–73, nonetheless finds Hobbes's idea of integrating politics with physical science premature. Strauss, *Political Philosophy of Hobbes,* p. 170, finds that Hobbes's science merely obfuscates his real moral philosophy, and Hobbes's traditional commentators have, in general, tended to find a dichotomy between the two.

30. *E.W.,* III, 43.

31. Ibid., p. 46. Also see Appendix, below.

32. Ibid., p. 51.

33. *Two Treatises of Government* (London, 1688), Bk. II, p. 189.

34. *E.W.,* I, xii.

35. Ibid., II, xv–xvi.

36. Ibid., II, xvi.

37. Ibid., II, xvii.

38. *E.W.*, III, 116–17.

39. Warrender, *Political Philosophy of Hobbes*, pp. 18–21, has a careful discussion of Hobbes's uses of "right."

40. *E.W.*, III, pp. 112,116; cf. *E.W.*, *II*, vii, 5–9. When Hobbes speaks of "mutual fear" among men, he does not mean simple fright, leading to flight. Fear comprehends "a certain foresight of future evil," which may lead to combat or prudence, but which remains the basis for society: "If [men] fight, civil society ariseth from victory; if they agree, from their agreement." *E.W.*, II, 6n.

41. *E.W.*, III, 116; *E.W.*, II, 16.

42. *E.W.*, III, 117.

43. Ibid., pp. 117–18.

44. The interpretation of the status of natural laws is central for an evaluation of Hobbes's moral philosophy, and a substantial literature has grown up around this question. For analyses and criticism of the various schools of thought that have developed on this, see Michael Oakeshott, "Moral Life in the Writings of Thomas Hobbes," in *Rationalism in Politics and Other Essays* (New York: Basic Books, 1962), pp. 264–83. Also, W. H. Greenleaf, "Hobbes: The Problem of Interpretation," in *Hobbes and Rousseau*, ed. Maurice Cranston and Richard S. Peters (New York: Doubleday, 1972), pp. 6–24.

45. *E.W.*, III, 115.

46. It cannot be denied that Hobbes, as previously mentioned, sometimes uses language that seems to indicate that natural laws do impose obligations in the same way proper laws do. One explanation for this (although there are others) is argued by Brian Barry, who finds such passages derived from an earlier concept of "natural obligation" which Hobbes dropped but failed to eradicate entirely from his writing in *Leviathan*. See Barry's "Warrender and his Critics," in *Hobbes and Rousseau*, pp. 37–65.

47. *E.W.*, III, 147.

48. Ibid., II, 85.

49. Ibid., III, 119.

50. Ibid., pp. 124–25. "Trust" and "hope" here are conclusions of calculations based on fear. There must be some first performer in order to leave the state of nature, but since he has no assurance that the other will perform, he does "but betray himself to his enemy." In such circumstances, "trust" must either mean gullibility, or a calculated risk taken to gain the benefits of peace. The third possibility has sometimes been suggested that the first performer was one of those men whom Hobbes called "generous Natures," an exceptional man who rises above the motivation of fear. See below, p. 121.

51. Ibid., pp. 130–31.

52. Ibid., p. 131.

53. Ibid. Hobbes makes a technical distinction between a commonwealth by institution and a commonwealth by acquisition. In the former, the sovereign power is established by everyone entering into covenants of mutual trust to always obey the sovereign; in the latter, a conquerer covenants to spare your life in return for your future obedience. This changes somewhat the role of force in bringing about the covenant, but not the obligations that derive from it. As second performer, the covenanted subject is still bound. See Barry, "Warrender and his Critics," pp. 53–55.

54. Ibid., p. 120.

55. Ibid., p. 126.

56. Ibid., p. 277. Religious belief, as one category of thought, is a free gift of God, which can be neither given nor taken away, and consequently it is not subject to covenants. Ibid., pp. 273, 493.

57. See the excellent analysis of Alan Gewirth, *Marsilius of Padua: The Defender of Peace*, I ("Records of Civilization," no. XLVI; New York: Columbia University Press, 1951), 54–63.

58. *E.W.*, III, 195–96.

59. See the careful argument of F. A. Olafson, "Thomas Hobbes and the Modern Theory of Natural Law," *Journal of the History of Philosophy*, IV (Jan. 1966), 1, 15–30.

60. George E. G. Catlin, *Thomas Hobbes as Philosopher, Publicist, and Man of Letters* (Oxford: Basil Blackwell, 1922), p. 40.

61. Richard Cumberland, *A Treatise on the Laws of Nature*, trans. John Maxwell (London: R. Phillips, 1727), I, 80.

62. *Mr. Hobbes's State of Nature Considered*, in *Dr. Eachard's Works* (London, 1705), pp. 39–40.

63. Sterling P. Lamprecht, "Hobbes and Hobbism," *American Political Science Review*, XXXIV (Feb. 1940), p. 31.

64. Warrender, *Political Philosophy of Hobbes*, has developed this point in lucid detail.

65. Hobbes is still usually interpreted this way. For a notable example, see C. H. McIlwain, *Constitutionalism and the Changing World* (New York: Macmillan Co., 1939).

66. *E.W.*, III, 345.

67. *A Brief View and Survey of the Dangerous and Pernicious Errors to Church and State in Mr. Hobbes's Book Entitled Leviathan* (London: Printed at the Theatre, 1676), p. 52.

68. Ibid., p. 60.

69. George H. Sabine, *A History of Political Theory* (3d rev. ed.; London: George G. Harrup & Co., 1951), p. 388.

70. Even in the pre-war period, anti-monarchical feeling was slow to develop, and not until late did the idea emerge that monarchy was incompatible with liberty (see G. P. Gooch, *English Democratic Ideas in the 17th Century*, 2d ed.; Cambridge: Cambridge University Press, 1927, p. 88). In the Restoration, all kinds of republicanism were discredited by rankling memories of the Cromwellian experiment, and monarchy only became an issue again with the possible Catholic succession of James II (Sabine, *History of Political Theory*, p. 436).

71. *The Anarchy of a Limited or Mixed Monarchy* (London, 1679), p. 78.

72. The author of *The Leviathan Heretical: or the Charge Exhibited in Parliament against Mr. Hobbes Justified* (1683), John Dowell, wrote that Oliver was so pleased with *Leviathan* that he offered Hobbes the place of Secretary, but no evidence has turned up to substantiate this unlikely-sounding offer.

73. *E.W.*, III, 195.

74. *The Works of the Most Reverend Father in God John Bramhall, D.D.* (Oxford: J. H. Parker, 1884), IV, 564.

75. *Patriarcha* (London: 1680), p. 93.

76. *Dangerous and Pernicious Errors*, p. 121.

77. John Bowles, *Hobbes and his Critics* (New York: Oxford University Press, 1952), surveys many more representative critics of Hobbes from the constitutionalist

viewpoint, emphasizing what he considers the inadequacy of Hobbes's "bleak utilitarianism" as a theory of society and his influence on the Austinians.

78. C. H. McIlwain, *Constitutionalism Ancient and Modern* (rev. ed.; Ithaca: Cornell University Press, 1947), p. 117.

79. *Reflections by the Lrd. Cheife Justice Hale on Mr. Hobbes His Dialogue of the Lawe,* in "Sir Matthew Hale on Hobbes: An Unpublished MS.," by Sir Frederick Pollock and W. S. Holdsworth, *The Law Quarterly Review,* XXXVII, 147 (July 1921), p. 301.

80. Richard Hooker, *Of the Laws of Ecclesiastical Polity* (London: J. M. Dent & Sons, 1907), I, 177.

81. *Patriarcha,* p. 91.

82. *E.W.,* III, 252.

83. The Huguenot *Vindicae Contra Tyrannos* is representative of contractarian thought based on this assumption. For a comparative discussion, see Goldsmith, *Hobbes's Science of Politics,* pp. 142–43.

84. *E.W.,* III, 257.

85. Ibid., p. 253.

86. So the argument by the Parliamentarian Henry Parker, for instance, in *Observator defended,* 2 Aug. 42, *Thomason Collection of Pamphlets,* vol. 114; quoted in Gooch, *English Democratic Ideas,* p. 92.

87. In a system of judicial review, this does not happen, of course, but then the judiciary becomes the true sovereign, at least intermittantly.

88. McIlwain, *Constitutionalism: Ancient and Modern,* p. 94.

89. See, for example, Chief Baron Fleming's comments in the *Bate's Case* (1607) and Attorney General Heath's decision on the *Five Knights Case* (1627).

90. F. D. Wormuth, *The Origins of Modern Constitutionalism* (New York: Harper & Bros., 1949), pp. 39–40.

91. Hale, *Reflections,* p. 296.

92. Wormuth, *Origins of Modern Constitutionalism,* p. 49.

93. *E.W.,* III, 206.

94. Ibid., 252; VI, 134.

95. Hale, *Reflections,* p. 302.

96. F. W. Maitland, *The Constitutional History of England* (Cambridge: Cambridge University Press, 1908), pp. 261–75.

97. Hale, *Reflections,* p. 288.

98. See *E.W.,* III, 336, where Hobbes describes a good law as one that is brief (diminishing the possibility of ambiguities in the words) and "perspicuous," by which he means a law that explains its meaning and intent.

99. *E.W.,* III, 265.

100. Hale, *Reflections,* p. 290.

101. *History of the Common Law* (4th ed.), p. 67, as cited in John C. Gray, *The Nature and Sources of the Law* (rev. ed.; New York: Macmillan Co., 1921), pp. 218–19.

102. Ibid., p. 308.

103. The most trenchant modern exponent of Hobbes's view, John Austin, has restated the position of the philosopher in a classical, if turgid, exposition of legal positivism. That "no law can be unjust," says Austin, is no pernicious paradox, but "a truism put in unguarded terms. His [Hobbes's] meaning is obviously this: that no *positive* law is legally unjust." And by *just* he means that something "accords with a given law.... And as that which is *just* conforms to a determinate *law,* justice is the

conformity of a given object to the same or similar measure. . . . And since such is the relative nature of justice and injustice, one and the same act may be just and unjust as tried by different measures." *The Province of Jurisprudence Determined, and the Uses of the Study of Jurisprudence* (New York: Noonday Press, 1934), pp. 260–61, n. 23.
104. Bramhall, *Works*, IV, 544.

Chapter V

1. According to Blackbourne's estimate in his *Vitae Hobbianae Auctarium, L.W.*, I, 1xix–1xxx, more than thirty works expressly devoted to refuting Hobbes appeared between 1655 and 1679; more than thirty others appeared between 1652 and 1679 which were clearly in opposition to him although not exclusively devoted to an attack against him. His list is not complete, and a further checklist can be consulted in S. I. Mintz, *The Hunting of Leviathan* (London: Cambridge University Press, 1962), pp. 157–60. See also Hugh Macdonald and Mary Hargreaves, *Thomas Hobbes: A Bibliography* (London: The Bibliographical Society, 1952).
2. Sabine, *History of Political Theory*, p. 205.
3. Louis Dudek, *Literature and the Press* (Toronto: Ryerson Press, 1960), p. 20.
4. Leo Strauss, "On the Spirit of Hobbes' Political Philosophy," in Brown, *Hobbes Studies*, p. 27, n. 43.
5. Aubrey reports that Hobbes said "he durst not write so boldly" as Spinoza did, and when it is assumed that this refers to Spinoza's religious writings—specifically, to the idea that there is no truth in revealed religion—Hobbes's Erastianism is regarded as tainted by "a specious display of respect" for religion and a source of ambiguity in his philosophy. See Robert J. McShea, *The Political Philosophy of Spinoza* (New York: Columbia University Press, 1968), pp. 154–55.
6. *B.L.*, I, 339.
7. Alexander Ross, *Leviathan Drawn out with a Hook* (1653), as cited in Bowle, *Hobbes and His Critics*, pp. 63–64.
8. *E.W.*, III, 346. The grounds of obligation are elsewhere rather differently derived, an ambiguity discussed by Warrender, *Political Philosophy of Hobbes*, Chaps. XIII and XIV.
9. Ibid. IV, 289–90.
10. Ibid., p. 292.
11. Ibid., p. 426; ibid., III, 350–52.
12. Ibid., III, ch. XXXIV.
13. Ibid., IV, 350.
14. Ibid., VI, 190.
15. Ibid., III, 378.
16. Ibid., pp. 493–94.
17. Bramhall, *Works*, IV, 540.
18. Ralph Cudworth, *The True Intellectual System of the Universe* (London: Printed by J. F. Dove for Richard Priestley, 1820), I, 110.
19. *E.W.*, III, 541.
20. Bramhall, *Works*, IV, 533; *E.W.*, IV, 341.
21. Bramhall, *Works*, IV, 531; *E.W.*, IV, 336.
22. *E.W.*, III, 711.

23. *E.W.*, II, 150.

24. *E.W.*, III, 146.

25. As pointed out by K. R. Minogue, "Hobbes and the Just Man," in *Hobbes and Rousseau*, ed. M Cranston and R. S. Peters, who notes that Hobbes "was a man of strong moral feeling who produced a philosophy whose ethical content is obscure," p. 70. See also Keith Thomas, "The Social Origins of Hobbes's Political Thought," in *Hobbes Studies*, ed. Brown.

26. Taylor, "Apology for Mr. Hobbes," pp. 135–36.

27. Cumberland, *Treatise on the Laws of Nature*, p. 39.

28. Ibid., p. 61.

29. Ibid., p. 41.

30. For more comprehensive discussions of this group see Cassirer, *Philosophy of the Enlightenment*, p. 81.; Willey, *Seventeenth Century Background*, pp. 139–205; and Mintz, *Hunting of Leviathan*, pp. 80–109.

31. Cudworth, *True Intellectual System of the Universe*, III, 514.

32. Ibid., I, 53.

33. Ibid., p. 54.

34. J. A. Passmore, *Ralph Cudworth: An Interpretation* (Cambridge: Cambridge University Press, 1951), pp. 58ff., presents a discussion to which I am much indebted.

35. Ibid., pp. 11–27.

36. Ibid., p. 83.

37. And still is being said: see John Plamenatz, "Mr. Warrender's Hobbes," *Political Studies*, V (1957), 295–308, rpt. in Brown, *Hobbes Studies*, pp. 73–87, where he argues that "God is superfluous" in Hobbes's system. A rejoinder from Warrender is also in Brown, ibid., pp. 89–100.

38. For the development of Hobbes's ideas on liberty and necessity between *De Cive* and *Leviathan* and Bramhall's influence on them, see Hood, *Divine Politics of Hobbes*, ch. iv.

39. G. Croom Robertson, *Hobbes* (Edinburgh: William Blackwood and Sons, 1886) has a more detailed discussion of this controversy with Bramhall. For another aspect of the dispute, see Marjorie H. Nicolson, "Milton and Hobbes," *Studies in Philology*, XXIII (October 1926), 405–33.

40. Bramhall's initial reply was published in 1655 under the title *A Defence of the True Liberty of Human Actions from Antecedent or Extrinsic Necessity;* the following year, Hobbes replied with *Questions concerning Liberty, Necessity and Chance*. In 1658, the Bishop issued his *Castigations of Mr. Hobbes's Animadversions,* to which was appended his *The Catching of Leviathan the Great Whale*. Hobbes's response to the latter, *An Answer* . . . . was his parting shot.

41. The debate goes on still in modern scholarship, an example of which can be found in Brown, *Hobbes Studies*, with the paired articles of J. Roland Pennock, "Hobbes's Confusing 'Clarity'—The Case of Liberty," and A. G. Wernham, "Liberty and Obligation in Hobbes."

42. *E.W.*, IV, 272–73; ibid., III, 47–49; ibid., V, 358–59.

43. Ibid., IV, 68–69.

44. Ibid., V, 433.

45. *Enchiridion Ethicum* (New York: The Facsimile Text Society, 1930), p. 175.

46. *E.W.*, V, 435.

47. Ibid., III, 197–98; ibid., V, 328–29.

48. Ibid., V, 203.
49. Ibid., IV, 252.
50. Ibid.
51. Ibid., p. 434.
52. Ibid., p. 203.
53. Ibid., p. 25.
54. Ibid., p. 455.
55. Clarendon, *Dangerous and Pernicious Errors*, p. 9.
56. Cumberland, *Treatise on the Laws of Nature*, p. 36.
57. Scargill petitioned the king for a letter to be readmitted to the University, and it was through his intervention that the procedure was smoothed out. A letter from Archbishop Sheldon, dated June 28, 1669, Lambeth House, to Dr. Spencer, Master of Corpus Christi College, advises that it would be prudent to readmit the student in the light of the king's letter, lest the Master of the college receive another. In all events, Scargill could be dismissed again should he suffer a relapse into Hobbism. B.M., *Harl. MSS. 7377*, fol. 1r. Spencer acquiesced to the reasoning, and the Archbishop wrote again to assure him that there would be no further pressure from the king. Ibid., fol. 1v.
58. Charles Ripley Gillett, *Burned Books: Neglected Chapters in British History and Literature* (New York: Columbia University Press, 1932), I, 406. The other doctrines he was cited for in articles seven and fourteen were:
   "7. Self-preservation is the fundamental law of nature, and supersedes the obligation of all others, whenever they stand in competition with it.
   "14. An Oath superadds no obligation to a pact, and a pact obliges no further than it is credited: and consequently if a Prince gives any indication that he does not believe the promises of fealty and allegiance made by any of his subjects, they are thereby freed from their subjection, and, notwithstanding their pacts and oaths may lawfully rebel against, and destroy their Sovereign." Ibid.
59. Ibid., p. 511, citing *Sermon Preached before the Lord Mayor November 5, 1683* (1683), pp. 28–29.
60. Gilbert Burnet, *History of His Own Time: from the Restoration of Charles II, to the Treaty of Peace at Utrecht, in the Reign of Queen Anne* (London: William Smith, 1838), p. 128.

Chapter VI

1. In the *Answer*, Hobbes notes that the ancients wrote dramas and epics in verse partly because they were meant to be sung, a custom he says "began to be revived in part, of late years in Italy." As a sidelight on these Paris years, it suggests that he heard, or heard about, opera there, where it had its first court performance in 1645, though Hobbes might have seen it in Italy, on his earlier trip to the Continent. Opera had not yet reached England, but would do so within a few years, Davenant's verse being the first to be set.
2. Spingarn, *Critical Essays*, I, lxviii.
3. Ibid., p. xxviii.
4. George Williamson, *The Donne Tradition: A Study in English Poetry from Donne to the Death of Cowley* (New York: Noonday Press, 1958), pp. 213–14.
5. Spingarn, *Critical Essays*, I, xxxii.

6. *E.W.*, IV, 443, 453.
7. Ibid., p. 451.
8. Ibid., p. 455.
9. Ibid., IV, 443–45.
10. Ibid., pp. 451–52.
11. Ibid.
12. Ibid., III, 4.
13. Ibid., p. 5.
14. Ibid., p. 6.
15. Ibid., I, 394.
16. Ibid., III, 6; Ibid., I, 398.
17. Ibid., III, 6.
18. Ibid., p. 57; also, I, 399.
19. Ibid.
20. Ibid., I, 399.
21. Ibid., III, 61.
22. Ibid., p. 56.
23. Ibid., pp. 61–62.
24. Ibid., p. 57.
25. Spingarn, *Critical Essays*, I, xxviii-xxx.
26. *E.W.*, III, 57.
27. *E.W.*, IV, 499.
28. Ibid., p. 448.
29. Ibid., III, 58.
30. Even C. D. Thorpe, *The Aesthetic Theory of Thomas Hobbes* (Russell & Russell: New York, 1964), p. 17, who has explored the full scope of "ornament" in Hobbes, apologizes for the sentence as overemphasizing one aspect of fancy's function—so accustomed have we become to thinking of ornament as a prettification.
31. *E.W.*, IV, 452.
32. E. W. Tayler (ed.), *Literary Criticism of Seventeenth Century England* (Alfred A. Knopf: New York, 1967), pp. 24–25, points out correctly that all the traditional parts of rhetoric are assigned by Hobbes to a psychological function, either fancy or judgment. But they are mutually dependent functions, not *opposing* functions, and it is slightly misleading to say that the parts of rhetoric were "collapsed, neatly enough" into them, for the lines are not so neatly drawn. Judgment cuts across the rhetorical lines and not only organizes, but is also the ultimate arbiter of fancy's work as well.
33. *E.W.*, X, iii.
34. Ibid., p. v.
35. On the relationship between Bacon's earlier suggestions and Hobbes's work, see Thorpe, *Aesthetic Theory of Hobbes*, p. 78.
36. Ibid., IV, 449–50. C. M. Dowlin, *Sir William Davenant's Gondibert, Its Preface, and Hobbes's Answer* (Philadelphia, 1934), has noted a similar passage in Puttenham's earlier *Arte of English Poesie*, to which Hobbes was probably indebted. But Hobbes also borrowed from himself, for there is a nearly parallel passage in *The Elements of Philosophy* (*E.W.*, I, 8; see also passages in *Human Nature*, *E.W.*, IV, 72 and *Leviathan*, *E.W.*, III, 113), in which philosophy is spoken of as the cause for all the "marvellous effects" here attributed to fancy. There is no contradiction, of course, since fancy achieves her effects by following philosophy's guidelines, as described in the passage quoted above.

37. Ibid., III, 58–59.

38. Ibid., IV, 75.

39. Ibid., II, 161–62. Aristotle's presence may be felt here, as in every place where Hobbes talks about rhetoric. See chapter 5 of the *Politics*, where Aristotle gives the same negative eminence to demagogues in his discussion of revolution.

40. Ibid., X, viii.

41. Ibid., p. vii.

42. Ibid., IV, 453.

43. Ibid., p. 455.

44. Ibid.

45. For the history of "admiration" in Renaissance criticism, see J. E. Spingarn, *Literary Criticism in the Renaissance* (New York: Harcourt, Brace and World, 1963 ed.), pp. 33–34. Hobbes may well never have read Minturno, their meanings are so disparate. A more likely source would be Aristotle's *Rhetoric*, which has a passage dealing with the pleasure inherent in wonder or admiration and which cites examples of imitations which give such pleasure (i, 11, 1371^{b}4-11).

46. *E.W.*, IV, 453.

47. Ibid., III, 45; also, ibid., IV, 50–51.

48. Ibid., IV, 453.

49. Ibid., p. 455.

50. *Timber, or Discoveries*, in Spingarn, *Critical Essays*, I, 38.

51. *E.W.*, IV, 453, 455.

52. Ibid., X, vii.

53. Ibid., IV, 447.

54. Ibid., p. 446.

55. Ibid.

56. Ibid., p. 454. Perhaps there is an echo here of Aristotle on riddles and barbarisms that result from trying to make speech nonprosaic (*Poetics*, 22, 1458^{a}21-30), and which apparently found its way into another Hobbes source, Cicero's *De Orat.*, III, xlii, 67–70, in a passage on metaphors: "This is a valuable stylistic ornament; but care must be taken to avoid obscurity—and in fact it is usually the way in which what are called riddles are constructed."

57. By Jonson in *Timber*, for instance; in Spingarn, *Critical Essays*, I, 39–40.

58. *E.W.*, VIII, xxiii; *De Orat.*, II, xiii, 58–60. It is well worth noting that Hobbes's criterion is the ratio of words to *thoughts* here, while Spratt's criterion for a plain style suited to science was famously phrased in terms of the ratio of words to *things*.

59. George Williamson, *The Senecan Amble: A Study in Prose Form from Bacon to Collier* (Chicago: University of Chicago Press, 1951), p. 216.

60. *E.W.*, IV, 454, 451.

61. Ibid., p. 455.

62. Douglas Bush, *English Literature in the Earlier Seventeenth Century: 1600–1660* ("Oxford History of English Literature": New York: Oxford University Press, 1945), p. 355.

63. *E.W.*, X, b$_2$.

64. *E.W.*, I, 2.

65. As cited in Williamson, *The Senecan Amble*, pp. 307–8.

66. *E.W.*, X, iv-v.

67. Ibid., III, 75.

68. Ibid., p. 79.
69. Ibid., p. 88.
70. Ibid., I, 402.
71. Ibid., III, 14.
72. Ibid., p. 712.
73. Ibid., VII, 350.
74. Ibid., III, 711.
75. Ibid., pp. 113–14. For purposes of comparison, a parallel passage may be found in the earlier *Philosophical Elements,* ibid., II, xv.
76. Ibid., III, 20.

Chapter VII

1. Laird, *Hobbes,* p. 115.
2. Aside from a record of his anatomical work with William Petty in Paris, it has been conjectured that he was present during some of William Harvey's dissections of the King's deer in the 1630s (Geoffrey Keynes, *The Life of William Harvey* [London: Oxford at the Clarendon Press, 1966], p. 388). Moreover, Hobbes seems to have worked with a considerable personal collection of optical instruments that he had gotten from Rome and Florence. Among the papers of the Duke of Devonshire, *Chatsworth MSS.,* E. 3, there is a note on the sale of Hobbes's "prospective glasses" dated April 13, 1659, which lists a large variety of lenses for telescopes with tubes ranging from 6 to 37 palms, and made by such respected scientists as Fontana, Torricelli, and Divini. Finally, Hobbes's scientific writings reveal a wide acquaintance with experiments by people like Torricelli and so-called common experiments.
3. *E.W.,* VII, 3.
4. Ibid., IV, 436.
5. *B.L.,* I, 371.
6. Ibid. The mention of Boyle does not appear in this edition, but in O. L. Dick's transcription from the Aubrey manuscripts in his *Brief Lives* (Ann Arbor: University of Michigan Press, 1957), p. 158.
7. Samuel Sorbière, in his *Relation d'un Voyage en Angleterre où sont touchées l'estat des Science, & de la Religion, & autres matieres curieuses* (Cologne: Pierre Michel, 1666), suggests that the king would have liked to have seen Hobbes enrolled as a member of the Society. The king agreed, he said, that Hobbes was "fort necessaire a l'Academie Royale: Car il y a peu de gens qui regardent les choses de plus pres que luy, & qui ayent apporte une aussi longue application a la Physique."
8. *E.W.,* III, 679.
9. Ibid., p. 671.
10. Ibid., pp. 3, 331–32, 670–87, passim.
11. Louis I. Bredvold, in *The Intellectual Milieu of John Dryden* (Ann Arbor: University of Michigan Press, 1934), p. 57, expresses the common opinion when he says that Hobbes "was incompetent enough as a mathematician to try to demonstrate the quadrature of the circle." But, as noted, mathematicians of the highest standing were attempting the same thing at the time, and it was no sign of incompetence until the task was proven to be an impossible one. Hobbes's competence may be faulted by the nature of his solution, but not for the attempt.

12. In his classic work on the subject, *Squaring the Circle: A History of the Problem* (Cambridge: Cambridge University Press, 1913), pp. 3–4, E. W. Hobson notes that the Greeks even had a name for the activity of the circle-squarer, *Tetragonizein*, which means to occupy oneself with the quadrature. Moreover, the tribe grew so profuse by 1775 that the Paris Academy tried to protect its officials' time, which would otherwise be wasted in examining papers by circle-squarers, by passing a resolution that no more such solutions would be examined, nor any dealing with the duplication of the cube, the trisection of an angle, or perpetual motion machines.

13. *E.W.*, VII, 224.

14. *Ibid.*, p. 225.

15. *Ibid.*, p. 353. Hobbes dedicated the *Six Lessons* to Henry Lord Pierrepont, Viscount Newark, a scientifically inclined nobleman who later became a fellow of the Royal Society.

16. This entire dispute is discussed in Robertson, *Hobbes*, pp. 167–85, to which I am indebted, while a more mathematical survey is in J. F. Scott, *The Mathematical Work of John Wallis: 1616–1703* (London: Taylor and Francis, Ltd., 1938).

17. Wallis, *Due Correction for Mr. Hobbes* . . . (Oxford: Leonard Lichfield, for Thomas Robinson, 1656), pp. 7, 124–25.

18. *E.W.*, IV, 440.

19. Ibid., VII, 427.

20. Sorbiére, *Relation d'une Voyage*, p. 79.

21. John Wallis, *Hobbius Heuton timorumenos. Or a Consideration of Mr. Hobbes His Dialogues* (Oxford: A. & L. Lichfield, for Samuel Thomson, 1662), p. 6.

22. *E.W.*, VII, 6.

23. *E.W.*, IV, 420; 416.

24. The 1666 work was *De Principiis et Ratiocinatione Geometrarum, contra Falsum Professorum Geometriae*, the content of which is sufficiently clear from the title. When Wallis refuted Hobbes's subsequent publication, *Quadratura circuli, Cubatio sphaerae, Duplicatio cubi*, Hobbes republished it with his own refutation in 1669. A reworked version of his proofs appeared in 1671 in his *Rosetum Geometricum, sive Propositiones Aliquot frustra antehac tentatae, cum Censura brevi Doctrinae Wallisianae, De Motu*. The geometrical "rose garden" received an answer by Wallis at the Royal Society in the same year, Hobbes having also delivered for their consideration *Three Papers* against the professor. When Wallis replied to the papers as well, Hobbes published them with *Considerations on Dr. Wallis's Answer to them*. In 1672, Hobbes reviewed the mathematical issues between himself and Wallis in a volume addressed to the Royal Society, the *Lux Mathematica*. . . , followed by two more works in 1674 and 1678 respectively, the *Principia et Problemata* . . . and the *Decameron Physiologicum*.

25. Wallis, *Hobbius Heuton timorumenos*, p. 155.

26. Montucla continues, as surprised by the savagery of the dispute as by Hobbes's persistent delusion that he had squared the circle and found the mean proportionals despite Wallis's refutations: "car nonseulement il crut avoir réussi à quarrer le cercle, et à trouver les deux proportionelles, mais ne vit jamais un pareil acharnement à le soutenir contre Wallis, qui prit la peine de le réfuter par plusieurs écrits." *Histoire des Recherches sur la Quadrature du Cercle* (rev. ed.; Paris: Bachelier Père et Fils, 1831), p. 78.

27. *E.W.*, I, 141.

28. Ibid., VII, 68.

29. Ibid., p. 330.

30. Florian Cajori, *A History of Mathematical Notation* (Chicago: Open Court Co., 1929), I, 426–30.

31. *E.W.*, VII, 329–30.

32. Christian Huygens, *Oeuvres Complètes* (The Hague: Martinus Nijhoff, 1888–), I, 334.

33. Bredvold, *Intellectual Milieu of Dryden*, p. 57.

34. Huygens, *Oeuvres Complètes*, XXII, 593.

35. Robert Boyle, *An Examen of Mr. T. Hobbes his Dialogus Physicus de Natura Aëris . . . .* (London: M. Flesher, 1682), "Preface."

36. Rigaud, *Correspondence*, I, 92–93.

37. *Ibid.*, p. 26.

38. Royal Society, *Letter Book*, T.I., letter of June 26, 1661.

39. *Due Correction for Mr. Hobbes . . .* , p. 2.

40. So Hobbes wrote in 1662, using the third person, "As for his reputation beyond the seas, it fades not yet." *E.W.*, IV, 435. See also his consciousness of his European audience in *Ibid.*, VII, 355.

41. See, for instance, Bishop Sprat, *History of the Royal Society*, reproduction of the 1667 edition, ed. J. I. Cope and H. W. Jones ("Washington University Studies"; St. Louis, Missouri: Washington University Press, 1958), pp. 124–29.

42. J. F. Scott, "John Wallis as a Historian of Mathematics," *Annals of Science*, I (July 15, 1936), 349.

43. B. M., *Birch MSS.* 4,292, fol. 3. Letter by Wallis to Mr. Tenison [Tonsion ?].

44. Royal Society, *Letter Books*, W.I. fols. 100, 123, 124–29.

45. Thomas Birch, *The History of the Royal Society* (London, 1746), I, 42; also in Royal Society, *Classified Papers*, I, item 14.

46. In the Royal Society copy of the *Journal Book*, III, 148, it is reported that "Mr. Colwal produced a paper, sent him by Mr. Brooke, concerning a young woman . . . that had lived without all meat and drink since March last. It was read and filed up by Order." There is no mention of Hobbes. But in the *Letter Book*, B.I. 129, Brooke writes Colwall that he received the case report from Hobbes and is merely forwarding it. The Hobbes letter itself is in the *Letter Book*, H.I. 105, where it has been catalogued and subsequently printed by Molesworth as addressed to Mr. Beale, for some reason. See *E.W.*, VII, 463, for the letter.

47. Royal Society, *Journal Book*, IV, 7 (copy).

48. *Ibid.*, fol. 63.

49. Hobbes's letter is in *E.W.*, VII, 465; Oldenburg's reply is in the Royal Society *Guard Books*, H. 3. 20.

50. Royal Society *Guard Books*, W. II. 4.

51. *The Correspondence of Henry Oldenburg*, ed. by A. Rupert Hall and Marie Boas Hall (Madison: The University of Wisconsin Press, 1965), I, 74–75; Royal Society, *Liber Epistolaris*, MM. I, f. 6.

52. Brandt, *Hobbes' Mechanical Conception of Nature*, p. 214.

53. B. M., *Egerton MSS.* 2231, fols. 193–94. From Hobbes in Hardwicke, Feb. 24, 1674, to Aubrey in London. This MS. is in a copyist's hand; another copy exists in Bodley, *MS. Aubrey*, 12, fol. 166.

54. L. I. Bredvold, *Intellectual Milieu of Dryden*, p. 57.

55. Huygens, *Oeuvres Complètes*, II, 296. The translation from the original Latin is based on Scott's, *Mathematical Work of Wallis*, pp. 170–71.

56. "Quamvis enim, prout tunc res erant, id omnino videbatur faciendum, (quando sub pratexta Magni Geometrae, qualem se venditabat ausus est, in Religionis negotio, incautis adolescentibus perperam sentiendi materiam subministaret;) ne tamen in Geometriae damnum id cedat, non jam videtur metuendum." John Wallis, *Opera Mathematica* (Oxford: Sheldonian Theatre, 1695), I, "Preface."

57. B.M. *Add. MSS. 32, 553,* f. 22. Letter of Thomas Barlow, L. Cott. Oxon., to Hobbes, 1656.

58. *Ibid.*

59. B.M., *Add. MSS. 32,553,* contain a series of letters from Stubbe to Hobbes, as well as the Barlow letter, all of them dealing with these university matters, political observations, Wallis and the translation.

60. Boyle, *Examen of Mr. T. Hobbes,* "Preface."

61. *Intellectual Milieu of Dryden,* p. 58.

62. Sprat, *History of the Royal Society,* pp. 348–49.

63. Boyle, *Examen of Mr. T. Hobbes,* "Preface."

64. Sprat, *History of the Royal Society,* p. 365.

65. *Ibid.,* p. 367.

66. So Sprat takes up in detail the role of experimental science in education. *Ibid.,* pp. 323–42.

67. *Ibid.,* p. 345.

68. Joseph Glanville, *Plus Ultra, or, the Progress and Advancement of Knowledge since the Days of Aristotle* ... (London: James Collins, 1668), p. 89.

69. *Ibid.,* "Preface."

70. See the letters in *Royal Society MSS,* G.I. 15, Glanville to Oldenburg, July 19, 1669, and W.I. 92, Wallis to Oldenburg, July 16, 1669.

71. Harcourt Brown, *Scientific Organizations in Seventeenth Century France* (Baltimore, 1934), pp. 256–57. As the editors of Sprat's *History* (Appendix B, p. 70) point out, Stubbe was a physician of some mark and Boyle remained friendly with him out of respect for his skill, despite his writings against the society.

72. A volume by T. Tenison, review in *Phil. Trans.* V (Oct. 1670), no. 64, pp. 2080–81.

73. B.M., *Egerton MSS. 2231,* fol. 204, Hobbes to Josias Pullen, Feb. 1, 1672.

74. Augustus De Morgan, *A Budget of Paradoxes,* ed. David Eugene Smith (2d ed., New York: Dover Publications, 1954), I, 109–10.

75. *Ibid.,* II, 80.

76. R. A. Hall, "Science, Technology and Utopia," in *Science and Society: 1600–1900,* ed. Peter Mathias (Cambridge: Cambridge University Press, 1972), p. 44.

77. B.M., *Add. MSS. 6,193,* fols. 68v.-69r; also printed in R. T. Gunther, "The Life and Work of Robert Hooke," *Early Science in Oxford* (Oxford: Printed for the Author, 1930), VI, 139.

78. Wallis, *Hobbius Heauton-timorumenos,* p. 2.

79. One of Pell's descriptions is printed in Laird, *Hobbes.,* pp. 26–27.

80. *Abraham Cowley; Poetry and Prose,* ed. L. C. Martin (Oxford: Clarendon Press, 1949), p. 45.

81. Letter by Sir Robert Southwell to James, 1st Duke of Ormond, Dec. 13, 1679, in *Hist. MSS. Comm., Ormonde Papers,* n.s. IV, p. 567.

Concluding Remarks

1. *E.W.*, X, x.

2. *L.W.*, V, 342.

3. Molesworth dates the *Historia Ecclesiastica* at "about 1670" (*L.W.*, V, 342) correctly; the date of its completion can, however, be established with the highest degree of certainty at 1671. When Hobbes's handwriting became illegible because of his tremor in the 1660's, one James Wheldon, a servant in the Cavendish household, became his amanuensis. In the account book of Wheldon's own personal finances, the following item appears: "*Sept. & Oct.*, 1671. At Chatsworth. Given me by Mr Hobbes for writing a book, *Historia Ecclesiastica Romana.* 1.0.0." *Chatsworth MSS.*, 19, H.

Chatsworth MSS, 19, H, Wheldon's detailed account books, offer some interesting side-lights on Hobbes. It has a draft of Hobbes's will, making Wheldon his executor, charging him to bury him decently "as an Executor ought to doe, and make a dinner for his frends." It also recommends to Wheldon's care one Elizabeth Alaby, purportedly an orphan that turned up in 1674 at the age of about five years. Hobbes left Elizabeth £100, recommending that she be married to one of Wheldon's sons "provided they liked one another, and that he was not a spendthrift." It also shows that between 1662 and 1679, Hobbes gave Wheldon some £400 for services and as gifts (including interest), and almost another £600 was given him in 1680, apparently as part of Hobbes's will and mostly for the upkeep of Elizabeth, although that must remain a surmise. Wheldon's own salary was £6 per annum and later £10, and he was the regular recipient of Hobbes's old cloaks, doublets, and other miscellaneous items, which he either used or sold.

4. *E.W.*, III, 314–15.

5. Ibid., p. 314.

6. Ibid., VII, 4.

7. Williamson, *The Senecan Amble*, pp. 294–96, 315.

8. Willey, *Seventeenth Century Background*, pp. 102, 117.

9. Hall, *The Scientific Revolution*, p. 192.

Selected Bibliography

Aaron, R. I., "A Possible Early Draft of Hobbes' *De Corpore,*" *Mind,* LIV (1945), 342–56.

"Additional Manuscripts of Sir Hervey Junkes Lloyd Bruce," *Historical Manuscripts Commission, Report on Manuscripts in Various Collections.* VII. London: H. M.'s Stationery Office, 1943.

Applebaum, Wilbur. "Boyle and Hobbes: A Reconsideration," *Journal of the History of Ideas,* XXV, 1 (Jan.-March, 1964), 117–19.

Aubrey, John. *'Brief Lives,' chiefly of Contemporaries, set down by John Aubrey, between the years 1669 & 1696.* Edited by Andrew Clark. 2 vols. Oxford: The Clarendon Press, 1898.

Austin, John. *The Province of Jurisprudence Determined, and the Uses of the Study of Jurisprudence.* New York: Noonday Press, 1934.

Barry, Brian. "Warrender and His Critics." In *Hobbes and Rousseau.* Edited by M. Cranston and R. S. Peters. Garden City, New York: Anchor Books, 1972.

Bickley, Francis. *The Cavendish Family.* Boston: Houghton Mifflin Company, 1914.

Birch, Thomas. *The History of the Royal Society.* 4 vols. London: 1746.

Bowle, John. *Hobbes and His Critics: A Study in Seventeenth Century Constitutionalism.* New York: Oxford University Press, 1952.

Boyle, Robert. *An Examen of Mr. T. Hobbes His Dialogus Physicus de Natura Aëris... With an Appendix touching Mr. Hobb's Doctrine of Fluidity and Firmness.* London: Printed by M. Flesher, for Richard Davis, 1682.

Bramhall, John. *The Works of the Most Reverend Father in God John Bramhall, D.D.* 5 vols. Oxford: J. H. Parker, 1884.

Brandt, Frithiof. *Thomas Hobbes' Mechanical Conception of Nature.* Copenhagen: Levin and Munksgaard, 1928.

Bredvold, Louis I. *The Intellectual Milieu of John Dryden: Studies in some Aspects of Seventeenth-Century Thought.* Ann Arbor: University of Michigan Press, 1934.

Brockdorff, Cay, Baron von. "Fünf ungedruckte Briefe von Jean Pierre de Martel an Thomas Hobbes," *Hobbes-Gesellschaft, Veröffentlichungen VI.* Kiel, 1937.

——. "Hobbes unter dem Protektorat," *Hobbes-Gesellschaft. Veröffentlichungen VI.* Kiel, 1937.

Brown, Harcourt. *Scientific Organisation in Seventeenth Century France.* Baltimore: History of Science Society Publications, 1934.

Brown, Keith C. (Editor). *Hobbes Studies.* Cambridge: Harvard University Press, 1965.

Brown, Stuart M., Jr. "Hobbes: The Taylor Thesis," *Philosophical Review,* LXVIII (July, 1959), 303–23.

Burnet, Gilbert. *History of His Own Time: From the Restoration of Charles II, to the Treaty of Peace at Utrecht in the Reign of Queen Ann.* London: William Smith, 1838.

Burtt, Edwin Arthur. *The Metaphysical Foundations of Modern Physical Science: a Historical and Critical Essay.* Revised edition. New York: Humanities Press, 1932.

Cajori, Florian. *A History of Mathematical Notation.* 2 vols. Chicago: Open Court Publishing Co., 1929.

Cassirer, Ernest. *The Philosophy of the Enlightenment.* Translated by F. C. A. Koelln and J. A. Pettegrove. Princeton: Princeton University Press, 1951.

Catlin, George E. G. *Thomas Hobbes as Philosopher, Publicist and Man of Letters.* Oxford: Basil Blackwood, 1922.

Cavendish, Charles. "The Pell Papers," British Museum, Birch MSS. 4278–80.

Cavendish Family. "Vere-Cavendish Papers," British Museum, Loan 29/235.

Clarendon, Edward, Earl of. *A Brief View and survey of the Dangerous and Pernicious Errors to Church and State, In Mr Hobbes's Book Entitled Leviathan.* Oxford: Printed at the Theater, 1676.

Cohen, I. Bernard. "A Lost Letter from Hobbes to Mersenne Found," *Harvard Library Bulletin,* I (1947), 112–13.

Coltman, Irene. *Private Men and Public Causes: Philosophy and Politics in the English Civil War.* London: Faber and Faber, 1962.

Crane, William G. *Wit and Rhetoric in the Renaissance: The Formal Bases of Elizabethan Prose Style.* New York: Columbia University Press, 1937.

Cranston, Maurice, and Peters, Richard S. (Editors). *Hobbes and Rousseau.* "Modern Studies in Philosophy." Garden City, New York: Anchor Books, 1972.

Cudworth, Ralph. *The True Intellectual System of the Universe. Wherein all the Reason and Philosophy of Atheism is Confuted and its Impossibility Demonstrated.* London: Printed by J. F. Dove for Richard Priestly, 1820.

Cumberland, Richard. *A Treatise of the Laws of Nature. To which is prefixed an Introduction . . . where the Usefulness of Revelation may appear.* Translated by John Maxwell. London: R. Phillips, 1727.

Curtis, Mark H. *Oxford and Cambridge in Transition: 1558–1642.* Oxford: The Clarendon Press, 1959.

De Beer, G. R. "Some Letters of Thomas Hobbes," *Notes and Records of the Royal Society,* VII (1950), 195–206.

De Morgan, Augustus. *A Budget of Paradoxes*. 2d edition. Edited by David Eugene Smith. 2 vols. New York: Dover Publications, 1954.

Descartes, René. *Philosophical Works of Descartes*. Translated by E. S. Haldane and G. R. T. Ross. 2 vols. Cambridge: Cambridge University Press, 1931.

Dewey, John. "The Motivation of Hobbes's Political Philosophy," *Studies in the History of Ideas*. New York: Columbia University Press, 1918, pp. 88–115.

Dowlin, Cornell March. *Sir William Davenant's Gondibert, its Preface, and Hobbes's Answer*. Philadelphia: University of Pennsylvania Press, 1934.

Eachard, John. *Dr. Eachard's Works*. London, 1705.

Eliot, T. S. "John Bramhall," *Selected Essays: 1917–1932*. New York: Harcourt, Brace and Co., 1932.

Filmer, Robert. *The Anarchy of a Limited or Mixed Monarchy*. London: 1679.

——. *Observations concerning the Originall of Government*. London: 1679.

——. *Patriarcha*. London: 1680.

Fitzmaurice, Lord Edmond. *The Life of Sir William Petty: 1623–1687*. London: John Murray, 1895.

Fujimura, Thomas H. *The Restoration Comedy of Wit*. Princeton: Princeton University Press, 1952.

Funkenstein, Amos. "Natural Science and Social Theory: Hobbes, Spinoza Vico," in *Giambattista Vico's Science of Humanity*. Edited by Giorgio Tagliacozzo and Donald P. Verene. Baltimore: Johns Hopkins University Press, 1976.

Fussner, F. Smith. *The Historical Revolution: English Historical Writing and Thought: 1580–1640*. New York: Columbia University Press, 1962.

Gierke, Otto. *Natural Law and the Theory of Society: 1500–1800*. Translated with an Introduction by Ernest Barker, 2 vols. Cambridge: Cambridge University Press, 1934.

Gillet, Charles R. *Burned Books: Neglected Chapters in British History and Literature*. 2 vols. New York: Columbia University Press, 1932.

Glanville, Joseph. *Plus Ultra. Or, The Progress and Advancement of Knowledge . . . Occasioned by a Conference with one of the Notional Way*. London: James Collins, 1668.

Goldsmith, M. M. *Hobbes's Science of Politics*. New York: Columbia University Press, 1966.

Gooch, G. P. *English Democratic Ideas in the Seventeenth Century*. 2d edition. Cambridge: Cambridge University Press, 1927.

Gray, John C. *The Nature and Sources of the Law*. Revised edition. New York: Macmillan Co., 1921.

Greene, Robert A. "Henry More and Robert Boyle on the Spirit of Nature," *Journal of the History of Ideas*, XXIII, 4 (Oct.-Dec., 1962), 451–74.

Hall, A. R. "Merton Revisited," *History of Science*, II (1963), 1–16.

———. *The Scientific Revolution: 1500–1800. The Formation of the Modern Scientific Attitude.* Boston: The Beacon Press, 1956.

Halliwell, James O. (Editor). *A Collection of Letters Illustrative of the Progress Of Science in England from the Reign of Queen Elizabeth to that of Charles the Second.* London: Printed for the Historical Society of Science by R. and J. E. Taylor, 1841.

Harrington, James. *Oceana.* Edited by S. B. Liljegren. Heidelberg: C. Winter, 1924.

Hartley, Harold. (Editor). *The Royal Society: Its Origins and Founders.* London: The Royal Society, 1960.

Heinrichs, T. A. "Language and Mind in Hobbes," *Yale French Studies,* No. 49, (1973), 56–70.

Hervey, Helen. "Hobbes and Descartes in the Light of some Unpublished Letters of the Correspondence between Sir Charles Cavendish and Dr. John Pell," *Osiris,* X (1952), 67–90.

Hobbes, Thomas. *The Elements of Law Natural and Political.* Edited by Ferdinand Tönnies. London: Simpkin, Marshall & Co., 1889.

———. *The English Works of Thomas Hobbes of Malmesbury.* Edited by Sir William Molesworth. 11 vols. London: Bohn, 1839–45.

———. "First Draught on Optiques," British Museum, Harleian MSS. 3,360.

———. Letter to Sir Charles Cavendish, British Museum, Harleian MSS. 6,796.

———. Letter to the Duke of Ormonde. "Ellis Papers," British Museum, Additional MSS. 28,927.

———. *Leviathan.* Edited by Michael Oakeshott. Blackwell's Political Texts. Oxford: Basil Blackwell, 1946.

———. *Leviathan.* Reprinted from the Edition of 1651, with an Essay by the late W. G. Pogson Smith. Oxford: The Clarendon Press, 1909.

———. Miscellaneous Letters to and from Hobbes. Bodleian Library, Rawlinson MSS. C. 232.

———. Miscellaneous Letters to and from Hobbes. Bodleian Library, Rawlinson MSS. D. 1104.

———. Miscellaneous: MSS. of some systematic works, correspondence, mathematical fragments, etc. Chatsworth Collection of the Duke of Devonshire.

———. *Opera Philosophica quae Latine Scripsit,* Collecta studio et labore Gulielmi Molesworth. 5 vols. Londini, 1839–45.

Hobson, E. W. *Squaring the Circle: A History of the Problem.* Cambridge: Cambridge University Press, 1913.

Höffding, Harold. *A History of Modern Philosophy: A Sketch of the History of Philosophy from the Close of the Renaissance to our own Day.* Translated by B. E. Meyer. 2 vols. New York: Dover Publications, 1955.

Hood, F. C. *The Divine Politics of Thomas Hobbes: An Interpretation of Leviathan.* Oxford: The Clarendon Press, 1964.

Hooke, Robert. Letter to Robert Boyle. British Museum, Additional MSS. 6,193.

Howell, Wilbur S. *Logic and Rhetoric in England, 1500–1700*. New York: Russell & Russell, 1961.

Huygens, Christian. *Oeuvres Complètes*. 20 vols. The Hague: Sociétè Hollandaise des Sciences, 1888–1950.

Hunton, Philip. *A Treatise on Monarchie . . . Done by an earnest Desirer of his Countrie's Peace*. Printed by John Bellamy and Ralph Smith in Corn-Hill, 1689.

Jacquot, Jean. "A Newly Discovered Manuscript of Hobbes," *Notes and Records of the Royal Society*, IX (1952), 188–95.

——. "Sir Charles Cavendish and his Learned Friends," *Annals of Science*, VIII (March, 1952), 13–27, and (June 1952) 175–91.

Jaeger, Werner. *Paideia: The Ideals of Greek Culture*. Translated by Gilbert Highet. 3 vols. New York: Oxford University Press, 1944.

Jones, R. F. *Ancients and Moderns: A Study of the Rise of the Scientific Movement in Seventeenth-Century England*. "Washington University Studies." 2d revised edition. St. Louis: Washington University Press, 1961.

——. "Science and Criticism in the Neo-Classical Age of English Literature," *Journal of the History of Ideas*, I, 4 (Oct. 1940), 381–412.

Krook, Dorothea. "Thomas Hobbes's Doctrine of Meaning and Truth," *Philosophy*, XXI (1956), 3–22.

Kyle, W. M. "British Ethical Theories: The Intuitionist Reaction Against Hobbes," *The Australasian Journal of Psychology and Philosophy*, V. (1927), 113–23.

Laird, John. *Hobbes*. London: Ernest Benn Limited, 1934.

Lamprecht, Sterling. "Hobbes and Hobbism," *American Political Science Review*, XXXIV (Feb. 1940), 31–53.

Landry, B. *Hobbes*. Paris: Librairc Félix Alcan, 1930.

Locke, John. *Two Treatises of Government*. London, 1688.

Lowrey, Charles E. *The Philosophy of Ralph Cudworth: A Study of the True Intellectual System of the Universe*. New York: Phillips & Hunt, 1884.

Lyons, Sir Henry. *The Royal Society: 1660–1940; A History of its Administration under its Charters*. Cambridge: Cambridge University Press, 1944.

MacDonald, Hugh, and Hargreaves, Mary. *Thomas Hobbes: A Bibliography*. London: The Bibliographical Society, 1952.

Macpherson, C. B. *The Political Theory of Possessive Individualism: Hobbes to Locke*. Oxford: The Clarendon Press, 1954.

Manuscripts of His Grace the Duke of Portland Preserved at Welbeck Abbey. Historical Manuscripts Commission, 13th Report, Appendix, Part II. London: H.M.'s Stationery Office, 1893.

McIlwain, Charles H. *Constitutionalism: Ancient and Modern*. Revised edition. Ithaca: Cornell University Press, 1947.

———. *Constitutionalism and the Changing World: Collected Papers of C. H. McIlwain.* New York: Macmillan Co., 1939.

Mersenne, Marin. *Correspondance du P. Marin Mersenne, Réligieux Minime.* Edited by Cornelis de Waard. Editions du Centre National de la Recherche Scientifique, 1960.

Milburn, D. Judson. *The Age of Wit: 1650–1750.* New York: Macmillan, 1966.

Mintz, Samuel I. "Hobbes, Galileo, and the Circle of Perfection," *Isis*, XLIII (1952), 98–100.

———. *The Hunting of Leviathan: Seventeenth-Century Reactions to the Materialism and Moral Philosophy of Thomas Hobbes.* London: Cambridge University Press, 1962.

More, Henry. *Enchiridion Ethicum.* The English translation of 1690, reproduced from the first edition. New York: The Facsimile Text Society, 1930.

Nicolson, Marjorie Hope. *Conway Letters.* New Haven: Yale University Press, 1930.

———. "The Early Stage of Cartesianism in England," *Studies in Philology*, XXVI (1929), 356–74.

———. "Milton and Hobbes," *Studies in Philology*, XXIII (1926), 405–33.

Oakeshott, Michael. "Moral Life in the Writing of Thomas Hobbes," in *Rationalism in Politics and Other Essays.* New York: Basic Books, 1962.

Olafson, Frederick A. "Thomas Hobbes and the Modern Theory of Natural Law," *Journal of the History of Philosophy*, IV, 1 (Jan. 1966), 15–30.

Oldenburg, Henry. *The Correspondence of Henry Oldenburg.* Edited by A. Rupert Hall and Marie Boas Hall. 3 vols. Madison: University of Wisconsin Press, 1965.

———. Letter to Hobbes. Royal Society "Guard Books," W. II. 4.

Passmore, John A. *Ralph Cudworth: An Interpretation.* Cambridge: Cambridge University Press, 1951.

Payne, Robert. Correspondence with Gilbert Sheldon. British Museum, Birch MSS. 4,162.

Pell, John. "The Pell Papers," British Museum, Birch MSS. 4278–80.

Peters, Richard. *Hobbes.* London: Penguin Books, 1956.

Petty, Sir William. *The Petty Papers: Some Unpublished Papers of Sir William Petty.* Edited from the Bowood Papers by the Marquis of Lansdowne. 2 vols. London: Constable and Co., 1928.

———. *The Petty-Southwell Correspondence: 1676–1687.* Edited from the Bowood Papers by the Marquis of Lansdowne. London: Constable and Co., Ltd., 1928.

Plamenatz, John. "Mr. Warrender's Hobbes," *Political Studies*, V. (1957), 298–308.

Pollock, Sr. Frederick, and Holdsworth, W. S. "Sir Matthew Hale on Hobbes: An Unpublished MS," *Law Quarterly Review*, XXXVII (1921), 274–303.

Powell, Anthony. *John Aubrey and his Freinds*. London: Eyre and Spottis-woode, 1948.

Randall, J. H., Jr. *Aristotle*. New York: Columbia University Press, 1960.

——. "Development of Scientific Method in the School of Padua," *Journal of the History of Ideas*, I, 2 (April 1940), 177–206.

Rigaud, Stephen Peter. *Correspondence of Scientific Men of the Seventeenth Century*. 2 vols. Oxford: Oxford University Press, 1841.

Robertson, George Croom. *Hobbes*. "Philosophic Classics for English Readers Series." Edinburgh: William Blackwood and Sons, 1886.

Sabine, George H. *A History of Political Theory*. 3d revised edition. London: George G. Harrup & Co., 1951.

Scott, John F. "John Wallis as a Historian of Mathematics," *Annals of Science*, I, 3 (July 15, 1936), 335–57.

——. *The Mathematical Work of John Wallis, D.D., F.R.S. (1616–1703)*. London: Taylor and Francis Ltd., 1938.

Sheldon, Gilbert. Correspondence. British Museum, Harleian MSS. 7,377.

Shillinglaw, Arthur T. "Hobbes and Ben Jonson," *London Times Literary Supplement*, April 18, 1936.

Skinner, Quentin. "The Context of Hobbes's Theory of Political Obligation," in *Hobbes and Rousseau*. Edited by M. Cranston and R. S. Peters. Garden City, New York: Anchor Books, 1972.

Sorbière, Samuel. *Relation d'un Voyage en Angleterre, où sont touchées l'estat des Science, & de la Religion, & autres matieres curieuses*. Cologne: Pierre Michel, 1666.

Spingarn, J. E. (Editor). *Critical Essays of the Seventeenth Century*. 3 vols. Bloomington: Indiana University Press, 1957. Vol. I: 1605–1650.

Sprat, Thomas. *History of the Royal Society*. A reproduction of the 1667 edition, edited by J. I. Cope and H. W. Jones. St. Louis: Washington University Press, 1958.

Stephen, Leslie. *Hobbes*. "English Men of Letters Series." London: Macmillan, 1904.

Strauss, Leo. *The Political Philosophy of Hobbes: Its Basis and Genesis*. Translated by Elsa M. Sinclair. Oxford: The Clarendon Press, 1936.

Stubbe, Henry, *et al*. Letters to Hobbes: 1664–1675, British Museum, Additional MSS. 32,553.

Syfret, R. H. "The Origins of the Royal Society," *Notes and Records of the Royal Society*, V, 2 (1948), 75–137.

——. "Some Early Critics of the Royal Society," *Notes and Records of the Royal Society*, VIII (1950), 20–64.

Sypher, G. Wylie. "Similarities between the Scientific and the Historical Revolutions at the End of the Renaissance," *Journal of the History of Ideas*, XXVI (July-Sept. 1965), 353–68.

Tayler, E. W. (Editor). *Literary Criticism of 17th Century England*. New York: Alfred A. Knopf, 1967.

Taylor, A. E. "An Apology for Mr. Hobbes," *Seventeenth Century Studies Presented to Sir Herbert Grierson.* New York: Oxford University Press, 1938.

Thorpe, Clarence D. *Aesthetic Theory of Thomas Hobbes.* Ann Arbor: University of Michigan Press, 1940.

Tönnies, Ferdinand. "Contributions à L'Histoire de la Pensée de Hobbes," *Archive de Philosophie,* XII, 81–84.

———. "Hobbes-Analekten," *Archiv für Geschichte der Philosophie,* XVII (1903), 291–317, and XIX (1906), 153–75.

———. "Siebzehn Briefe des Thomas Hobbes an Samuel Sorbière, nebst Briefen Sorbière's, Mersenne's, U. Aa.," *Archiv für Geschichte der Philosophie,* III (1889).

———. *Thomas Hobbes—der Mann und der Denker.* Osterwieck/Harz und Leipzig: U. W. Zickfeldt, 1912.

Vaughan, Robert. *The Protectorate of Oliver Cromwell and the State of Europe during the early part of the reign of Louis XIV.* 2 vols. London, 1838.

Wallis, John. *A Defense of the Royal Society and the Philosophical Transactions . . . In a Letter to the Right Honourable William Lord Viscount Brounker.* London: n.p., 1678.

———. *Due Correction for Mr. Hobbes: Or Schoole Discipline, for not saying his Lessons . . . By the Professor of Geometry.* Oxford: By Leonard Lichfield, Printer to the University for Tho: Robinson, 1656.

———. *Hobbius Heauton-timorumenos: Or a consideration of Mr. Hobbes his Dialogues; In an Epistolary Discourse Addressed to the Honourable Robert Boyle, Esq.* Oxford: By A. & L. Lichfield, for Samuel Thomson, 1662.

———. *Letters to Henry Oldenburg.* Royal Society, "Letter Book," W. I.

———. *Opera Mathematica.* Oxford: Sheldonian Theatre, 1695.

Ward, Seth. *In Thomae Hobbii Philosophiam Exercitatio Epistolica, cui subjicitur Appendicula ad calumnias ab eodem Hobbio (in sex Documentis nuperrime editis) in authorem congestas, responsoria.* Oxford: 1656.

Warrender, Howard. *The Political Philosophy of Hobbes: His Theory of Obligation.* Oxford: The Clarendon Press, 1961.

———. "A Reply to Mr. Plamenatz," in *Hobbes Studies.* Edited by Keith Brown. Cambridge: Harvard University Press, 1965.

Watkins, J. W. N. "Philosophy and Politics in Hobbes," *Philosophic Quarterly,* V (1955), 125–46.

———. *Hobbes's System of Ideas: A Study in the Political Significance of Philosophic Theories.* Revised edition. London: Hutchinson University Library, 1973.

Weiss, Samuel A. "Hobbism and Restoration Comedy," unpublished doctoral dissertation, Columbia University, 1953.

Willey, Basil. *The English Moralists.* New York: W. W. Norton, 1964.

———. *The Seventeenth Century Background: Studies in the Thought of the Age in Relation to Poetry and Religion.* New York: Columbia University Press, 1934.

Williamson, George. *The Senecan Amble: A Study in Prose Form from Bacon to Collier.* Chicago: University of Chicago Press, 1951.

Wilson, John W. *The Court Wits of the Restoration.* Princeton: Princeton University Press, 1948.

Wolin, Sheldon. *Politics and Vision: Continuity and Innovation in Western Political Thought.* Boston: Little, Brown & Co., 1960.

Wood, Anthony. *Athenae Oxonienses.* Edited by Philip Bliss. 4 vols. London: Printed for Rivington, . . . Payne *et al.*, 1813–1820.

Wormuth, F. D. *The Origins of Modern Constitutionalism.* New York: Harper & Bros., 1949.

Yule, G. Udney. "John Wallis, D.D., F.R.S.: 1616–1703," *Notes and Records of the Royal Society,* II (1939), 74–82.

Index

Accidents, 69–70, 72
Amyot, Jacques, 201n.12, 202n.18
Anaxagoras, 23
Appetites. *See* Passions
Aristotle
—on "admiration," 220n.45
—on history, 38, 50
—idea of art, 148
—on poetry: and verse, 139; and history, 50; principles of, codified, 134
—on rhetoric: 40–41; related to dialectic, 40, 45, 203n.35; the *Rhetoric*, 27, 66; opposed to Sophists, 40–41; related to politics, 40, 45; influences Hobbes, 51, 220n.39
—on the state, 65, 96
Aristotelianism, 29, 168
Atheism
—Cudworth's purported, 124, 181
—Hobbes's purported. *See* Hobbes, reputation as atheist
—and science and materialism, 123, 180–81
Atomism, 123–24; atomists, 77, 166
Aubrey, John, 11, 18, 30, 51, 54, 66–67, 76, 79, 82, 114, 167, 176–77, 184, 191, 200n.2, 201n.24, 216n.5
Austin, John, 215n.103
Ayton (*or* Aytoun), Robert, 67

Bacon, Sir Francis, 16, 33, 139, 148, 158, 175, 201n.24
Barlow, Thomas, 179
Barrow, Isaac, 177
Barry, Brian, 213n.46
Baxter, Richard, 130
Beaugrand, Jean de, 74, 209n.88
Beaumont, Francis, 15
Berkeley, George, 166
Berkeley, Sir Robert, 108
Blackbourne, Richard, 200n.2
Blount, Thomas, 27
Bodin, Jean, 21

Bolton, Edward, 38
Boole, George, 185
Boyle, Robert, 167, 171, 174, 180–83, 187, 194
Bramhall, John (Bishop of Derry), 102, 111, 116, 118–19, 125–28, 170
Brandt, Frithiof, 78, 177, 208n.84
Bredvold, Louis I., 174, 178, 181, 221n.11
Brooke, Joseph, 176
Brouncker, William, Viscount, 176
Bruce, A., 174
Burnet, Bishop Gilbert, 132
Bush, Douglas, 156

Cambridge Platonists (*see also* names of individual philosophers), 121–25
Case of Ship-Money (1638), 108
Cassirer, Ernst, 63
Causes (*see also* Hobbes, on causes)
—in geometry, 62–63
—in history, 46–49, 57
—meaning of, in Hobbes, 72
—necessary and sufficient, 70, 126
—of will, 126
Cavendish, Sir Charles, 67–68, 78–81, 207n.54
Cavendish, William (first Earl of Devonshire), 30, 33
Cavendish, William (second Earl of Devonshire), 30–35, 37
Cavendish, William (third Earl of Devonshire), 34, 37, 66, 74, 86, 167
Cavendish, William (fourth Earl of Devonshire), 86, 130–32
Cavendish, William (Earl of Newcastle), 67–68, 74–75, 79, 81, 125
Cavendish family, 18, 30, 33–34, 52, 66, 68, 186, 210n.1
Charles I (King of England), 74–75, 106, 125
Charles II (King of England), 15, 84, 100–101, 129, 167, 170–72, 176, 183, 221n.7

235

Miriam M. Reik is a graduate of Sarah Lawrence College (1960); she holds the M.A. degree from Wayne State University (1962) and the Ph.D. from Columbia University (1967). She has enjoyed a varied career as a college professor, political and science writer, and journalist, and is presently engaged in independent research and writing.

The book was designed by Gary Gore. The typeface for the text and display is Palatino designed by Hermann Zapf about 1950. Initial letters on chapter opening pages and display type on title page is Vivaldi script.

The text is printed on S.D. Warren's "66" paper. The book is bound in Columbia Mills Fictionette cloth over binders' boards. Manufactured in the United States of America.